**The Stamford Streets AZ**

# The

# Stamford

# Streets

# AZ

Database

Lev M Vozchikov

The Stamford Streets AZ full hypertext singular database is presenting the geographical regional merge. Transportation handbook print of 2014. All rights reserved.

**The Stamford Streets AZ**

© Copyright 2014. All rights reserved. Any part of this book may not reproduce and store in a retrieval system or transmit by any means without written permission of the author. Paperback book printed on acid-free paper in the U.S.A.

# The Stamford Streets AZ

**The**

**Stamford Streets**

**AZ**

Annotation … 4

Copyrights … 5

A….6  B…..21  C…..60  D…..101  E…..127

F…..142 G…..162 H…..178 I…..216 J…..222

K…..229  L…..237  M…..261  N…..290

O…..301 P…..315 Q…..334 R…..336 S….364

T…..416  U…..432  V…..436  W…..443

Y…..485 Z…..486

# The Stamford Streets AZ

## Annotation

Stamford, CT regional merge The Greenwich Streets AZ is guide through 1400 streets Stamford highway structure. Follow highway substructure, stay within connected area, route trip, track local resources.

**Street name**
  Sub streets: **streets within internal regional merge.**
  External streets:
**Straight, left, right: streets within external regional merge.**
  External streets:
**Straight, left, right: streets within external regional merge.**

Singular database support full hypertext linked streets structure. In this edition added new streets to the known. Web enabled data design perfectly improve eBook user fast view.

# The Stamford Streets AZ

## Copyrights

Printed edition *The Stamford Streets AZ by Lev M Vozchikov* © Copyright 2008. Second edition 2014. All rights reserved. Paperback format 5 x 8 inch 488 pages include handbook end user guided annotation. No one part of this publication may not be retrieve, copied in any means without written permission. Annotation end user guided. Author encourages reader welcome suggestion.

# The Stamford Streets AZ

## A

**Abel Av**

Straight: Coolidge Av, first left: Treat Av, second left: Holcomb Av, first right: Rock Spring Rd, Puritan La
Straight: Kennedy La, straight: Hope St, first left: Faucett St, second left: Rock Spring Rd, third left: Plymouth Rd, first right: Frisbee St, second right: Treat Av, third right: Glenbrook Rd

**Aberdeen St**
Sylvandale Av

Straight: Ferris Av, first left: West Av, first right: Harvard Av
Straight: Boston Post Rd 1, first left: Harvard Av, second left: Alvord La, third left: Myano La, first right: West Av, second right: Diaz St, third right: Virgil St

**Acosta St**
Depinedo Av

Straight: West Av, Burr St, first left: Stillwater Av, first right: Tuttle St, second right: Leslie St, third right: Nobile St, Moore St

# The Stamford Streets AZ

**Acre View Dr**
Daffodil Rd, Cricket La

Straight: High Ridge Rd 137, Hoyclo Rd, first left: Cedar Wood Rd, second left: Pinner La, third left: Skymeadow Dr, Bartlett La, first right: Hoyclo Rd, Bracchi Dr, second right: Hickory Rd, third right: Hickory Rd


**Adams Av**
Vista St, Green St, Chestnut St

Straight: W Broad St, first left: Schuyler Av, second left: Hanrahan St, third left: Mill River St, first right: Oak Hill St, second right: Stephen St, third right: Anderson St
Straight: W North St, Powell Pl, first left: Hillside Av, second left: Woodcliff St, Anderson St, third left: Hinckley Av, first right: North St, second right: Hollywood Ct, third right: W Washington Av


**Akbar Rd**

Straight: MacGregor Dr, first left: Akbar Rd, first right: W Hill Rd
Straight: MacGregor Dr, first right: Akbar Rd, second right: W Hill Rd

# The Stamford Streets AZ

**Albert Pl**

Straight: Edward Pl, first left: Todd La, first right: Whistler Pl

**Albin Rd**

Straight: Cove Rd, first left: Island Heights Dr, second left: Weed Av, third left: Weed Cir, first right: Euclid Av, second right: Dora St, third right: Dean St, fourth right: Seaside Av
Straight: Neponsit St, Webster Rd, first left: Dora St, first right: Andover Rd, second right: Island Heights Dr, third right: Cambridge Rd

**Alden St**

Straight: Stillwater Av, first left: Smith St, second left: Boston Post Rd, first right: Spruce St, second right: Spruce St, third right: Fairfield Av, fourth right: Finney La

**Alexandra Dr**
Eliot La

Straight: High Ridge Rd 137, first left: Ingleside Dr, second left: Briar Brae

# The Stamford Streets AZ

Rd, third left: Briar Brae Rd, first right: Sunset Rd, second right: Hickory Rd, third right: Hickory Rd, fourth right: Bracchi Dr, Hoyclo Rd

**Alfred La**

Straight: Doral Farms Rd, first left: Farm Hill Rd, second left: Farm Hill Rd, third left: Roxbury Rd, first right: Roxbury Rd, second right: Farm Hill Rd, third right: Farm Hill Rd

**Algonquin Av**

Straight: Rippowam Rd, first left: Ponus Av, second left: Mohegan Av, third left: Shippan Av, first right: Wampanaw Rd
Straight: Iroquois Rd, Wampanaw Rd, first left: Rippowam Rd, second left: Algonquin Av, first right: Ponus Av, second right: Mohegan Av, third right: Shippan Av

**Allison Rd**
Beach View Dr

Straight: Kenilworth Dr W, first left: Beach View Dr, Kenilworth Dr E, first right: Soundview Av

# The Stamford Streets AZ

Straight: Kenilworth Dr E, first left: Soundview Av, first right: Beach View Dr, Kenilworth Dr W

**Alma Rock Rd**

Straight: High Ridge Rd 137, first left: N Stamford Rd, second left: Skymeadow Dr, Bartlett La, third left: Pinner La, first right: N Stamford Rd, second right: Brookdale Rd, third right: Bird Song La

**Alpine St**
Jay Rd, Rushmore Cir, Ken Ct

Straight: Dunn Av, first left: Dunn Av Ext, second left: High Ridge Rd 137, first right: Peak St, second right: Derry St, third right: Winter St
Straight: Cedar Heights Rd, first left: Cedar Circle, second left: Shadow Ridge Rd, third left: Dunn Av, first right: Apple Tree La, second right: Duke Dr, third right: Clay Hill Rd

**Alton Rd**
Marie Pl, Tioga Pl, Norman Rd

# The Stamford Streets AZ

Straight: Pine Tree Dr, first right: Apple Tree Dr, second right: Boxwood Dr, third right: Upland Rd
Straight: Upland Rd, first left: Norman Rd, second left: Pine Tree Dr, third left: Strawberry Hill Av, Fieldstone La, first right: Burdick St, second right: Bellmere Av, Belltown Rd


**Alvord La**

Straight: Boston Post Rd 1, first left: Harvard Av, second left: Aberdeen St, third left: West Av, first right: Myano La, second right: Whitmore La, third right: Havemeyer La
Straight: Catoona La, first left: Myano La, second left: Whitmore La, third left: Havemeyer La


**Amelia Pl**
Durant St

Straight: Bonner St, straight: Selleck St, Irving Av, first left: Durant St, Montauk Dr, first right: Vassar Av
Straight: Betts Av, straight: Selleck St, first left: West Av, first right: Durant St, Montauk Dr

# The Stamford Streets AZ

**Amherst Ct**

Straight: Amherst Pl, first right: Woodridge Dr S

**Amherst Pl**
Warwick La, Amherst Ct

Straight: Woodridge Dr S, first left: Bridle Path Rd, Long Ridge Rd 104

**Anderson St**
Vista St, Chestnut St, W North St, Grandview Av

Straight: W Broad St, first left: Stephen St, second left: Oak Hill St, third left: Adams Av, fourth left: Schuyler Av, first right: Wright St, second right: Hinckley Av, third right: Hubbard Av
Straight: Ivy St, first left: Hubbard Ct, Woodcliff St, first right: Powell Pl

**Andover Rd**

Straight: Neponsit St, Island Heights Dr, first left: Cambridge Rd, first right: Webster Rd, Albin Rd, second right: Dora St

# The Stamford Streets AZ

Straight: Middlebury St, first left: Webster Rd, second left: Webb Av, Dora St, first right: Cambridge Rd

**Ann St**

Straight: Richmond Hill Av, Taylor St, first left: Rose Park, second left: Mission St, third left: Greenwich Av, first right: Spruce St, second right: Fairfield Av, third right: Boston Post Rd 1, Wilson St
Straight: Boston Post Rd, first left: Spruce St, second left: Hazel St, Spruce St, third left: Fairfield Av, first right: Rose Park, second right: Stillwater Av, third right: Greenwich Av, W Main St

**Annie Pl**

Straight: West Av, first left: Sylvandale Av, Leon Pl, second left: Ferris Av, third left: Piave St, first right: Boston Post Rd 1, second right: Nurney St, third right: Minor Pl

# The Stamford Streets AZ

**Anthony St**

Straight: Liberty St, first left: Boston Post Rd 1, first right: Stillwater Av

**Apple Tree Dr**
Holbrook Dr

Straight: Pine Tree Dr, first left: Boxwood Dr, second left: Upland Rd, first right: Alton Rd

**Apple Valley Rd**

Straight: Mayapple Rd, first left: Rock Rimmon Rd, first right: Tanglewood La, second right: Boulderol Rd, third right: Country Club Rd

**Applebee Rd**

Straight: Benstone St, first right: Oaklawn Av

**Aquila Rd**

Straight: Island Heights Dr, first left: Cove Rd, first right: Island Heights

# The Stamford Streets AZ

Cir, second right: Andover Rd, Cambridge Rd, Neponsit St

**Arbor Rd**

Straight: Bartlett La, first right: High Ridge Rd 137, Skymeadow Dr, N Stamford Rd
Straight: Don Bob Rd

**Archer La**
Lancer La

Straight: Clay Hill Rd, first left: Arden La, first right: Timber La, second right: Cedar Heights Rd

**Arden La**

Straight: Clay Hill Rd
Archer La, Timber La
Straight: Cedar Heights Rd, first left: Rapids Rd, second left: Wire Mill Rd, first right: Duke Dr, second right: Apple Tree La

# The Stamford Streets AZ

**Ardmore Rd**

Straight: Harvard Av, first left: Brown House Rd, Warshaw Pl, second left: Selleck St, first right: Baxter Av, E 6 Governor John Davis Lodge Tpke I-95, second right: Grenhart Rd, E 6 Governor John Davis Lodge Tpke I-95, third right: Ferris Av
Straight: West Av, first left: Baxter Av, second left: Grenhart Rd, third left: Piave St, first right: Warshaw Pl, second right: Orlando Av, third right: Selleck St

**Ardsley Rd**
Van Buren Circle

Straight: Holcomb Av, first left: Coolidge Av, second left: Cowan Av, third left: Hillandale Av, first right: Van Buren Circle, second right: Strawberry Hill Av
Straight: Rock Spring Rd, first left: Strawberry Hill Av, Strawberry Hill Ct, first right: Mayflower Av, second right: Treat Av, third right: Puritan La, Coolidge Av, fourth right: Hope St

**Arlington Rd**
Valley Rd, Fenway St

# The Stamford Streets AZ

Straight: Glenbrook Rd, Daskam Pl, first left: Lafayette St, second left: Hope St, third left: Wenzel Terrace, first right: Boston Post Rd 1, Clarks Hill Av
Straight: Underhill St, first right: Hillandale Av


**Arnold Dr**

Joan Rd


**Arrow Head Dr**

Straight: Den Rd, first left: Old Orchard La, second left: Flint Rock Rd, third left: Hardesty Rd, first right: Long Ridge Rd 104


**Arthur Pl**

Straight: Glenbrook Rd, first left: Cowing Pl, second left: Kirkham Pl, Church St, third left: Crescent St, first right: Courtland Av 106, second right: Research Dr, third right: Oakdale Rd
Straight: Crescent St, first left: Taylor Reed Pl, first right: Glenbrook Rd

# The Stamford Streets AZ

## Ashton Rd

Straight: Beechwood Rd, first left: Crystal Lake Rd, first right: Hartswood Rd
Straight: Crystal Lake Rd, first left: Wilder Rd, first right: Beechwood Rd

## Aspen La

Straight: Frost Pond Rd, first left: Cascade Rd

## Atlantic St

Washington Blvd, Walter Wheeler Dr, Lipton Pl, Woodland Av, Lipton Pl, Henry St, Rockland Pl, Station Pl, Manhattan St, S State St, E 8 Governor John Davis Lodge Tpke I-95, N State St, Federal St, Tresser Blvd 1, Bell St, Bank St, Town Center Dr, Main St, Luther St, Broad St

Straight: Bedford St, Broad St, first left: Summer St, second left: Franklin St, third left: Washington Blvd 137, first right: Landmark Sq, second right: Greyrock Pl, third right: Suburban Av, fourth right: Grove St
Straight: Washington Blvd, first left: Crosby St, second left: Pacific St, first right: Pulaski St, second right: W

# The Stamford Streets AZ

Henry St, Henry St, third right: Station Pl

## Auldwood Rd

Straight: Shippan Av, first left: Downs Av, second left: Lanark Rd, third left: Chesterfield Rd, first right: Lanell Dr, second right: Mitchell St, third right: Wallace St
Straight: Ocean Dr N, first right: Lanark Rd, second right: Chesterfield Rd

## Austin Av

Straight: Duncanson St, Borglum St, first left: Berges Av, first right: Travis Av
Straight: Reynolds Av, first left: Travis Av, first right: Berges Av

## Autumn La

Straight: Toms Rd, first left: Dale Pl, second left: Overbrook Dr, third left: Deleo Dr, first right: Central St, second right: Summit Pl, third right: Belltown Rd

# The Stamford Streets AZ

**Avery St**

Straight: Charles St, first left: Dean St, first right: Horton St, second right: George St
Straight: Cove Rd, first left: Horton St, second left: George St, third left: Hobbie St, first right: Seaside Av, second right: Dean St, third right: Dora St


**Avon La**

Straight: Hope St, first left: Barnstable La, second left: Hartford Av, Castle Ct, third left: Chatfield St, first right: Short Hill St, second right: Omega Dr, third right: Clearview Av, fourth right: Largo Dr


**Ayres Dr**

Straight: Lewis Rd, first left: Nichols Av, first right: Hartswood Rd
Straight: Meadowpark Av N, first left: Swampscott Rd, second left: Hartswood Rd, first right: Nichols Av, second right: Meadowpark Av W, Meadowpark Av E

# The Stamford Streets AZ

## B

**Baker Pl**

Straight: Brook Run La, first left: Long Ridge Rd 104, first right: Lakeview Dr


**Barncroft Rd**
Overhill Rd

Straight: Roxbury Rd, first left: Doral Farms Rd, first right: Munko Dr, second right: Den Rd, third right: Roxbury Terrace
Straight: Barncroft Rd, Barncroft Rd


**Bangall Rd**
Constance La

Straight: Riverbank Rd, first left: Thunder Hill Dr, second left: Cow Path Dr, Westover Rd, Roxbury Rd, first right: Windward La, second right: Fawnfield Rd, third right: June Rd
Straight: Den Rd, first left: Hardesty Rd, second left: Flint Rock Rd, third left: Old Orchard La, first right: Barclay Dr, second right: E 33 Merritt Pkwy 15, CT15

# The Stamford Streets AZ

**Bank St**

Straight: Atlantic St, first left: Town Center Dr, second left: Main St, third left: Luther St, first right: Bell St, second right: Tresser Blvd 1, third right: Federal St
Straight: Main St, Clark St, Summer St, W Park Pl, first left: Washington Blvd 137, second left: Rippowam Pl, third left: Clinton Av, first right: Atlantic St

**Barclay Dr**
Willoughby Rd

Straight: Den Rd, first left: E 33 Merritt Pkwy 15, CT15, first right: Constance La, Bangall Rd, second right: Hardesty Rd, third right: Flint Rock Rd

**Barholm Av**
Hilltop Av, Sunset St

Straight: Weed Hill Av, first left: Upper Haig Av, second left: Bouton St W, third left: Estwick Pl, first right: Hilltop Av, second right: Newfield Av

# The Stamford Streets AZ

**Barmore Dr E**

Pamlynn Rd, Barmore Dr W

Straight: Barmore Dr, Barmore Dr W, first left: Vine Rd, first right: Barmore Dr E


**Barmore Dr W**

Straight: Barmore Dr, Barmore Dr E, first left: Pamlynn Rd, second left: Barmore Dr W, first right: Vine Rd
Straight: Barmore Dr E, first right: Pamlynn Rd, second right: Barmore Dr, Barmore Dr W


**Barmore Dr**

Straight: Vine Rd, first left: Pamlynn Rd, second left: Brandywine Rd, third left: Malvern Rd, first right: Vine Pl, second right: Kane Av, third right: High Ridge Rd
Straight: Barmore Dr W, Barmore Dr E, first left: Barmore Dr E, first right: Pamlynn Rd, second right: Barmore Dr W

## The Stamford Streets AZ

### Barn Hill Rd

Straight: E Middle Patent Rd, first left: Cherry Hill Rd, second left: Taconic Rd, first right: Ledge Rd, second right: Hidden Valley Way, third right: Hope's Farm La

### Barnes Rd W

Straight: Barnes Rd, first right: Long Ridge Rd 104

### Barnes Rd
Barnes Rd W

Straight: Long Ridge Rd 104, first left: Buckingham Dr, Roxbury Rd, Stillwater Rd, second left: Clover Hill Dr, third left: Three Lakes Dr, first right: Loughran Av, second right: Maltbie Av, third right: Vineyard La

### Barnstable La

Straight: Hope St, first left: Hartford Av, Castle Ct, second left: Chatfield St, third left: Riverbend Dr S, first right: Avon La, second right: Short Hill Rd, third right: Omega Dr

# The Stamford Streets AZ

**Barrett Av**

Straight: Silver Hill La, first left: Cody Dr, second left: Fara Dr, third left: Pepper Ridge Rd, first right: Case Rd, Brinkerhoff Av
Straight: Turner Rd, first left: Brinkerhoff Av, second left: Newfield Av, Belltown Rd, first right: Cody Dr, second right: Pepper Ridge Rd, third right: High Clear Dr

**Barry Pl**

Straight: Melrose Pl, straight: Fairfield Av, first left: Liberty Pl, second left: Sunnyside Av, third left: Selleck St, first right: Congress St, second right: Claremont St, third right: Barry Pl
Straight: Fairfield Av, first left: Claremont St, second left: Congress St, first right: Burwood Av, second right: Dee La, third right: Top Gallant Rd, fourth right: Hendrie Ct

**Bartina La**
Brodwood Dr

Straight: Westover Rd, first left: Westview La, second left: Summit Ridge

# The Stamford Streets AZ

Rd, third left: W Hill Rd, first right: Westover La, second right: Westover Av, third right: Mianus Rd, fourth right: W Glen Dr
Straight: W Hill Rd, first left: W Hill Circle, second left: Wyndover La, third left: Wesgate Dr, first right: Westview La, second right: Westover Rd

**Bartlett La**
Arbor Rd

Straight: High Ridge Rd 137, Skymeadow Dr, first left: N Stamford Rd, second left: Alma Rock Rd, third left: N Stamford Rd, first right: Pinner La, second right: Cedar Wood Rd, third right: Hoyclo Rd, Acre View Dr

**Baxter Av**
West Av, E6 Governor John Davis Lodge Tpke I-95, Southwood Dr, Southfield Village Ct, Southfield Village Ct, Wilson St

Straight: Fairfield Av, first left: Jackson St, second left: First Stamford Pl, third left: Madison Pl, first right: Pressprich St, second right: Selleck St
Straight: Harvard Av, E6 Governor John Davis Lodge Tpke I-95, first left: Brown

# The Stamford Streets AZ

House Rd, Warshaw Pl, second left: Selleck St, first right: Grenhart Rd, E 6 Governor John Davis Lodge Tpke I-95, second right: Ferris Av, third right: Commerce Rd

**Bayberrie Dr**
Emery Dr, Westover Rd, Halliwell Dr

Straight: Indian Hill Rd, first left: Westover Rd, first right: Emery Dr E
Straight: Starin Dr, first left: Palmers Hill Rd, first right: Westover Rd

**Beach View Dr**

Straight: Allison Rd, first left: Kenilworth Dr W, first right: Kenilworth Dr E
Straight: Kenilworth Dr W, Kenilworth Dr E, first left: Allison Rd, second left: Soundview Av, first right: Allison Rd, second right: Soundview Av

**Beal St**

Straight: Congress St, first left: Fairfield Av, second left: Claremont St, third left: Fairfield Av, Barry Pl,

# The Stamford Streets AZ

first right: Noble St, second right: Keith St, third right: Carlisle Pl
Straight: Burwood Av, first left: Noble St, second left: Keith St, third left: Silver St, first right: Claremont St, second right: Fairfield Av

**Bedford St**
Spring St, Prospect St, Forest St, Walton Pl, North St, Dolsen Pl, Hoyt St, Oak St, 1st St, 2nd St, 3 rd St, 4th St, 5th St, 6th St, Chester St, Urban St, Marlou La, Locust La

Straight: Long Ridge Rd, Summer St, High Ridge Rd 137, first left: Hoover Av, second left: Forest Lawn Av, third left: 8th St, first right: Cold Spring Rd, second right: Halpin Av, third right: Oaklawn Av
Straight: Broad St, Atlantic St, first left: Landmark Sq, second left: Greyrock Pl, third left: Suburban Av, first right: Summer St, second right: Franklin St, third right: Washington Blvd 137, W Broad St

**Beechwood Rd**
Ashton Rd

# The Stamford Streets AZ

Straight: Crystal Lake Rd, first left: Ashton Rd, second left: Wilder Rd
Straight: Hartswood Rd, first left: Southwest Dr, second left: High Ridge 137, first right: Meadowpark Av N, Swampscott Rd, second right: Lewis Rd


**Beehler St**

Straight: Guernsey Av, first left: Federal St, first right: N State St
Straight: Washington Blvd, first left: Richmond Hill Av, first right: Division St


**Bel Aire Dr**
Hollow Oak La

Straight: High Ridge Rd 137, first left: Swampscott Rd, second left: Emma Rd, third left: Nichols Av, first right: Hartswood Rd, second right: Brandt Rd, third right: Maplewood Pl
Straight: Rolling Wood Dr, first right: Little Hill Dr, second right: Hollow Oak La, third right: Berrian Rd


**Belden St**
Manor St, Harbor St

# The Stamford Streets AZ

Straight: Pacific St, first left: Dyke La, second left: Washington Blvd, first right: Crosby St, second right: Remington St, third right: E Walnut St, Walter Wheeler Dr
Straight: Elmcroft Rd, first left: Remington St, second left: E Walnut St, third left: Woodland Pl, first right: Rugby St, second right: Dyke La

**Bell St**

Straight: Washington Blvd 137, first left: Tresser Blvd, Tresser Blvd 1, second left: Division St, third left: Richmond Hill Av, first right: Rippowam Pl, second right: Main St, third right: W Park Pl, fourth right: Whittaker Pl
Straight: Atlantic St, first left: Bank St, second left: Town Center Dr, third left: Main St, first right: Tresser Blvd, Tresser Blvd 1, second right: Federal St, third right: N State St, E 8 Governor John Davis Lodge Tpke I-95

**Bellmere Av**
Norman Rd

Straight: Belltown Rd, Upland Rd, first left: Burdick St, second left: Alton Rd, third left: Norman Rd, first right:

# The Stamford Streets AZ

Leonard St, second right: Francis Av, third right: Fairland St


**Belltown Rd**
Burdick St, Bellmere Av, Leonard St, Francis Av, Fairland St, Toms Rd, Ledge La, Pershing Av

Straight: Newfield Av, Turner Rd, first left: Ogden Rd, second left: Hirsch Rd, third left: Newfield Ct, first right: Todd La, second right: Case Rd, Swan La, third right: Sanford La
Straight: Upland Rd, Alton Rd, first left: Norman Rd, second left: Tioga Pl, third left: Marie Pl


**Bend of River La**

Straight: W Glen Dr, Benenson Dr, first left: Shelter Dr, second left: Serenety La, third left: Daffodil La, first right: W Bank La, second right: Westover Rd


**Bennett St**
Palmer St, Knickerbocker Av

Straight: Lawton Av, first left: Tower Av, first right: Woodledge Rd, second

# The Stamford Streets AZ

right: Birchwood Rd, third right: Woodbury Av
Straight: Hope St, first left: Fahey St, second left: Northill St, third left: Cushing St, first right: Largo Dr, second right: Clearview Av, third right: Omega Dr

**Bennington Ct**

Straight: W Haviland La, first left: Haviland Rd, first right: Chestnut Hill Rd

**Benstone St**
Applebee Rd

Straight: Oaklawn Av, first left: Stanwick Pl, second left: Camore St, third left: Dartley St, first right: Northwoods Rd, second right: Cantwell Av, Old North Stamford Rd, third right: Halpin Av

**Bentwood Dr**

Straight: Erskine Rd, first left: Jonathan Dr, second left: Gun Club Rd, third left: Long Ridge Rd 104, first right: Riverbank Rd

# The Stamford Streets AZ

**Berges Av**
Borglum St

Straight: Reynolds Av, first left: Austin Av, second left: Travis Av

**Berkeley St**

Straight: Pulaski St, first left: Water St, second left: Greenwich Av, first right: Washington Blvd

**Berrian Rd**
Rolling Wood Dr, Woods End Rd, Idlewood Dr, Pepper Ridge Rd

Straight: Little Hill Dr, first left: Janice Rd, first right: Hollow Oak La, second right: Rolling Wood Dr, third right: Idlewood Dr

**Bertmor Dr**

Straight: Club Rd, first left: Newfield Av, first right: Kerr Rd, second right: Sandy La, third right: Malvern Rd

# The Stamford Streets AZ

**Betts Av**

Straight: Selleck St, first left: West Av, second left: Outlook St, third left: Harvard Av, first right: Montauk Dr, second right: Irving Av, Bonner St, third right: Vassar Av
Straight: Amelia Pl, first left: Durant St, second left: Bonner St

**Big Oak Cir**

Straight: Big Oak Rd, first left: Wake Robin La, first right: Twin Hills Rd, second right: Big Oak La, Red Fox Rd

**Big Oak La**

Straight: Big Oak Rd, Red Fox Rd, first left: Wake Robin La, second left: Wire Mill Rd, Studio Rd, first right: White Fox Rd

**Big Oak Rd**
Twin Hills Rd, Big Oak Cir

Straight: Wake Robin La, first left: Red Fox Rd, first right: Four Brooks Rd

# The Stamford Streets AZ

Straight: Red Fox Rd, Big Oak La, first left: White Fox Rd, first right: Wake Robin La, second right: Wire Mill Rd


**Birch St**

Straight: Waterbury Av, first left: Mathews St, first right: Boston Post Rd 1, Hamilton Av
Straight: Weed Av, first left: Boston Post Rd 1, first right: Holly Cove Cir, second right: Mathews St, third right: Weed Cir, fourth right: Cove Rd


**Birchwood Rd**
Tower Av

Straight: Crestview Av, first left: Bon Air Av, Northwood Rd, first right: Woodbury Av, second right: Klondike Av, third right: Haig Av
Straight: Lawton Av, first left: Woodbury Av, second left: Knapp St, Sleepy Hollow La, first right: Woodledge Rd, Lawton Av


**Bird Song La**

Straight: High Ridge Rd 137, first left: Brookdale Rd, second left: N Stamford

# The Stamford Streets AZ

Rd, third left: Alma Rock Rd, first right: Interlaken Rd, second right: Scofieldtown Rd, third right: Meredith La, fourth right: Diamondcrest La

**Bishop La**

Straight: Selleck St, first left: Betts Av, second left: Montauk Dr, Durant St, first right: West Av, second right: Outlook St

**Bittersweet La**
Quails Trail

Straight: Woodbine Rd, first left: Round Lake Rd, second left: Cedar Wood Rd, third left: Brushwood Rd, first right: Fernwood Dr, second right: Reservoir La, third right: Ingleside Dr
Straight: Thornwood Rd, first left: Brushwood Rd

**Blachley Rd**
Daycroft Rd, Daycroft Rd, Courtland Circle, E9 Governor John Davis Lodge Tpke I-95

Straight: Boston Post Rd 1, first left: Maher Rd, second left: Seaton Rd,

# The Stamford Streets AZ

Noroton Hill Pl, third left: Lawn Av, first right: Standish Rd, second right: E9 Governor John Davis Lodge Tpke I-95, third right: Courtland Av 106, E9 Governor John Davis Lodge Tpke I-95 Straight: Cove Rd, Willowbrook Av, first left: Duffy St, second left: Hobbie St, third left: George St, first right: Ranson St, Cove Rd, second right: Van Buskirk Av, third right: Dale St

**Black Rock Rd**

Straight: Trinity Pass, first left: Ponus Ridge, second left: Rolling Meadows, Lower Trinity Pass, third left: Trinity La, first right: Calass La, second right: High Ridge Rd 137

**Black Twig Pl**

Straight: McIntosh Rd, first left: McIntosh Ct, second left: Winesap Rd, first right: Russet Rd, second right: Mayapple Rd

# The Stamford Streets AZ

**Blackberry Dr E**

Straight: Blackberry Dr, first left: Mill Valley La, first right: Happy Hill Rd

**Blackberry Dr**
Mill Valley La, Blackberry Dr E

Straight: Happy Hill Rd, first left: Breezy Hill Rd

**Blackwood La**
Opper Rd, Deming La

Straight: Wire Mill Rd, first left: High Ridge Rd 137, first right: Gutzon Borglum Rd, second right: Studio Rd, third right: Red Fox Rd

**Blue Ridge Dr**

Straight: High Ridge Rd 137, first left: Diamondcrest La, second left Meredith La, third left: Scofieldtown Rd, first right: Perna La, second right: Pine Hill Terrace, third right: Marva La

# The Stamford Streets AZ

### Blue Rock Dr

Straight: Quarry Rd, first left: Greenbrier La, second left: Chapin La, third left: Lakeside Dr, first right: New England Dr

### Blue Spruce La

Straight: Taconic Rd, first left: Cherry Hill Rd, second left: E Middle Patent Rd, third left: Stanwich Club, first right: Banksville Av

### Blueberry Dr
Pond Rd, Skyview Dr

Straight: Pond Rd, first left: Hemlock Dr, second left: Stillwater Rd, first right: Blueberry Dr, second right: Skyview Dr
Straight: W Hill Rd, first left: Wesgate Dr, second left: Wyndover La, third left: W Hill Cir, first right: Greenleaf Dr, second right: Stony Brook Dr, third right: Carriage Dr

### Bon Air Av
Northwood Rd, Crestview Av, Northwood Rd, Buena Vista St

## The Stamford Streets AZ

Straight: Buena Vista St, Clearview Av, first left: Tower Av, second left: Knickerbocker Av, third left: Hope St, first right: Cady St, second right: Southill St
Straight: Tower Av, first left: Lawton Av, second left: Birchwood Rd, third left: Woodbury Av, first right: Palmer St, second right: Clearview Av

**Bonner St**

Straight: Amelia Pl, first right: Durant St, second right: Betts Av
Straight: Selleck St, Irving Av, first left: Durant St, Montauk Dr, second left: Betts Av, third left: West Av, first right: Vassar Av, second right: Fairfield Av, third right: Fairfield Av, fourth right: Orchard St, fifth right: Greenwich Av, Southfield Av

**Borglum St**

Straight: Berges Av, first left: Reynolds Av
Straight: Austin Av, Duncanson St, first left: Travis Av

# The Stamford Streets AZ

**Boston Post Rd 1, CT 06902**
Broad St, Lindale St, Crandall St, Glenbrook Rd, Clarks Hill Av, Daly St, Lafayette St, Quintard Terrace, N State St, Crystal St, Myrtle Av, Maple Av, Lincoln Av, Lockwood Av, Grant Av, Lawn Av, Seaton Rd, Noroton Hill Pl, Maher Rd, Blachley Rd, Standish Rd, E 9 Governor John Davis Lodge Tpke I-95, E 9 Governor John Davis Lodge Tpke I-95, Courtland Av 106, E 9 Governor John Davis Lodge Tpke I-95, E 9 Governor John Davis Lodge Tpke I-95, E 9 Governor John Davis Lodge Tpke I-95, Seaside Av, Home Ct, Houston Terrace, Hamilton Av, Waterbury Av, Weed Av, Brookside Dr, Purdy La, Hillside Av, Oakland Terrace, Catalpa St, Hollow Tree Ridge Rd, Hampton Rd, Weeds Landing, Gardiner St, Seagate Rd, Salt Box La, Lighthouse Way, Beach Dr, Coachlamp La, Outlook Dr, Duffy's La, Dubois St, Hedge Row, Nearwater La

Straight: Stamford Plaza 1, Elm St, Grove St, first left: N State St, E 8 Governor John Davis Lodge Tpke I-95, second left: S State St, E 8 Governor John Davis Lodge Tpke I-95, third left: Elm Ct, first right: E Main St, Grove St

# The Stamford Streets AZ

## Boston Post Rd 1

Whitmore La, Myano La, Alvord La, Harvard Av, Aberdeen St, West Av, Diaz St, Virgil St, Victory St, Liberty St, Roosevelt Av, Wilson St, Richmond Hill Av, High St, Fairfield Av, Hazel St, Spruce St, Spruce St, Ann St, Rose Park, Stillwater Av, W Main St, Greenwich Av, Clinton Av

Straight: E Putnam Av, Havemeyer La, Laddin Rock Rd, first left: Ferris Dr, Midbrook La, second left: Chasmar Rd, Deepwoods La, first right: Hassake Rd, second right: Stuart Dr, third right: Halsey Dr
Straight: Tresser Blvd, Clinton Av, first left: Main St, first right: Division St, second right: Richmond Hill Av

## Boulder Brook Dr

Straight: Hunting Ridge Rd, first left: Long Ridge Rd 104, first right: Surrey Rd, second right: Erickson Dr, third right: Lawrence Hill Rd

# The Stamford Streets AZ

**Boulderol Rd**

Straight: Mayapple Rd, Country Club Rd, first left: Country Club Rd, second left: Russet Rd, third left: High Ridge Rd 137, first right: Tanglewood La, second right: Apple Valley Rd, third right: Rock Rimmon Rd

**Bouton St**

Straight: Highview Av, first left: Columbus Pl, second left: Woodway Rd, first right: Mead St, second right: Cerretta St, third right: Camp Av
Straight: Bouton St W, Hope St, first left: Mead St, second left: Minivale Rd, third left: Weed Hill Av, first right: Woodway Rd, second right: Robinhood Rd, third right: Putter Dr

**Bouton Circle**

Straight: Bouton St W, first left: Gaymoor Dr, second left: Sunset St, third left: Minivale Rd, first right: Weed Hill Av

# The Stamford Streets AZ

### Bouton St W
Bouton Cir, Gaymoor Dr, Sunset St, Minivale Rd, Old Colony Rd, Prudence Dr

Straight: Bouton St, Hope St, first left: Woodway Rd, second left: Robinhood Rd, third left: Putter Dr, first right: Mead St, second right: Minivale Rd, third right: Weed Hill Av
Straight: Weed Hill Av, first left: Estwick Pl, second left: Ridgeway St, third left: Hickory Way, first right: Upper Haig Av, second right: Barholm Av, third right: Hilltop Av

### Bowen St

Straight: Hartford Av, first left: Knickerbocker Av, first right: Hope St, Castle Ct

### Boxwood Dr
Holbrook Dr

Straight: Pine Tree Dr, first left: Upland Rd, first right: Apple Tree Dr, second right: Alton Rd

# The Stamford Streets AZ

## Bracchi Dr

Straight: High Ridge Rd 137, Hoyclo Rd, first left: Hoyclo Rd, Acre View Dr, second left: Cedar Wood Rd, third left: Pinner La, first right: Hickory Rd, second right: Hickory Rd, third right: Sunset Rd

## Bracewood Dr

Straight: Bedford St, first left: Urban St, second left: 6th St, Chester St, third left: 5th St, first right: Marlou La, second right: Locust La, third right: Summer St, Long Ridge Rd, High Ridge Rd

## Broad St

Franklin St, Summer St, Atlantic St, Bedford St, Landmark Sq, Greyrock Pl, Suburban Av, Grove St, Pleasant St, Boston Post Rd 1

Straight: Boston Post Rd 1, first left: Lindale St, second left: Crandall St, third left: Glenbrook Rd, Clarks Hill Av, first right: Elm St, Stamford Plaza 1

Straight: Washington Blvd 137, W Broad St, first left: Whittaker Pl, second

## The Stamford Streets AZ

left: W Park Pl, third left: Main St, first right: North St, second right: Linden Pl, Hoyt St, third right: 2nd St, fourth right: 2nd St, fifth right: Bridge St


**Broad Brook La**

Straight: Ponus Ridge, Hope St, W Cross Rd, first left: Woodway Ridge La, second left: Running Brook La, first right: Eden Rd, E Cross Rd, second right: Slice Dr


**Bradley Pl**

Straight: Snow Crystal La, first left: Wild Horse Rd, second left: Sun Dance Rd, first right: Corn Cake La
Straight: High Ridge Rd 137, first left: Donata La, second left: Merriman Rd, third left: Vine Rd, first right: Tally Ho La, second right: Maplewood Pl, third right: Brandt Rd


**Branch La**

Straight: Riverbank Dr, first left: Riverbank Rd, first right: Shelter Rock Rd

# The Stamford Streets AZ

**Brandt Rd**

Straight: Warchol La
Straight: High Ridge Rd 137, first left: Maplewood Pl, second left: Tally Ho La, third left: Bradley Pl, first right: Hartswood Rd, second right: Bel Aire Dr, third right: Swampscott Rd


**Brandywine Rd**

Straight: Vine Rd, first left: Malvern Rd, second left: Pepper Ridge Rd, third left: Kerr Rd, first right: Pamlynn Rd, second right: Barmore Dr, third right: Vine Pl, fourth right: Kane Av


**Brantwood La**

Straight: Willard Terrace, first right: High Ridge Rd 137
Straight: High Ridge Rd, first left: Opper Rd, second left: Willard Terrace, third left: Wire Mill Rd, first right: Marva La, second right: Pine Hill Terrace, third right: Perna La


**Breezy Hill Rd**
Happy Hill Rd

# The Stamford Streets AZ

Straight: Rock Rimmon Rd, first left: Mayapple Rd, second left: Rock Meadow La, third left: Pond View La, first right: Golden Farm Rd, second right: Ridge Brook Dr, third right: Mill Rd

**Briar Brae Rd**
Shady La, Briar Wood Trail

Straight: High Ridge Rd 137, Ingleside Dr, first left: Russet Rd, second left: Flora Pl, third left: Laurel Rd, fourth left: Mayapple Rd, first right: Ingleside Dr, second right: Alexandra Dr, third right: Sunset Rd
Straight: Rock Rimmon Rd, first left: Saddle Hill Rd, second left: Dads La, Rock Rimmon Rd, E Hunting Ridge Rd, first right: Mill Rd, second right: Ridge Brook Dr, third right: Golden Farm Rd, fourth right: Breezy Hill Rd

**Briar Wood Trl**

Straight: Briar Brae Rd, first left: Rock Rimmon Rd, first right: Shady La, second right: High Ridge Rd 137

# The Stamford Streets AZ

## Briarwood La

Straight: Dogwood La, first left: Webbs Hill Rd, first right: Dogwood Ct, second right: Webbs Hill Rd

## Bridge St
Hubbard Av, Woodmere Rd, Riverside Av, Washington Blvd 137, Woodside Green

Straight: Stillwater Rd, first left: Halliwell Dr, second left: Palmers Hill Rd, E Gaynor Brennan Golf Course, third left: Connecticut Av, first right: Knoblock La, second right: Cold Spring Rd, third right: Pond Rd
Straight: Summer St, first left: 7th St, second left: 8th St, third left: Forest Lawn Av, first right: 6th St, second right: 5th St, third right: 4th St

## Bridle Path Rd

Straight: Three Lakes Dr, first left: Long Ridge Rd 104, first right: Elaine Dr
Straight: Woodridge Dr S, first left: Amherst Pl, second left: Elaine Dr, first right: Long Ridge Rd 104

# The Stamford Streets AZ

**Brighton Pl**

Straight: S Lindsey Av, first left: Crane Rd N, first right: Rome Pl, second right: Oaklawn Av

**Brightside Dr**

Straight: Hobson St, first left: Shippan Av, first right: Ocean Dr E, second right: Rockledge Dr, third right: Sea Beach Dr
Straight: Fairview Av, first left: Ocean Dr E, second left: Ocean View Dr, first right: Shippan Av, second right: Cresthill Pl, third right: Stamford Av

**Brinkerhoff Av**

Straight: Case Rd, Silver Hill La, first right: Newfield Av, Swan La
Straight: Turner Rd, first left: Newfield Av, Belltown Rd, first right: Barrett Av, second right: Cody Dr, third right: Pepper Ridge Rd

**Brodwood Dr**
Caprice Dr

# The Stamford Streets AZ

Straight: Bartina La, first left: W Hill Rd, first right: Westover Rd
Straight: Greenleaf Dr, first right: W Hill Rd


**Brook Run La**
Baker Pl, Lakeview Dr

Straight: Long Ridge Rd 104, first left: River Ridge Ct, second left: Stark Pl, third left: Terrace Av, first right: Wishing Well La, second right: Woodridge Dr S, third right: Three Lakes Dr


**Brookdale Dr**

Straight: Brookdale Rd, first left: Bud La, second left: Scofieldtown Rd, first right: High Ridge Rd 137


**Brookdale Rd**
Brookdale Dr, Bud La

Straight: Scofield Rd, first left: Chestnut Hill Rd, second left: Georgian Ct, third left: Campbell Dr, first right: Haviland Rd, second right: Rock Rimmon Rd, third right: Hannahs Rd, fourth right: Skymeadow Dr

# The Stamford Streets AZ

Straight: High Ridge Rd 137, first left: N Stamford Rd, second left: Alma Rock Rd, third left: N Stamford Rd, first right: Bird Song La, second right: Interlaken Rd, third right: Scofieldtown Rd, fourth right: Meredith La


**Brookhollow La**

Straight: Old Mill La, first left: Westover Rd, first right: Mill Brook Rd


**Brooklawn Av**
Center St

Straight: Frisbee St, Frisbie St, first right: Faucett St
Straight: Howes Av, first left: Nash Pl, second left: Pierce Pl, third left: Glenbrook Rd, first right: Hope St


**Brookside Dr**
River View Dr

Straight: Hamilton Av, first left: De Bera La, second left: E 9 Governor John Davis Lodge Tpke I-95, third left: Cove View Dr, first right: Hamilton Ct, second right: King St, third right: Midland Av, Courtland Hill St

# The Stamford Streets AZ

## Brookvale Pl

Straight: Wood Ridge Dr, first left: Ridge Park Av, first right: Rosano Rd, Ridge Park Av
Straight: Meadowpark Av E, first left: Meadowpark Av S, Meadowpark Av W, first right: Meadowpark Av W, Meadowpark Av N


## Brown Av

Straight: West St, first left: Mission St, first right: Greenwich Av


## Brown House Rd
Selleck St, Rosa Hartman Park, Harding Rd, Kensington Ct

Straight: Forest Av, Despoilation Alley, first left: Harding Rd, first right: Fairfield Av, second right: Rockland Pl, third right: Sound Beach Av


## Brownley Dr
Deacon Hill Rd, Wood La

Straight: High Ridge Rd 137, first left: Unity Rd, second left: Lakeview Dr, third left: Loveland Rd W, fourth left: Longview Av, first right: Colony Ct,

# The Stamford Streets AZ

High Clear Dr, second right: High Ridge Rd, third right: High Ridge Rd, fourth right: Terrace Av


**Brundage St**

Straight: Knapp St, first left: Gilford St, second left: Carroll St, third left: Hope St, Greenway St, first right: Sleepy Hollow La, Lawton Av
Straight: Mulberry St, first left: Ridgeway St, first right: Elmer St, second right: Carroll St, third right: Hope St


**Brushwood Rd**

Straight: Woodbine Rd, first left: Pinewood Rd, second left: Mather Rd, third left: Woodbine Way, first right: Cedar Wood Rd, second right: Round Lake Rd, third right: Bittersweet La
Straight: Thornwood Rd, first left: Bittersweet La


**Buckingham Ct**

Straight: Buckingham Dr, first left: Long Ridge Rd 104, first right: Warwick La

# The Stamford Streets AZ

**Buckingham Dr**
Warwick La, Buckingham Ct

Straight: Roxbury Rd, Long Ridge Rd 104, first left: Stillwater Rd, second left: Clover Hill Dr, third left: Three Lakes Dr, first right: Barnes Rd, second right: Loughran Av, third right: Maltbie Av


**Bud La**

Straight: Brookdale Rd, first left: Scofieldtown Rd, first right: Bartlett Arboretum and Gardens, second right: Brookdale Dr


**Buena Vista St**
Bon Air Av

Straight: Woodbury Av, first left: St Charles Av, Marian St, first right: Crestview Av, second right: Tower Av, thirst right: Lawton Av
Straight: Bon Air Av, Clearview Av, first left: Tower Av, second left: Palmer St, third left: Bon Air Av, first right: Cady St, second right: Southill St

# The Stamford Streets AZ

**Bungalow Park**

Straight: Seaside Av, first left: Webb Av, second left: E 9 Governor John Davis Lodge Tpke I-95, third left: E 9 Governor John Davis Lodge Tpke I-95, fourth left: Boston Post Rd, first right: Mathews St, second right: Sylvan Knoll Rd, third right: Cove Rd
Straight: Hearthstone Ct


**Burdick St**

Straight: Newfield Av, first left: Crane Rd, Strawberry Hill Av, first right: Oaklawn Av, second right: Francis Av, third right: Fairland St
Straight: Belltown Rd, Upland Rd, first left: Bellmere Av, second left: Leonard St, third left: Francis Av, first right: Alton Rd, second right: Norman Rd, third right: Pine Tree Dr


**Burley Av**

Straight: Southfield Av, first left: Sunnyside Av, second left: Taff Av, third left: Homestead Av, first right: McClurg Av, second right: Wells Av, third right: Congress St

## The Stamford Streets AZ

Straight: Carlisle Pl, straight: Carlisle Pl

**Burns Rd**

Straight: Wallacks Dr, first right: Soundview Av

**Burr St**

Straight: West Av, Acosta St, first left: Tuttle St, second left: Nobile St, Moore St, third left: Minor Pl, third left: Nurney St, fourth left: Boston Post Rd, West Av, first right: Stillwater Av
Straight: Corbo Terrace, first left: Stillwater Av, first right: Tuttle St

**Burwood Av**
Claremont St, Beal St, Noble St, Keith St, Silver St

Straight: Southfield Av, first left: Congress St, second left: Wells Av, third left: McClurg Av, first right: Top Gallant Rd, Davenport Dr, second right: Cook Rd, third right: Hickory Dr
Straight: Fairfield Av, first left: Dee La, second left: Top Gallant Rd, third

# The Stamford Streets AZ

left: Hendrie Ct, first right: Barry Pl, second right: Claremont St, third right: Congress St


**Butternut La**
Butternut Pl

Straight: Malibu Rd
Straight: Long Ridge Rd 104, first left: Chestnut Hill Rd, second left: Hunting Ridge Rd, third left: Stone Hill Dr, first right: Hazard La, second right: Den Rd, third right: Midrocks Dr


**Butternut Pl**

Straight: Butternut La, first left: Malibu Rd, first right: Long Ridge Rd 104, Chestnut Hill Rd


**Buxton Farm Rd**

Straight: High Ridge Rd 137, E 35 Merritt Pkwy 15, CT15, first left: E 35 Merritt Pkwy 15, CT15, second left: Dunn Av, third left: Square Acre Dr, first right: E 35 Merritt Pkwy 15, CT15, second right: High Ridge Rd, third right: E 35 Merritt Pkwy 15, CT15, fourth right: Wire Mill Rd

# The Stamford Streets AZ

Straight: Turn Of River Rd, first left: High Ridge Park, first right: Sterling Lake La, second right: Intervale Rd, third right: Talmadge La

**Bateman Way**

Straight: Dyke La, first left: Harbor St, first right: Elmcroft Rd

# The Stamford Streets AZ

## C

**Cady St**

Straight: Woodbury Av, first left: St Charles Av, Marian St, first right: Buena Vista St, second right: Crestview Av, third right: Tower Av
Straight: Clearview Av, first left: Buena Vista St, Bon Air Av, second left: Tower Av, third left: Knickerbocker Av, fourth left: Hope St

**Calass La**

Straight: Trinity Pass, first left: Black Rock Rd, second left: Ponus Ridge, third left: Rolling Meadows, Lower Trinity Pass, first right: High Ridge Rd 137

**Caldwell Av**
Ranson St

Straight: Van Buskirk Av, first left: Sachem Pl, second left: East Av, first right: Cove Rd
Straight: Willowbrook Av, first left: Cove Rd, Blachley Rd, first right: Uncas Rd, second right: Hale St, third right: Wascussee La E

# The Stamford Streets AZ

**Cambridge Rd**
Middlebury St

Straight: Mathews St, first left: Waterbury Av, second left: Houston Terrace, third left: Webb Av, first right: Weed Av
Straight: Neponsit St, Andover Rd, Island Heights Dr


**Camelot Ct**

Straight: Hope St, first left: Deep Spring La, second left: Nottingham Dr, third left: Mary Violet Rd, fourth left: Putter Dr, first right: Slice Dr, second right: Eden Rd, E Cross Rd, third right: Broad Brook La, W Cross Rd


**Camore St**

Straight: Oaklawn Av, first left: Dartley St, second left: Dann Dr, third left: Sherwood Rd, first right: Stanwick Pl, second right: Benstone St, third right: Northwoods Rd, fourth right: Cantwell Av, Old North Stamford Rd
Straight: Edice Rd, straight: Dartley St, first right: Oaklawn Av

# The Stamford Streets AZ

**Camp Av**
Ryan St, Highview Av, Garland Dr, St John's Cemetery, Greenwood Av, Hoyt St 106, Spring Grove St, Jackson Pl, Petticoat La

Straight: Hollow Tree Ridge Rd, first left: Wheat La, second left: Natures Way, third left: Allwood Rd, first right: Stephanie Av, second right: Nolen La, third right: Christie Hill Rd
Straight: Hope St, first left: Knapp St, Greenway St, second left: Hyde St, third left: Cushing St, fourth left: Northill St, first right: Mulberry St, second right: Weed Hill Av, third right: Minivale Rd


**Campbell Dr**

Straight: Scofieldtown Rd, first left: Georgian Ct, second left: Chestnut Hill Rd, third left: Brookdale Rd, first right: Woodley Rd, second right: Middle Ridge Rd, third right: Janes La, fourth right: Old Logging Rd


**Canal St**
Henry St, Market St, Dock St, Jefferson St, S State St, E 7 Governor John Davis Lodge Tpke I-95, N State St

# The Stamford Streets AZ

Straight: Ludlow St, first right: Ludlow Pl, second right: Cedar St, third right: Woodland Av, Pacific St
Straight: Stamford Forum 1, Stamford Plaza 1, Greyrock Pl, first left: Tresser Blvd, Town Center Dr, first right: Grove St, Elm St, Boston Post Rd 1

## Canfield Dr
Cogswell La

Straight: Westover Rd, first left: Nathan Hale Dr, second left: High Line Trail, first right: Canfield Dr, second right: Long Close Rd, third right: Merriebrook La, fourth right: Long Close Rd
Straight: Westover Rd, first left: Canfield Dr, second left: Nathan Hale Dr, third left: High Line Trail, first right: Long Close Rd, second right: Merriebrook La, third right: Long Close Rd

## Cantwell Av
Reed Pl

Straight: Dubois St, first left: Halpin Av, second left: High Ridge Rd 137

# The Stamford Streets AZ

Straight: Oaklawn Av, Old North Stamford Rd, first left: Northwoods Rd, second left: Benstone St, third left: Stanwick Pl, first right: Halpin Av, second right: High Ridge Rd 137

**Caprice Dr**

Straight: Brodwood Dr, first left: Greenleaf Dr, first right: Bartina La

**Carlisle Pl**
Liberty Pl, McClurg Av, Wells Av

Straight: Congress St, first left: Silver St, second left: Southfield Av, first right: Keith St, second right: Noble St, third right: Beal St, fourth right: Fairfield Av
Straight: Burley Av, straight: Southfield Av, first left: Sunnyside Av, second left: Taff Av, third left: Homestead Av, first right: McClurg Av, second right: Wells Av, third right: Congress St, fourth right: Burwood Av

**Carolina Rd**

Straight: Delaware Av, straight: W Broad St, first left: Stillwater Av, first

# The Stamford Streets AZ

right: Merrell Av, second right: Rachelle Av, Shelburne Rd, third right: St George Av
Straight: Merrell Av, first left: W Broad St, first right: Edison Rd, second right: Stillwater Av

## Carriage Dr S

Straight: Carriage Dr, first right: Carriage Dr S, second right: W Hill Rd
Straight: Carriage Dr, first left: Carriage Dr S, first right: W Hill Rd

## Carriage Dr
Carriage Dr S, Carriage Dr S

Straight: W Hill Rd, first left: Green Tree La, second left: Dancy Dr, third left: MacGregor Dr, first right: Stony Brook Dr, second right: Greenleaf Dr, third right: Blueberry Dr

## Carrington Dr

Straight: Stanwich Rd, first left: Stag La, second left: Carissa La, third left: Londonderry Dr, first right: Tod La, second right: Meeting House Rd, third right: Crown La

# The Stamford Streets AZ

**Carroll St**
Knapp St

Straight: Northill St, first left: Knickerbocker Av, second left: Hope St, first right: Palmer St, second right: Woodledge Rd
Straight: Mulberry St, first left: Elmer St, second left: Brundage St, third left: Ridgeway St, first right: Hope St

**Carter Dr**
Tupper Dr

Straight: Soundview Av, first left: Wascussee La, second left: Tupper Dr, third left: McMullen Av, first right: Willowbrook Av, second right: Soundview Ct, third right: Soundview Dr

**Cascade Ct**

Straight: Cascade Rd, first left: N Stamford Rd, first right: Pembroke Dr, second right: Michael Rd, third right: Frost Pond Rd, fourth right: Woodbine Rd

**Cascade Rd**
Woodbine Rd, Frost Pond Rd, Michael Rd, Pembroke Dr, Cascade Ct

# The Stamford Streets AZ

Straight: Ponus Ridge, first left: Four Winds La, second left: Greenley Rd, third left: Clearview La, first right: Wahackme Rd, second right: Arrowhead Trail, third right: Winfield La
Straight: N Stamford Rd, first left: Lakeside Dr, second left: High Ridge Rd 137, first right: High Ridge Rd 137

**Case Rd**

Straight: Newfield Av, Swan La, first left: Sanford La, second left: Denicola Rd, third left: Megan La, first right: Todd La, second right: Turner Rd, Belltown Rd, third right: Hirsch Rd, fourth right: Newfield Ct
Straight: Brinkerhoff Av, Silver Hill La, first left: Turner Rd, first right: Barrett Av, second right: Cody Dr, third right: Fara Dr

**Castle Ct**

Straight: Hope St, Hartford Av, first left: Chatfield St, second left: Riverbend Dr S, third left: Edgewood Av, fourth left: Viaduct Rd, first right: Barnstable La, second right: Avon La, third right: Short Hill St, fourth right: Omega Dr

# The Stamford Streets AZ

**Catoona La**
Alvord La, Myano La, Whitmore La

Straight: Havemeyer La, first left: Halsey Dr, second left: Stuart Dr, third left: Hassake Rd, fourth left: Boston Post Rd 1, E Putnam Av 1, Laddin Rock Rd, first right: MacArthur Dr, second right: Northridge Rd, third right: Palmer Hill Rd


**Cedar Cir**

Straight: Cedar Heights Rd, first left: Shadow Ridge Rd, second left: Dunn Av, third left: High Ridge Rd 137, first right: Alpine St, second right: Apple Tree La, third right: Duke Dr


**Cedar Heights Rd**
Rapids Rd, Clay Hill Rd, Duke Dr, Apple Tree La, Alpine St, Cedar Circle, Shadow Ridge Rd, Dunn Av

Straight: Wire Mill Rd, first left: Cedar Tree La, Hunting La, second left: Long Ridge Rd 104, first right: Four Brooks Rd, second right: Linwood La, third right: Red Fox Rd
Straight: High Ridge Rd 137, Turn Of River Rd, first left: Olga Dr, second

## The Stamford Streets AZ

left: Square Acre Dr, third left: Dunn Av, first right: Vine Rd, second right: Merriman Rd, third right: Donata La, fourth right: Bradley Pl

**Cedar St**
Ludlow St

Straight: Stone St, first right: Woodland Pl
Straight: Henry St, first left: Pacific St, second left: Garden St, third left: Atlantic St, first right: Canal St

**Cedar Tree La**

Straight: Wire Mill Rd, Hunting La, first left: Cedar Heights Rd, second left: Four Brooks Rd, third left: Linwood La, fourth left: Red Fox Rd, first right: Long Ridge Rd 104

**Cedar Wood Rd**
Pinewood Rd

Straight: Woodbine Rd, first left: Round Lake Rd, second left: Bittersweet La, third left: Fernwood Dr, first right: Brushwood Rd, second right: Pinewood Rd, third right: Mather Rd

# The Stamford Streets AZ

Straight: High Ridge Rd 137 first left: Pinner La, second left: Bartlett La, Skymeadow Dr, third left: N Stamford Rd, first right: Hoyclo Rd, Acre View Dr, second right: Bracchi Dr, Hoyclo Rd, third right: Hickory Rd, fourth right: Hickory Rd

**Center St**
Hallmark Pl, Faucett St, Morris St, Scofield Av, Goodwin St, Rose St, Center Terrace

Straight: Frisbee St, Brooklawn Av, first left: Howes Av, first right: Frisbie St, second right: Hope St
Straight: Church St, first left: Hope St, second left: Pine Hill Av, first right: Elm Tree Pl, second right: Parker Av, third right: Kirkham Pl, fourth right: Glenbrook Rd

**Center Ter**

Straight: Center St, first left: Rose St, second left: Goodwin St, third left: Scofield Av, first right: Church St

# The Stamford Streets AZ

**Central St**

Straight: Leonard St, first left: Dale Pl, first right: Summit Pl, second right: Belltown Rd
Straight: Toms Rd, first left: Summit Pl, second left: Belltown Rd, first right: Autumn La, second right: Dale Pl, third right: Overbrook Dr

**Cerretta St**
Columbus Pl

Straight: Highview Av, first left: Camp Av, first right: Mead St, second right: Bouton St, third right: Columbus Pl
Straight: Garland Dr, straight: Camp Av, first left: St John's Cemetery, second left: Greenwood Av, third left: Hoyt St 106, first right: Highview Av, second right: Ryan St, third right: Hope St

**Chapin La**

Straight: Quarry Rd, first left: Lakeside Dr, first right: Greenbrier La, second right: Blue Rock Dr, third right: New England Dr

# The Stamford Streets AZ

**Charles Mary La**

Straight: Hubbard Av, first left: Vuono Dr, second left: Grandview Av, third left: W North St, first right: Prince Pl, second right: Pellom Pl, third right: Woodmere Rd


**Charles St**
Avery St, Horton St

Straight: Dean St, straight: Cove Rd, first left: Seaside Av, second left: Avery St, third left: Horton St, first right: Dora St, second right: Euclid Av, third right: Albin Rd
Straight: George St
Robin St, Martin St, Elmwood St
Straight: Cove Rd, first left: Hobbie St, second left: Duffy St, third left: Blachley Rd, first right: Horton St, second right: Avery St, third right: Seaside Av


**Chatfield St**
Edgewood Av

Straight: Ridgewood Av, first left: Cleveland St, first right: Elizabeth Av
Straight: Hope St, first left: Hartford Av, Castle Ct, second left: Barnstable

# The Stamford Streets AZ

La, third left: Avon La, first right: Riverbend Dr S, second right: Edgewood Av, third right: Viaduct Rd

**Chatham Rd**

Straight: E Hunting Ridge Rd, first left: Dads La, Rock Rimmon Rd, second left: Saddle Hill Rd, third left: Briar Brae Rd, first right: Falmouth Rd, second right: Quaker Ridge Rd, third right: Heritage La

**Cherry Hill Rd**

Straight: Taconic Rd, first left: E Middle Patent Rd, second left: Stanwich Club, third left: Farms Rd, first right: Blue Spruce La, second right: Banksville Av
Straight: E Middle Patent Rd, first left: Barn Hill Rd, second left: Ledge Rd, first right: Taconic Rd

**Cherry St**

Straight: Elm St, Elm Ct, first left: S State St, E7 Governor John Davis Lodge Tpke I-95, E7 Governor John Davis Lodge Tpke I-95, second left: E7 Governor John

# The Stamford Streets AZ

Davis Lodge Tpke I-95, third left: N State St, E8 Governor John Davis Lodge Tpke I-95, fourth left: Stamford Plaza 1, Boston Post Rd 1, first right: Myrtle Av, Jefferson St, second right: Wardwell St, third right: Shippan Av, Cove Rd
Straight: Jefferson St, first left: Magee Av, second left: Halloween Blvd, third left: Elm St, Myrtle Av, first right: Harbor View Av, second right: Meadow St, third right: Canal St, Dock St

**Chester St**

Straight: Bedford St, 6th St, first left: 5th St, second left: 4th St, first right: Urban St, second right: Marlou La, third right: Locust La
Straight: Revonah Av, first left: Urban St, second left: Revonah Circle, third left: East La, first right: 5th St, second right: 4th St, third right: 3rd St

**Chesterfield Rd**

Straight: Shippan Av, first left: Ralsey Rd, second left: Gurley Rd, third left: Sagamore Rd, first right: Lanark Rd,

## The Stamford Streets AZ

second right: Downs Av, third right: Auldwood Rd, fourth right: Lanell Dr
Straight: Ocean Dr N
Lanark Rd, Auldwood Rd

**Chestnut Hill La**

Straight: Chestnut Hill Rd, first left: Jordan La, second left: W Haviland La, third left: Eagle Dr, first right: Webbs Hill Rd, second right: Long Ridge Rd 104, Butternut La

**Chestnut Hill Rd**
Webbs Hill Rd, Chestnut Hill La, Jordan La, W Haviland La, Eagle Dr, Ethan Allen La

Straight: Long Ridge Rd 104, Butternut La, first left: Hazard La, second left: Den Rd, third left: Midrocks Dr, first right: Hunting Ridge Rd, second right: Stone Hill Dr, third right: Partridge Rd
Straight: Scofieldtown Rd, first left: Brookdale Rd, second left: Haviland Rd, third left: Rock Rimmon Rd, first right: Georgian Ct, second right: Campbell Dr, third right: Woodley Rd

# The Stamford Streets AZ

**Chestnut St**

Straight: Adams Av, first left: W North St, Powell Pl, first right: Green St, second right: Vista St, third right: W Broad St
Straight: Anderson St, first left: Vista St, second left: W Broad St, first right: W North St, Woodcliff St

**Church St**
Center St, Elm Tree Pl, Parker Av, Kirkham Pl

Straight: Pine Hill Av, Hope St, first left: Rose St, second left: Colonial Rd, third left: Scofield Av, Pilgrim Walk, first right: Glendale Dr, second right: Union St, third right: Douglas Av
Straight: Glenbrook Rd, first left: Cowing Pl, second left: Arthur Pl, third left: Courtland Av 106, first right: Crescent St, second right: Scofield Av, third right: Windell Pl

**Cider Mill Rd**

Straight: Sawmill Rd, first left: Long Ridge Rd 104, first right: Wind Mill Circle, second right: Mill Stone Circle,

## The Stamford Streets AZ

third right: Dundee Rd, fourth right: Mill Stream Rd

**Claremont St**

Straight: Fairfield Av, first left: Barry Pl, second left: Burwood Av, third left: Dee La, fourth left: Top Gallant Rd, first right: Congress St, second right: Melrose Pl, third right: Liberty Pl
Straight: Burwood Av, first left: Beal St, second left: Noble St, third left: Keith St, first right: Fairfield Av

**Clark St**
Main St, W Park Pl, Summer St, Main St, Banks St

Straight: Main St, W Park Pl, Summer St, Main St, Banks St, first left: Washington Blvd 137, first right: Atlantic St

**Clarks Hill Av**

Straight: Boston Post Rd 1, Glenbrook Rd, first left: Crandall St, second left: Lindale St, third left: Broad St, fourth left: Grove St, Elm St, first

# The Stamford Streets AZ

right: Daly St, second right: Lafayette St, third right: Quintard Terrace, fourth right: N State St
Straight: N State St
Daly St, Lafayette St, S State St
Straight: Boston Post Rd 1, first left: Quintard Terrace, second left: Lafayette St, first right: Crystal St, second right: Myrtle Av, third right: Maple Av

**Clay Hill Rd**
Archer La, Timber La

Straight: Arden La
Straight: Cedar Heights Rd, first left: Rapids Rd, second left: Wire Mill Rd, third left: Cedar Tree La, Hunting La, first right: Duke Dr, second right: Apple Tree La, third right: Alpine St, fourth right: Cedar Circle

**Clearview Av**
Cady St, Buena Vista St, Bon Air Av, Tower Av, Knickerbocker Av

Straight: Southill St, straight: Knickerbocker Av
Straight: Hope St, first left: Largo Dr, second left: Bennett St, third left: Fahey St, first right: Omega Dr, second

# The Stamford Streets AZ

right: Short Hill St, third right: Avon La

## Cleveland St

Straight: Edgewood Av, first left: Chatfield St, first right: Hope St
Straight: Ridgewood Av, first right: Chatfield St, second right: Elizabeth Av

## Clifford Av
Rome Pl

Straight: Oaklawn Av, first left: Jamroga La, second left: Pepper Ridge Rd, third left: Vanech Dr, first right: Lindsey Av, second right: Dorlen Rd, third right: Newfield Av

## Clinton Av
Division St, Tresser Blvd 1, Boston Post Rd 1

Straight: Main St, first left: W Main St, Mill River St, first right: Rippowam Pl, second right: Washington Blvd 137, third right: W Park Pl, Summer St, Bank St, Clark St
Straight: Richmond Hill Av, first left: Washington Blvd, first right: Greenwich

# The Stamford Streets AZ

Av, second right: Mission St, third right: Rose Park


**Clorinda Ct**

Straight: Elaine Dr, first left: Florence Ct, second left: Woodridge Dr S, first right: Three Lakes Dr


**Clovelly Rd**
Scott Pl, Penzance Rd

Straight: Lafayette St, first left: Daskam Pl, Crystal St, second left: Boston Post Rd 1, third left: N State St, fourth left: E 8 Governor John Davis Lodge Tpke I-95, first right: Glenbrook Rd
Straight: Glenbrook Rd, first left: Hope St, second left: Lafayette St, third left: Arlington Rd, Daskam Pl, first right: Hamilton Av, second right: Howes Av, third right: Ely Pl, fourth right: Frankel Pl


**Clover Hill Dr**
Long Hill Dr, Evergreen Ct

Straight: Stillwater Rd, first left: River Hill Dr, second left: London La,

# The Stamford Streets AZ

third left: Stillview Rd, first right: Skyview Dr, second right: Logan's Run, third right: Westwood Rd, fourth right: Long Hill Dr, fifth right: Roxbury Rd, Long Ridge Rd 104
Straight: Long Ridge 104, first left: Stillwater Rd, Roxbury Rd, Buckingham Dr, second left: Barnes Rd, third left: Loughran Av, first right: Three Lakes Dr, second right: Woodridge Dr S, third right: Wishing Well La


**Club Circle**

Straight: Club Rd, first right: Malvern Rd, second right: Sandy La, third right: Kerr Rd


**Club Rd**
Bertmor Dr, Kerr Rd, Sandy La, Malvern Rd, Club Circle

Straight: Newfield Av, first left: Knox Rd, second left: Weed Hill Av, third left: Sterling Farms Golf Club, fourth left: Newfield Dr, first right: Vine Rd, second right: Gray Farms Rd, third right: Megan La, fourth right: Denicola Rd

# The Stamford Streets AZ

## Coachlamp La

Straight: Westover Rd, first left: Palmers Hill, first right: Sycamore Terrace, second right: Emery Dr E, third right: Bayberrie Dr

## Cody Dr

Straight: Turner Rd, first left: Barrett Av, second left: Brinkerhoff Av, third left: Newfield Av, first right: Pepper Ridge Rd, second right: High Clear Dr, third right: Sherwood Rd
Straight: Silver Hill La, first left: Fara Dr, second left: Pepper Ridge Rd, third left: Deer La, first right: Barrett Av, second right: Case Rd, Brinkerhoff Av

## Cogswell La

Straight: Canfield Dr, first left: Westover Rd, first right: Westover Rd

## Colahan St

Straight: Stillwater Av, first left: Liberty St, second left: Stillwater Pl, third left: Finney La, first right:

# The Stamford Streets AZ

Virgil St, second right: Merrell Av, third right: Corbo Terrace, fourth right: West Av

**Cold Spring Rd**
Severance Dr, Windsor Rd, Severance Dr, Windsor Rd, Washington Blvd 137, Travis Av, Old Barn Rd S, Randall Av, Long Ridge Rd 104

Straight: Stillwater Rd, first left: Knobloch La, Knoblock La, second left: Bridge St, third left: Halliwell Dr, first right: Pond Rd, second right: Stillview Rd, third right: London La, fourth right: River Hill Dr
Straight: High Ridge Rd 137, first left: Halpin Av, second left: Oaklawn Av, third left: Cross Rd, first right: Long Ridge Rd, Bedford St, Summer St

**Coleton Rd**

Straight: Hunting Ridge Rd, first left: Long Ridge Rd, first right: Boulder Brook Dr, second right: Surrey Rd, third right: Erickson Dr

**Colonial Rd**
Mayflower Av, Pilgrim Walk

# The Stamford Streets AZ

Straight: Strawberry Hill Av, first left: 5th St, second left: Hackett Circle, third left: Rock Spring Rd, fourth left: Strawberry Hill Ct, first right: Holbrook Dr, second right: Fieldstone La, Upland Rd, third right: Crane Rd, Newfield Av
Straight: Hope St, first left: Rose St, second left: Pine Hill Av, Church St, third left: Glendale Dr, first right: Pilgrim Walk, Scofield Av, second right: Plymouth Rd, third right: Rock Spring Rd, fourth right: Faucett St

**Colony Ct**

Straight: High Ridge Rd 137, High Clear Dr, first left: Brownley Dr, second left: Unity Rd, third left: Lakeview Dr, first right: High Ridge Rd, second right: Terrace Av, third right: McClean Av

**Columbus Pl**
Overlook Pl, River Pl

Straight: Cerretta St, first left: Garland Dr, first right: Highview Av
Straight: Highview Av, first left: Bouton St, second left: Mead St, third

# The Stamford Streets AZ

left: Cerretta St, first right: Woodway Rd

**Commerce Rd**

Straight: Harvard Av, first left: Boston Post Rd 1, first right: Ferris Av, second right: Grenhart Rd, E 6 Governor John Davis Lodge Tpke I-95, third right: Baxter Av, E 6 Governor John Davis Lodge Tpke I-95, fourth right: Ardmore Rd

**Congress St**
Silver St, Carlisle Pl, Keith St, Noble St, Beal St

Straight: Southfield Av, first left: Wells Av, second left: McClurg Av, third left: Burley Av, first right: Burwood Av, second right: Top Gallant Rd, Davenport Dr, third right: Cook Rd
Straight: Fairfield Av, first left: Claremont St, second left: Barry Pl, third left: Burwood Av, first right: Melrose Pl, second right: Liberty Pl, third right: Sunnyside Av

**Connecticut Av**
Myano La

# The Stamford Streets AZ

Straight: Stillwater Av, first left: Palmers Hill Rd, E Gaynor Brennan Golf Course, second left: Halliwell Dr, Bridge St, third left: Knobloch La, fourth left: Knoblock La, first right: W Broad St, second right: Oxford Ct, third right: Progress Dr, fourth right: West Av

## Connecticut Turnpike I-95

### South
E6: Harvard Av, Baxter Av, West Av, E7: Greenwich Av, S State St, E7: S State St, Canal St, E8: S State St, E8: Guernsey Av, S State St, Atlantic St, Elm St, Lafayette St, E9: Seaside Av, E9: Boston Post Rd 1, Seaside Av

### North
E9: Hamilton Av, Boston Post Rd 1, E8: Courtland Av 106, Boston Post Rd 1, Blachley Rd, E8: Maple Av, Myrtle Av, N State St, Lafayette St, Elm St, N State St, E8: Washington Blvd, N State St, E7: Canal St, E8: Atlantic St, N State St, Guernsey Av, E6: Grenhart Rd, West Av, Harvard Av

## Constance La
Bangall Rd

# The Stamford Streets AZ

Straight: Den Rd, first left: Hardesty Rd, second left: Flint Rock Rd, third left: Old Orchard La, first right: Barclay Dr, second right: E33 Merritt Pkwy 15, CT15

**Cook Rd**

Straight: Southfield Av, first left: Hickory Dr, second left: Eureka Terrace, first right: Top Gallant Rd, Davenport Dr, second right: Burwood Av, third right: Congress St
Straight: Davenport Dr, first left: Southfield Av, second left: Dolphin Cove Quay third left: Gatehouse Rd, first right: Eureka Terrace

**Coolidge Av**
Treat Av, Abel Av

Straight: Holcomb Av, first left: Cowan Av, second left: Hillandale Av, first right: Ardsley Rd, second right: Van Buren Circle, third right: Strawberry Hill Av
Straight: Rock Spring Rd, Puritan La, first left: Treat Av, second left: Mayflower Av, third left: Ardsley Rd, first right: Hope St

# The Stamford Streets AZ

**Coopers Pond Rd**
Stone Wall Dr

Straight: Lakeview Dr, first left: Stone Wall Dr, second left: High Ridge Rd 137, first right: Brook Run La

**Corbo Terrace**
Burr St

Straight: Tuttle St, straight: West Av first left: Leslie St, second left: St Nobile St, Moore St, third left: Minor Pl, fourth left: Nurney St, first right: Acosta St, Burr St, second right: Stillwater Av
Straight: Stillwater Av, first left: West Av, second left: Progress Dr, third left: Oxford Ct, first right: Merrell Av, second right: Virgil St, third right: Colahan St

**Corn Cake La**

Straight: Snow Crystal La, first left: Bradley Pl, second left: Wild Horse Rd, third left: Sun Dance Rd

**Country Club Rd**
Coventry Rd, Rolling Ridge Rd

# The Stamford Streets AZ

Straight: Mayapple Rd, first left: Russet Rd, second left: High Ridge Rd 137, first right: Boulderol Rd, second right: Tanglewood La, third right: Apple Valley Rd

**Court St**
W Washington Av

**Courtland Av 106**
Seaton Rd, Hamilton Av, Tremont Av, Fairmont Av, Lenox Av, Taylor Reed Pl, Maple Tree Av, Glen Terrace

Straight: Boston Post Rd 1, E9 Governor John Davis Lodge Tpke I-95, first left: E9 Governor John Davis Lodge Tpke I-95, second left: E9 Governor John Davis Lodge Tpke I-95, third left: Seaside Av, first right: Standish Rd, second right: Blachley Rd, third right: Maher Rd
Straight: Glenbrook Rd 106, first left: Arthur Pl, second left: Cowing Pl, third left: Church St, Kirkham Pl, first right: Research Dr, second right: Oakdale Rd, third right: Fresh Meadows La, Middlesex Rd

**Courtland Circle**
Daycroft Rd, Courtland Circle

# The Stamford Streets AZ

Straight: Blachley Rd, first left: Daycroft Rd, second left: Daycroft Rd, third left: Cove Rd, Willowbrook Av, first right: E9 Governor John Davis Lodge Tpke I-95, second right: Boston Post Rd


**Courtland Hill St**
Midland Av, Fairmont Av

Straight: Hamilton Av, first left: King St, second left: Hamilton Ct, third left: Brookside Dr, first right: Field St, second right: Courtland Av, third right: Maitland Rd, fourth right: Sutton Dr, Judy La
Straight: Lenox Av, first left: Midland Av, second left: Courtland Av 106


**Cousins Rd**

Straight: Larkspur Rd, first left: Hannahs Rd, first right: Very Merry Rd, second right: Skymeadow Dr


**Cove Rd**
Frederick St, Lockwood Av, Soundview Av, Leeds St, St Benedict Circle, Raymond St, Dale St, Van Buskirk Av, Cove Rd, Cove Rd, Ranson St, Blachley Rd,

# The Stamford Streets AZ

Willowbrook Av, Duffy St, Hobbie St, George St, Horton St, Avery St, Seaside Av, Dean St, Dora St, Euclid Av, Albin Rd, Island Heights Dr

Straight: Elm St, Shippan Av, first left: Wardwell St, second left: Hanover St, third left: Park St, first right: Frederick St, second right: Warren St
Straight: Weed Av
Weed Circle, Mathews St, Holly Cove Circle, Birch St
Straight: Boston Post Rd 1, first left: Hamilton Av, Waterbury Av, second left: Houston Terrace, first right: Brookside Dr, second right: Purdy La

**Cove View Dr**

Straight: Hamilton Av, first left: Boston Post Rd 1, Waterbury Av, first right: E9 Governor John Davis Lodge Tpke I-95, second right: De Bera La, third right: Brookside Dr, fourth right: Hamilton Ct

**Coventry Rd**
Rolling Ridge Rd

# The Stamford Streets AZ

Straight: Country Club Rd, first right: Rolling Ridge Rd, second right: Mayapple Rd

**Cow Path Dr**

Straight: Westover Rd, Riverbank Rd, Roxbury Rd, first left: Thunder Hill Dr, second left: Bangall Rd, third left: Windward La, first right: Old Mill La, second right: Winding Brook La

**Cowan Av**

Straight: Holcomb Av, first left: Hillandale Av, first right: Coolidge Av, second right: Ardsley Rd, third right: Van Buren Circle, fourth right: Strawberry Hill Av
Straight: Treat Av, first left: Coolidge Av, second left: Rock Spring Rd, first right: Hillandale Av, second right: Hope St

**Cowing Ct**

Straight: Cowing Pl, first left: Glenbrook Rd, first right: Cowing Terrace

# The Stamford Streets AZ

**Cowing Pl**
Cowing Terrace, Cowing Ct

Straight: Glenbrook Rd, first left: Arthur Pl, second left: Courtland Av 106, third left: Research Dr, first right: Church St, second right: Crescent St, third right: Scofield Av


**Cowing Terrace**

Straight: Cowing Pl, first left: Cowing Ct, second left: Glenbrook Rd


**Crab Apple Pl**

Straight: Winesap Rd, first left: Russet Rd, first right: McIntosh Rd, second right: Merriland Rd, Shady La


**Craig Ct**

Straight: High Ridge Rd 137, first left: Fairway Dr, second left: Raiding Stable Trail, third left: Trinity Pass, first right: Pound Ridge Country Club, second right: Old Snake Hill Rd, third right: Old Snake Hill Rd, fourth right: Upper Shad Rd

# The Stamford Streets AZ

**Crandall St**

Straight: Harding Av
Straight: Boston Post Rd 1, first left: Lindale St, second left: Broad St, third left: Elm St, Stamford Plaza 1, first right: Glenbrook Rd, Clarks Hill Av, second right: Daly St, third right: Lafayette St

**Crane Rd N**
Crane Rd

Straight: Crane Rd, first left: Newfield Av, Strawberry Hill Av

**Crane Rd**
Crane Rd N

Straight: Crane Rd N, first right: Crane Rd
Straight: Newfield Av, Strawberry Hill Av, first left: Burdick St, second left: Oaklawn Av, third left: Francis Av, first right: Fieldstone La, Upland Rd, second right: Holbrook Dr, third right: Colonial Rd

**Crescent St**
Arthur Pl

# The Stamford Streets AZ

Straight: Glenbrook Rd, first left: Scofield Av, second left: Windell Pl, third left: Frankel Pl, first right: Church St, Kirkham Pl, second right: Cowing Pl, third right: Arthur Pl
Straight: Taylor Reed Pl, first left: Courtland Av 106, Maple Tree Av

## Cresthill Pl

Straight: Fairview Av, first left: Shippan Av, second left: Brightside Dr, third left: Ocean Dr E, fourth left: Ocean View Dr, first right: Stamford Av, second right: Van Rensselaer Av, third right: Ocean Dr W
Straight: Sound Av, first left: Stamford Av, first right: Shippan Av

## Crestview Av
Klondike Av, Woodbury Av, Birchwood Rd

Straight: Bon Air Av, first left: Northwood Rd, second left: Tower Av, first right: Northwood Rd, second right: Clearview Av, Buena Vista St
Straight: Haig Av, first left: St Charles Av, second left: Joffre Av, third left: Pershing Av, first right: Gray Farms Rd, second right: Nyselius Pl, third right: Dagmar Pl

# The Stamford Streets AZ

**Crestwood Dr**
Hazelwood La, Hazelwood La, Dannell Dr

Straight: Pepper Ridge Rd, first left: Pepper Ridge Rd Pl, second left: Fawn Dr, third left: Harvest Hill La, first right: Kensington Rd, second right: White Birch La, third right: Silver Hill La
Straight: Dannell Dr, first left: Loveland Rd, second left: Woods End Rd, third left: High Ridge Rd 137, Mercedes La, first right: Crestwood Dr

**Cricket La**

Straight: Acre View Dr, first right: Daffodil Rd, second right: High Ridge Rd 137, Hoyclo Rd

**Crofts La**

Straight: Haviland Rd, first left: Hunting Ridge Rd, first right: Haviland Dr, second right: Wellington Dr, third right: E Hunting Ridge Rd, fourth right: W Haviland La

# The Stamford Streets AZ

**Crosby St**

Straight: Washington Blvd, first left: Pacific St, first right: Atlantic St, second right: Pulaski St, third right: W Henry St, Henry St
Straight: Pacific St, first left: Remington St, second left: Walter Wheeler Dr, E Walnut St, third left: Woodland Pl, first right: Belden St, second right: Dyke La, third right: Washington Blvd

**Cross Country Trail**

Straight: Haviland Rd, first left: Haviland Ct, second left: Deerfield Dr, third left: Hickory Farm, first right: W Haviland La, second right: E Hunting Ridge Rd, third right: Wellington Dr

**Cross Rd**

Straight: High Ridge Rd 137, first left: Dubois St, second left: McClean Av, third left: Terrace Av, first right: Oaklawn Av, second right: Halpin Av, third right: Cold Spring Rd
Straight: Long Ridge Rd 104, first left: Cold Spring Rd, Cold Spring Rd 137, second left: High Ridge Rd, Summer St,

# The Stamford Streets AZ

Bedford St, first right: McClean Av, second right: Terrace Av, third right: Stark Pl, fourth right: River Ridge Ct

**Crystal Lake Rd**
Beechwood Rd, Ashton Rd, Wilder Rd

**Crystal St**
Culloden Rd, Hundley Ct, Peveril Rd, Quintard Terrace

Straight: Daskam Pl, Lafayette St, first left: Boston Post Rd 1, second left: N State St, third left: E8 Governor John Davis Lodge Tpke I-95, first right: Clovelly Rd, second right: Glenbrook Rd Straight: Boston Post Rd 1, first left: Myrtle Av, second left: Maple Av, third left: Lincoln Av, first right: N State St, second right: Quintard Terrace, third right: Lafayette St

**Culloden Rd**
Scott Pl, Penzance Rd, Hamilton Av, Ely Pl

Straight: Crystal St, first left: Boston Post Rd 1 (E Main St), first right: Hundley Ct, Peveril Rd, second right:

# The Stamford Streets AZ

Quintard Terrace, third right: Lafayette St, Daskam Pl
Straight: Frankel Pl, straight: Glenbrook Rd, first left: Ely Pl, second left: Howes Av, third left: Hamilton Av, first right: Windell Pl, second right: Scofield Av, third right: Crescent St


**Cumming Park Rd**

Straight: Shippan Av, first left: Seaview Av, second left: Magee Av, Harbor Dr, third left: Lindstrom Rd, first right: Park St, second right: Hanover St


**Cummings Av**

Straight: Park St, first left: Frederick St, first right: Shippan Av
Straight: Wardwell St, first left: Shippan Av, second left: Elm St, first right: Frederick St, second right: Soundview Av


**Cummings Point Rd**
Gatehouse Rd

Straight: Shore Rd, Fairfield Av, first left: Tomac La, second left: Tomac Av,

# The Stamford Streets AZ

third left: Tait Rd, Ford La, first right: Hendrie Ct, second right: Top Gallant Rd, third right: Dee La

**Cushing St**

Straight: Hope St, Northill St, first left: Bennett St, second left: largo Dr, third left: Clearview Av, first right: Hyde St, second right: Knapp St, Greenway St, third right: Camp Av

**Custer St**

Straight: Lawn La, Helen Pl, first left: Leroy Pl, second left; Hamilton Av, first right: Trumbull Gate, second right: Sherman St
Straight: Sheridan St, Lincoln Av

**Cypress Dr**
New England Dr

# The Stamford Streets AZ

## D

**Dads La**
E Hunting Ridge Rd

Straight: Rock Rimmon Rd, first left: Saddle Hill Rd, second left: Briar Brae Rd, third left: Mill Rd, first right: Ridge Tree La, second right: Pin Oak Circle, third right: Rock Rimmon Dr

**Daffodil Rd**

Straight: Acre View Dr, first left: High Ridge Rd 137, Hoyclo Rd

**Dagmar Pl**
Dagmar Rd

Straight: Haig Av, first left: Knox Rd, Upper Haig Av

**Dagmar Rd**

Straight: Nyselius Pl, first left: Haig Av
Straight: Dagmar Pl, first right: Haig Av

# The Stamford Streets AZ

**Dairy View La**

Straight: Davenport Ridge La, first left: Davenport Ridge Rd, Zora La

**Dale Pl**

Straight: Toms Rd, first left: Autumn La, second left: Central St, third left: Summit Pl, first right: Overbrook Dr, second right: Deleo Dr, third right: Rutz St
Straight: Leonard St, first right: Central St, second right: Summit Pl, third right: Belltown Rd

**Dale St**
St Benedict Circle, Cove Rd, Ursula Pl, Ursula Pl, Woodrow St, William St, Lillian St

Straight: Frank St
Lockwood Av
Straight: Maple Av, first left: Gregory St, second left: William St, third left: Warren St, first right: E8 Governor John Davis Lodge Tpke I-95, second right: Boston Post Rd 1

# The Stamford Streets AZ

## Daly St

Straight: Boston Post Rd 1, first left: Glenbrook Rd, Clarks Hill Av, second left: Crandall St, third left: Lindale St, first right: Lafayette St, second right: Quintard Terrace, third right: N State St
Straight: N State St, first left: Lafayette St, second left: S State St, third left: Boston Post Rd 1, first right: Clarks Hill Av

## Dancy Dr

Straight: W Hill Rd, first left: Green Tree La, second left: Carriage Dr, third left: Stony Brook Dr, first right: MacGregor Dr, second right: Drum Hill La, third right: W Hill La

## Dann Dr
Turner Rd

Straight: Oaklawn Av, first left: Sherwood Rd, second left: Vanech Dr, third left: Pepper Ridge Rd, first right: Fairfield Memorial Park Cemetery, second right: Dartley St, third right: Camore St

# The Stamford Streets AZ

Straight: High Clear Dr, first left: Unity Rd, second left: Kijek St, third left: High Ridge Rd 137, Colony Ct, first right: Turner Rd


**Dannell Dr**
Crestwood Dr, Loveland Rd, Woods End Rd

Straight: Crestwood Dr, first left: Pepper Ridge Rd, first right: Hazelwood La, second right: Hazelwood La, third right: Dannell Dr
Straight: High Ridge Rd 137, Mercedes La, first left: Knollwood Av, second left: Longview Av, third left: Loveland Rd W, first right: Yale Ct, second right: Janice Rd, third right: Ridge Park Av


**Dartley St**
Edice Rd

Straight: Oaklawn Av, first left: Fairfield Memorial Park Cemetery, second left: Dann Dr, third left: Sherwood Rd, first right: Camore St, second right: Stanwick Pl, third right: Benstone St

# The Stamford Streets AZ

**Daskam Pl**

Straight: Lafayette St, Crystal St, first left: Clovelly Rd, second left: Glenbrook Rd, first right: Boston Post Rd 1, second right: N State St, third right: E8 Governor John Davis Lodge Tpke I-95
Straight: Glenbrook Rd, Arlington Rd, first left: Boston Post Rd 1, Clarks Hill Av, first right: Lafayette St, second right: Hope St, third right: Clovelly Rd


**Davenport Dr**
Cook Rd, Hickory Dr, Eureka Terrace

Straight: Southfield Av, Top Gallant Rd, first left: Cook Rd, second left: Hickory Dr, third left: Eureka Terrace, first right: Burwood Av, second right: Congress St, third right: Wells Av


**Davenport Farm La E**
Davenport Farm La N

Straight: Davenport Ridge Rd, first left: Thornridge Dr, second left: Skyview La, third left: Ponus Ridge, first right: Thornridge Dr, second

# The Stamford Streets AZ

right: Davenport Farm La W, third right: Jeanne Ct

**Davenport Farm La N**

Straight: Davenport Farm La E, first right: Davenport Ridge Rd
Straight: Davenport Farm La W, first left: Davenport Farm La S, second left: Davenport Ridge Rd

**Davenport Farm La S**

Straight: Davenport Farm La W, first left: Davenport Farm La N, first right: Davenport Ridge Rd

**Davenport Farm La W**
Davenport Farm La N, Davenport Farm La S

Straight: Davenport Ridge Rd, first left: Thornridge Dr, second left: Davenport Farm La E, third left: Thornridge Dr, first right: Jeanne Ct, second right: Zora La, Davenport Ridge La, third right: Lakeside Dr, Newfield Av

# The Stamford Streets AZ

**Davenport Ridge La**
Dairy View La

Straight: Davenport Ridge Rd, Zora La, first left: Lakeside Dr, Newfield Av, first right: Jeanne Ct, second right: Davenport Farm La W, third right: Thornridge Dr

**Davenport Ridge Rd**
Skyview La, Thornridge Dr, Davenport Farm La E, Thornridge Dr, Davenport Farm La W, Jeanne Ct, Zora La, Davenport Ridge La

Straight: Lakeside Dr, Newfield Av, first left: N Meadows La, second left: Eden Rd, third left: Wedgemere Rd, first right: Interlaken Rd, second right: Quarry Rd, third right: N Stamford Rd, Cascade Rd
Straight: Ponus Ridge, first left: Thurton Dr, second left: Frogtown Rd, third left: Bartling Dr, first right: Adams La, second right: Sagamore Trail, third right: Skyview La

**Davenport St**

Straight: Selleck St

## The Stamford Streets AZ

Greenwich Av, Southfield Av, Orchard St, Fairfield Av, Fairfield Av, Vassar Av, Irving Av, Bonner St, Durant St, Montauk Dr, Betts Av, West Av, Outlook St, Harvard Av
Straight: Brown House Rd, first left: Harding Rd, second left: Kensington Ct, first right: Harvard Av, Warshaw Pl
Straight: Greenwich Av, first left: Milton St, second left: Selleck St, third left: Homestead Av, first right: Pulaski St, second right: First Stamford Pl, third right: S State St, E7 Governor John Davis Lodge Tpke I-95

**Daycroft Rd Cir**

Straight: Blachley Rd, first left: Daycroft Rd, second left: Cove Rd, Willowbrook Av, first right: Daycroft Rd, second right: Courtland Circle, third right: E9 Governor John Davis Lodge Tpke I-95
Straight: Blachley Rd, first left: Daycroft Rd, second left: Cove Rd, first right: Courtland Circle, second right: E 9 Governor John Davis Lodge Tpke I-95, third right: Boston Post Rd 1

# The Stamford Streets AZ

## Daycroft Rd

Straight: Courtland Circle, first left: Blachley Rd, first right: Courtland Circle

## De Bera La

Straight: Hamilton Av, first left: Brookside Dr, second left: Hamilton Ct, third left: King St, first right: E 9 Governor John Davis Lodge Tpke I-95, second right: Cove View Dr, third right: Boston Post Rd 1

## Deacon Hill Rd

Straight: Brownley Dr, first right: Wood La, second right: High Ridge Rd 137

## Dean St

Straight: Cove Rd, first left: Horton St, second left: George St, third left: Hobbie St, first right: Dora St, second right: Euclid Av, third right: Albin Rd
Straight: Charles St
Avery St, Horton St
Straight: George St

# The Stamford Streets AZ

**Dee La**

Straight: Fairfield Av, first left: Burwood Av, second left: Barry Pl, third left: Claremont St, first right: Top Gallant Rd, second right: Hendrie Ct, third right: Shore Rd, Cummings Point Rd

**Deep Spring La**
Old Well Rd

Straight: Hope St, first left: Camelot Ct, second left: Slice Dr, third left: Eden Rd, E Cross Rd, first right: Nottingham Dr, second right: Mary Violet Rd, third right: Putter Dr

**Deep Valley Rd**
High Valley Way

Straight: Riverbank Rd, first left: Farms Rd, second left: Rocky Rapids Rd, third left: Wildwood Rd, first right: Ridgecrest Rd, second right: Riverbank Dr, third right: June Rd

# The Stamford Streets AZ

**Deep Valley Trl**

Straight: Deep Valley Rd, first left: High Valley Way, second left: Riverbank Rd

**Deepwood Rd**

Straight: Eagle Dr, first left: Chestnut Hill Rd

**Deer La**

Straight: Silver Hill La, first left: Pepper Ridge Rd, second left: Fara Dr, third left: Cody Dr, first right: Loveland Rd W
Straight: White Birch La, first left: Loveland Rd, second left: Lantern Circle, third left: Dannell Dr, first right: Pepper Ridge Rd

**Deer Meadow La**

Straight: Jonathan Dr, first left: S Brook Dr, first right: Erskine Rd

# The Stamford Streets AZ

### Deerfield Dr

Straight: Haviland Rd, first left: Hickory Farm, second left: Spinning Wheel La, third left: Scofieldtown Rd, first right: Haviland Ct, second right: Cross Country Trail, third right: W Haviland La

### Delaware Av

Straight: Carolina Rd: straight: Merrell Av, first left: W Broad St, first right: Edison Rd, second right: Stillwater Av Straight: W Broad St, first left: Stillwater Av, second left: Connecticut Av, third left: Palmers Hill Rd, E Gaynor Brennan Golf Course, first right: Merrell Av, second right: Rachelle Av, third right: Shelburne Rd

### Deleo Dr

Straight: Toms Rd, first left: Overbrook Dr, second left: Dale Pl, third left: Autumn La, first right: Rutz St, second right: Derwin St, third right: Hope St

# The Stamford Streets AZ

**Delwood Rd**

Straight: Rock Rimmon Rd, first left: Mayapple Rd, second left: Breezy Hill Rd, third left: Golden Farm Rd, first right: Pond View La, second right: Winslow Dr, third right: Old Long Ridge Rd


**Deming La**

Straight: Blackwood La, first left: Opper Rd, second left: Wire Mill Rd


**Den Rd**
Arrow Head Dr, Old Orchard La, Flint Rock Rd, Hardesty Rd, Constance La, Bangall Rd, Barclay Dr

Straight: Long Ridge Rd 104, first left: Hazard La, second left: Butternut La, third left: Chestnut Hill Rd, first right: Midrocks Dr, second right: Northwood La, third right: Webbs Hill Rd, fourth right: E34 Merritt Pkwy 15, CT15
Straight: E33 Merritt Pkwy 15, CT15


**Den Rd**
Walter La, Doolittle Rd

# The Stamford Streets AZ

Straight: E33 Merritt Pkwy 15, CT15
Straight: Roxbury Rd, first left: Munko Dr, second left: Barncroft Rd, third left: Doral Farms Rd, first right: Roxbury Terrace, second right: Westover Rd, third right: Cow Path Dr, Riverbank Rd

**Denicola Rd**

Straight: Newfield Av, first left: Megan La, second left: Gray Farms Rd, third left: Vine Rd, first right: Sanford La, second right: Case Rd, Swan La, third right: Todd La

**Denise Dr**
Denise Pl

Straight: Fawn Dr, first left: Pepper Ridge Rd

**Denise Pl**

Straight: Denise Dr, first right: Fawn Dr

# The Stamford Streets AZ

**Depinedo Av**

Straight: Nobile St, first left: West Av, Moore St
Straight: Acosta St, first right: West Av, Burr St

**Derry St**

Straight: Dunn Av, first left: Peak St, second left: Alpine St, third left: Dunn Av Ext, first right: Winter St, second right: Dunn Ct, third right: Finch St

**Derwin St**

Straight: Toms Rd, first left: Rutz St, second left: Deleo Dr, third left: Overbrook Dr, first right: Hope St
Straight: Glen Av, Glendale Dr, first left: Hope St, first right: Rutz St

**Diamondcrest La**

Straight: High Ridge Rd 137, first left: Meredith La, second left: Scofieldtown Rd, third left: Interlaken Rd, first right: Blue Ridge Dr, second right: Perna La, third right: Pine Hill Terrace

# The Stamford Streets AZ

Straight: Redmont Rd, straight: Opper Rd, first left: High Ridge Rd 137, first right: Blackwood La

**Diaz St**
Piave St

Straight: Boston Post Rd 1, first left: West Av, second left: Aberdeen St, third left: Harvard Av, first right: Virgil St, second right: Victory St, third right: Liberty St
Straight: Grenhart Rd, first left: Victory St, first right: West Av, E 6 Governor John Davis Lodge Tpke I-95, second right: Harvard Av, E 6 Governor John Davis Lodge Tpke I-95

**Division St**
Clinton Av

Straight: Washington Blvd, first left: Tresser Blvd 1, second left: Bell St, third left: Rippowam Pl, first right: Richmond Hill Av, second right: N State St, E 8 Governor John Davis Lodge Tpke I-95, third right: S State St

# The Stamford Streets AZ

**Dock St**

Straight: John St
Manhattan St
Straight: Market St
Straight: Jefferson St, Canal St, first left: S State, E 7 Governor John Davis Lodge Tpke I-95, second left: N State St, E 7 Governor John Davis Lodge Tpke I-95, third left: Stamford Forum 1, Stamford Plaza 1, first right: Market St, second right: Henry St, third right: Ludlow St


**Dogwood Ct**
Honey Hill Rd

Straight: Dogwood La, first left: Webbs Hill Rd, first right: Briarwood La, second right: Webbs Hill Rd


**Dogwood La**
Dogwood Ct, Briarwood La

Straight: Webbs Hill Rd, first left: Pheasant La, second left: Long Ridge Rd, first right: Dogwood La, second right: Jeffrey La, third right: Lynam Rd
Straight: Webbs Hill Rd, first left: Dogwood La, second left: Pheasant La, third left: Long Ridge Rd, first right:

# The Stamford Streets AZ

Jeffrey La, second right: Lynam Rd, third right: Huckleberry Hollow, fourth right: Chestnut Hill Rd

**Dolphin Cove Quay**
Flying Cloud Rd, Half Moon Way, Joshua Slocum Dock, Gypsy Moth Landing

Straight: Top Gallant Rd, first left: Gatehouse Rd, second left: Fairfield Av, first right: Southfield Av, Davenport Dr

**Dolsen Pl**

Straight: North St, first left: Bedford St, second left: Prospect St, first right: Summer St, second right: Franklin St, third right: Washington Blvd 137 Straight: Bedford St, first left: Hoyt St, second left: Oak St, third left: 1st St, first right: North St, second right: Walton Pl, third right: Forest St, fourth right: Prospect St, Spring St

**Don Bob Rd**
Arbor Rd

# The Stamford Streets AZ

## Donald Rd

Straight: Gray Farms Rd, first left: Newfield Av, first right: Mitzi Rd, second right: Haig Av
Straight: Mitzi Rd, straight: Gray Farms Rd, first left: Donald Rd, second left: Newfield Av, first right: Haig Av

## Donata La

Straight: Vine Pl, first right: Saxon Ct
Straight: High Ridge Rd 137, first left: Bradley Pl, second left: Tally Ho La, third left: Maplewood Pl, first right: Merriman Rd, second right: Vine Rd, third right: Turn Of River Rd, Cedar Heights Rd

## Doolittle Rd
Pakenmer Rd, MacArthur La

Straight: Den Rd, first left: Roxbury Rd, first right: Walter La, second right: E33 Merritt Pkwy 15, CT15

## Dora St
Neponsit St

# The Stamford Streets AZ

Straight: Webb Av, Middlebury St, first right: Webster Rd, second right: Andover Rd, third right: Cambridge Rd
Straight: Cove Rd, first left: Euclid Av, second left: Albin Rd, third left: Island Heights Dr, first right: Dean St, second right: Seaside Av, third right: Avery St

**Doral Farms Rd**
Farm Hill Rd, Farm Hill Rd, Alfred La

Straight: Roxbury Rd, first left: Barncroft Rd, second left: Munko Dr, third left: Den Rd, first right: Overhill Rd, second right: W Hill Rd, third right: Stillwater Rd, Long Ridge Rd 104, Buckingham Dr

**Doris La**
Briar Wood Trail

Straight: Briar Brae Rd, first left: Rock Rimmon Rd, first right: Shady La, second right: High Ridge Rd 137

**Dorlen Rd**

Straight: Oaklawn Av, first left: Newfield Av, first right: Lindsey Av,

# The Stamford Streets AZ

second right: Clifford Av, third right: Jamroga La, fourth right: Pepper Ridge Rd

**Dorset La**

Straight: Regent Ct, first left: Woodway Rd

**Douglas Av**

Straight: Hope St, first left: Union St, second left: Glendale Dr, third left: Pine Hill Av, Church St, first right: Glen Av, second right: Toms Rd, third right: Viaduct Rd

**Downs Av**
Ralph St, Whittaker St

Straight: Shippan Av, first left: Auldwood Rd, second left: Lanell Dr, third left: Mitchell St, first right: Lanark Rd, second right: Chesterfield Rd, third right: Ralsey Rd

# The Stamford Streets AZ

**Drum Hill La**

Straight: W Hill Rd, first left: W Hill Rd, second left: Roxbury Rd, first right: MacGregor Dr, second right: Dancy Dr, third right: Green Tree La

**Dryden St**

Straight: Virgil St, first left: Minor Pl, second left: Stillwater Av, first right: Boston Post Rd 1

**Dubois St**
Halpin Av, Cantwell Av

Straight: High Ridge Rd 137, first left: Cross Rd, second left: Oaklawn Av, third left: Halpin Av, first right: McClean Av, second right: Terrace Av, third right: High Ridge Rd, fourth right: Colony Ct, High Clear Dr

**Duck Way**

Straight: Stillwater Rd, first left: Pond Rd, second left: Stillview Rd, first right: Cold Spring Rd, second right: Knoblock La, third right: Bridge St

# The Stamford Streets AZ

**Duffy St**
Givens Av, Palmer Av

Straight: Sylvan Knoll Rd
Straight: Cove Rd, first left: Hobbie St, second left: George St, third right: Horton St, first right: Blachley Rd, Willowbrook Av, second right: Ranson St, Cove Rd, third right: Cove Rd, fourth right: Van Buskirk Av

**Duke Dr**
Jay Rd

Straight: Cedar Heights Rd, first left: Apple Tree La, second left: Alpine St, third left: Cedar Circle, first right: Clay Hill Rd, second right: Rapids Rd, third right: Wire Mill Rd

**Dulan Dr**

Straight: Mill Rd, first left: Mill Spring La, second left: Mohawk Trail, third left: Old Long Ridge Rd, first right: Gatewood Rd, second right: Rock Rimmon Rd

# The Stamford Streets AZ

**Duncanson St**

Straight: Travis Av, first right: Reynolds Av, second right: Cold Spring Rd
Straight: Borglum St, Austin Av, first left: Reynolds Av, first right: Berges Av


**Dundee Rd**
Forestwood Dr, Timber Mill Rd

Straight: Sawmill Rd, first left: Mill Stream Rd, first right: Mill Stone Circle, second right: Wind Mill Circle, third right: Cider Mill Rd, fourth right: Long Ridge Rd 104


**Dunn Av Ext**

Straight: Dunn Av, first left: High Ridge Rd 137, first right: Alpine St, second right: Peak St, third right: Derry St


**Dunn Av**
Finch St, Dunn Ct, Winter St, Derry St, Peak St, Alpine St, Dunn Av Ext

# The Stamford Streets AZ

Straight: Cedar Heights Rd, first left: High Ridge Rd, Turn Of River Rd, first right: Shadow Ridge Rd, second right: Cedar Circle, third right: Alpine St
Straight: High Ridge Rd 137, first left: E 35 Merritt Pkwy 15, CT15, Buxton Farm Rd, E 35 Merritt Pkwy 15, CT15, second left: High Ridge Rd, third left: E 35 Merritt Pkwy 15, CT15, fourth left: Wire Mill Rd, first right: Square Acre Dr, second right: Olga Dr, third right: Cedar Heights Rd, Turn Of River Rd

## Dunn Ct

Straight: Dunn Av, first left: Winter St, second left: Derry St, third left: Peak St, first right: Finch St, second right: Cedar Heights Rd

## Durant St

Straight: Amelia Pl, first left: Bonner St, second left: Selleck St, Irving Av, first right: Betts Av, second right: Selleck St
Straight: Selleck St, Montauk Dr, first left: Betts Av, second left: West Av, third left: Outlook St, first right: Bonner St, Irving Av, second right: Vassar Av, third right: Fairfield Av

# The Stamford Streets AZ

**Dyke La**
Harbor St, Manor St

Straight: Pacific St, Washington Blvd, first left: Washington Blvd, first right: Belden St, second right: Crosby St, third right: Remington St
Straight: Elmcroft Rd
Rugby St, Belden St, Remington St, E Walnut St
Straight: Woodland Pl, first left: Stone St, second left: Pacific St, first right: Woodland Cemetery

**Dzamba Grove**

Straight: Somerset La, first right: Hampton La, second right: Perna La

# The Stamford Streets AZ

## E

### E Cross Rd

Straight: Eden Rd, Hope St, first left: Slice Dr, second left: Camelot Ct, third left: Deep Spring La, first right: Broad Brook La, W Cross Rd, second right: Woodway Ridge La, Ponus Ridge
Straight: Hawks Hill Rd, first left: W Cross Rd, second left: Ponus Ridge


### E Gaynor Brennan Golf Course

Straight: Stillwater Rd, Palmers Hill Rd, first left: Connecticut Av, second left: W Broad St, first right: Halliwell Dr, Bridge St, second right: Knobloch La


### E Hunting Ridge Rd
Hillsbury La, Heritage La, Quaker Ridge Rd, Falmouth Rd, Chatham Rd

Straight: Haviland Rd, first left: W Haviland La, second left: Cross Country Trail, third left: Haviland Ct, first right: Wellington Dr, second right: Haviland Dr, third right: Crofts La
Straight: Dads La, Rock Rimmon Rd, first right: Ridge Tree La, second right: Pin Oak Circle, third right: Rock Rimmon Dr

# The Stamford Streets AZ

**E Main St**
Suburban Av, Grove St, Elm St

Straight: Greyrock Pl, first left: Stamford Forum, Stamford Plaza 1, Canal St, first right: Broad St, second right: Forest St, third right: Grove St


**E Main St**
Broad St, Lindale St, Crandall St, Glenbrook Rd, Clarks Hill Av, Daly St, Lafayette St, Quintard Terrace, N State St, Crystal St, Myrtle Av, Maple Av, Lincoln Av, Lockwood Av, Grant Av, Lawn Av, Seaton Rd, Noroton Hill Pl, Maher Rd, Blachley Rd, Standish Rd, E9 Governor John Davis Lodge Tpke I-95, E9 Governor John Davis Lodge Tpke I-95, Courtland Av, E9 Governor John Davis Lodge Tpke I-95, E9 Governor John Davis Lodge Tpke I-95, Seaside Av, Home Ct, Houston Terrace, Hamilton Av, Waterbury Av, Weed Av, Brookside Dr, Purdy La

Straight: Main St, straight: Elm St, Grove St, Stamford Plaza
Straight: Darien Post Rd, Purdy La


**E Middle Patent Rd**
Cherry Hill Rd, Barn Hill Rd, Ledge Rd, Hidden Valley Way, Hope's Farm La,

# The Stamford Streets AZ

Mianus River Rd, St Marys Church Rd, Hickory Kingdom Rd, Cedar Hill Rd, Rustling La, Little Town La

Straight: Taconic Rd, first left: Stanwich Club, second left: Farms Rd, third left: N Stanwich Rd, first right: Cherry Hill Rd, second right: Blue Spruce La, third right: Banksville Av
Straight: Middle Patent Rd, Rustling La, Little Town La

**E Ridge Rd**
Midrocks Dr

**E Walnut St**

Straight: Walter Wheeler Dr, Pacific St, first left: Remington St, second left: Crosby St, third left: Belden St, first right: Woodland Pl, second right: Woodland Av, Ludlow St, third right: Henry St
Straight: Elmcroft Rd, first left: Woodland Pl, first right: Remington St, second right: Belden St, third right: Rugby St

**Eagle Dr**
Deepwood Rd

# The Stamford Streets AZ

Straight: Chestnut Hill Rd, first left: W Haviland La, second left: Jordan La, third left: Chestnut Hill La, first right: Ethan Allen La, second right: Scofieldtown Rd

**East Av**

Straight: Van Buskirk Av, first left: Sachem Pl, second left: Caldwell Av, third left: Cove Rd
Straight: Soundview Av, first left: James St, second left: McMullen Av, third left: Tupper Dr, first right: McMullen Av, second right: Limerick St, third right: Wardwell St

**East La**
West La

Straight: Revonah Av, Revonah Circle, Urban St, first left: Revonah Circle S, first right: Bedford St
Straight: West La
Northwoods Rd, Toilsome Brook Rd
Straight: East La, first left: West La, first right: Revonah Circle

# The Stamford Streets AZ

### Easthill Rd

Straight: Ridgecrest Rd, first left: Riverbank Rd, first right: Rocky Rapids Rd

### Eastover Rd

Straight: Shadow La, Intervale Rd E, first left: Newfield Av, first right: Intervale Rd, Newfield Dr

### Echo Hill Dr

Straight: Long Ridge Rd 104, first left: Old Long Ridge Rd, second left: Rockrimmon Country Club, third left: White Birch Rd, fourth left: Lower Shad Rd, first right: N Lake Dr, second right: Parsonage Rd, third right: Erskine Rd, fourth right: Grey Birch Rd

### Eden La

Straight: Eden Rd, first left: Newfield Av, first right: Parry Rd, second right: Twin Brook Dr, third right: Woodbrook Dr

# The Stamford Streets AZ

### Eden Rd
Eden La, Parry Rd, Twin Brook Dr, Woodbrook Dr, Old Well Rd, Friars La

Straight: Newfield Av, first left: Wedgemere Rd, second left: White Oak La, third left: Emerald La, first right: N Meadows La, second right: Lakeside Dr, Davenport Ridge Rd
Straight: Hope St, E Cross Rd, first left: Broad Brook La, W Cross Rd, Ponus Ridge, first right: Slice Dr, second right: Camelot Ct, third right: Deep Spring La, fourth right: Nottingham Dr

### Edgewood Av
Cleveland St

Straight: Hope St, first left: Riverbend Dr S, second left: Chatfield St, third left: Hartford Av, Castle Ct, first right: Viaduct Rd, second right: Toms Rd, third right: Glen Av
Straight: Chatfield St, first left: Ridgewood Av, first right: Hope St

### Edice Rd

Straight: Dartley St, first right: Oaklawn Av

# The Stamford Streets AZ

Straight: Camore St, straight: Oaklawn Av, first left: Dartley St, second left: Fairfield Memorial Park Cemetery, third left: Dann Dr, first right: Stanwick Pl, second right: Benstone St, third right: Northwoods Rd

**Edison Rd**

Straight: Shelburne Rd, first left: W Broad St, Rachelle Av
Straight: Merrell Av, first left: Stillwater Av, first right: Carolina Rd, second right: W Broad St

**Edward Pl**
Albert Pl, Whistler Pl

Straight: Todd La, first left: Maryanne La, second left: Pershing Av, third left: Haig Av, first right: Newfield Av

**Eighth St, 8th St**
Weil St

Straight: Summer St, first left: Hoover Av, second left: Bedford St, Long Ridge Rd, High Ridge Rd, first right: 7th St, second right: Bridge St, third right: 6th St

# The Stamford Streets AZ

Straight: Waterford La
7th St


**Elaine Dr**
Clorinda Ct, Florence Ct, Woodridge Dr S

Straight: Three Lakes Dr, first right: Bridle Path Rd, second right: Long Ridge Rd 104


**Eliot La**

Straight: Alexandra Dr, first right: High Ridge Rd 137


**Elizabeth Av**
Selby Pl, Ridgewood Av

Straight: Marian St, first right: St Charles Av, Woodbury Av
Straight: Knickerbocker Av, first left: Hartford Av, second left: St Charles Av, third left: Southill St


**Eljays La**

Straight: Winding Brook La, first right: Westover Rd

# The Stamford Streets AZ

**Elm Ct**

Straight: Elm St, first left: Cherry St, second left: Jefferson St, Myrtle Av, third left: Wardwell St, first right: S State St, E 8 Governor John Davis Lodge Tpke I-95, second right: N State St, E 8 Governor John Davis Lodge Tpke I-95, third right: Stamford Plaza 1, Boston Post Rd 1

**Elm St**
N State St, E 8 Governor John Davis Lodge Tpke I-95, S State St, E 8 Governor John Davis Lodge Tpke I-95, Elm Ct, Cherry St, Jefferson St, Myrtle Av, Wardwell St

Straight: Grove St, Boston Post Rd 1, Stamford Plaza 1, first left: Greyrock Pl, Canal St, second left: Tresser Blvd, Town Center Dr, first right: Broad St, second right: Lindale St, third right: Crandall St
Straight: Shippan Av, Cove Rd, first left: Frederick St, second left: Warren St, first right: Wardwell St, second right: Hanover St, third right: Park St

# The Stamford Streets AZ

**Elm Tree Pl**

Straight: Union St, first left: Hope St, first right: Kirkham Pl
Straight: Church St, first left: Parker Av, second left: Kirkham Pl, third left: Glenbrook Rd, first right: Center St, second right: Hope St, Pine Hill Av

**Elmbrook Dr**
Marie Pl, Tioga Pl

Straight: Glendale Circle, Glendale Rd, first right: Greenfield Rd, second right: Greenfield Rd
Straight: Pine Hill Av, first left: Hope St, Church St

**Elmcroft Rd**
Rugby St, Belden St, Remington St, E Walnut St

Straight: Woodland Pl, first left: Stone St, second left: Pacific St, first right: Woodland Cemetery
Straight: Dyke La
Harbor St, Manor St
Straight: Pacific St, first left: Washington Blvd, first right: Belden St, second right: Crosby St, third right: Remington St

# The Stamford Streets AZ

**Elmer St**

Straight: Mulberry St, first left: Carroll St, second left: Hope St, first right: Brundage St, second right: Ridgeway St
Straight: Weed Hill Av, first left: Hickory Way, second left: Ridgeway St, third left: Estwick Pl, first right: Sterling Pl, second right: Hope St


**Elmwood St**

Straight: George St, first left: Cove Rd, Hobbie St, first right: Martin St, second right: Robin St, third right: Horton St, Charles St
Straight: Ferro Dr, straight: Hale St, Martin St, first left: George St, second left: Horton St, first right: Willowbrook Pl, Willowbrook Ct, second right: Willowbrook Av


**Ely Pl**

Straight: Culloden Rd, first left: Frankel Pl, first right: Hamilton Av, second right: Penzance Rd, third right: Scott Pl, fourth right: Crystal St
Straight: Glenbrook Rd, first left: Howes Av, second left: Hamilton Av,

# The Stamford Streets AZ

third left: Clovelly Rd, first right: Frankel Pl, second right: Windell Pl, third right: Scofield Av


**Emerald La**

Straight: Newfield Av, first left: Intervale Rd E, Sweet Briar Rd, second left: Newfield Dr, third left: Sterling Farms Golf Club, first right: White Oak La, second right: Wedgemere Rd, third right: Eden Rd


**Emery Dr E**
Westover Rd, Halliwell Dr, Indian Hill Rd

Straight: Emery Dr, first left: Palmers Hill Rd, first right: Bayberrie Dr
Straight: Knobloch La, first left: W Rock Trail


**Emery Dr**
Emery Dr E

Straight: Palmers Hill Rd, first left: Westover Rd, second left: Stillwater Rd, E Gaynor Brennan Golf Course, first right: Starin Dr, second right:

# The Stamford Streets AZ

Havemeyer La, third right: Hillcrest Park Rd
Straight: Bayberrie Dr, first left: Starin Dr, first right: Westover Rd, second right: Halliwell Dr, third right: Indian Hill Rd

**Emma Rd**

Straight: High Ridge Rd 137, first left: Swampscott Rd, second left: Bel Aire Dr, third left: Hartswood Rd, first right: Nichols Av, second right: Ridge Park Av, third right: Janice Rd

**Erickson Dr**

Straight: Hunting Ridge Rd, first left: Lawrence Hill Rd, second left: Wildwood Rd, Konandreas Dr, third left: Haviland Rd, first right: Surrey Rd, second right: Boulder Brook Dr, third right: Long Ridge Rd

**Erskine Rd**
Bentwood Dr, Jonathan Dr, Gun Club Rd, Long Ridge Rd 104

Straight: Old Long Ridge Rd, first left: Heming Way, second left: Parsonage Rd,

# The Stamford Streets AZ

third left: Rock Rimmon Rd, first right: Shag Bark Rd, second right: Mill Rd, third right: Hunting Ridge Rd
Straight: Riverbank Rd, first left: Trailing Rock Rd, second left: Harpsichord Tpke, third left: Laurel Ledge Rd, first right: Wildwood Rd, second right: Rocky Rapids Rd, third right: Farms Rd

**Estwick Pl**

Straight: Weed Hill Av, first left: Bouton St W, second left: Upper Haig Av, third left: Barholm Av, first right: Ridgeway St, second right: Hickory Way, third right: Elmer St

**Ethan Allen La**

Straight: Chestnut Hill Rd, first left: Eagle Dr, second left: W Haviland La, third left: Jordan La, first right: Scofieldtown Rd

**Euclid Av**

Straight: Wallacks La, straight: Soundview Av, first right: Wallacks Dr,

# The Stamford Streets AZ

second right: Kenilworth Dr E, third right: Kenilworth Dr W
Straight: Cove Rd, first left: Dora St, second left: Dean St, third left: Seaside Av, first right: Albin Rd, second right: Island Heights Dr, third right: Weed Av

**Eureka Terrace**

Straight: Davenport Dr, first left: Hickory Dr
Straight: Southfield Av
Hickory Dr, Cook Rd, Top Gallant Rd, Davenport Dr, Burwood Av, Congress St, Wells Av, McClurg Av, Burley Av, Sunnyside Av, Taff Av, Homestead Av
Straight: Selleck St, Greenwich Av, first left: Orchard St, second left: Fairfield Av, first right: Davenport St

**Evergreen Ct**

Straight: Clover Hill Dr, first left: Long Ridge Rd 104, first right: Long Hill Dr, second right: Stillwater Rd

# The Stamford Streets AZ

## F

**Fahey St**

Straight: Hope St, first left: Bennett St, second left: Largo Dr, third left: Clearview Av, first right: Northill St, second right: Cushing St, third right: Hyde St


**Fairfield Av**
Hazel St, Boston Post Rd 1, Richmond Hill Av, Richmond Pl, Perry St, Hall Pl, Taylor St, Madison Pl, First Stamford Pl, Jackson St, Baxter Av, Pressprich St, Selleck St, Sunnyside Av, Liberty Pl, Melrose Pl, Congress St, Claremont St, Barry Pl, Burwood Av, Dee La, Top Gallant Rd, Hendrie Ct

Straight: Shore Rd, Cummings Point Rd, first left: Gatehouse Rd, first right: Tomac La, second right: Tomac Av, third right: Tait Rd, Ford La
Straight: Stillwater Av, first left: Finney La, second left Stillwater Pl, third left: Liberty St, first right: Spruce St, second right: Alden St, third right: Smith St

# The Stamford Streets AZ

**Fairland St**
Hornez St

Straight: Newfield Av, first left: Francis Av, second left: Oaklawn Av, third left: Burdick St, first right: Dorlen Rd, second right: Newfield Ct, third right: Hirsch Rd
Straight: Belltown Rd, first left: Toms Rd, second left: Ledge La, third left: Pershing Av, first right: Francis Av, second right: Leonard St, third right: Bellmere Av

**Fairfield Memorial Park Cemetery**

Straigt: Oaklawn Av, first left: Dartley St, second left: Camore St, first right: Dann Dr, second right: Sherwood Rd

**Fairmont Av**
Midland Av

Straight: Courtland Av 106, first left: Tremont Av, second left: Hamilton Av, third left: Seaton Rd, first right: Lenox Av, second right: Taylor Reed Pl, Maple Tree Av, third right: Glen Terrace
Straight: Courtland Hill St, first left: Lenox Av, first right: Midland Av, Hamilton Av

# The Stamford Streets AZ

**Fairview Av**
Ocean Dr W, Van Rensselaer Av, Stamford Av, Cresthill Pl, Shippan Av, Brightside Dr, Ocean Dr E

Straight: Ocean View Dr


**Fairview Ct**

Straight: Houston Terrace, first left: Mathews St, first right: Boston Post Rd


**Fairway Dr**
Greens Circle

Straight: High Ridge Rd 137, first left: Craig Ct, second left: Pound Ridge Country Club, third left: Old Snake Hill Rd, fourth left: Old Snake Hill Rd, first right: Riding Stable Trail, second right: Trinity Pass, third right: Mayapple Rd


**Falmouth Rd**

Straight: E Hunting Ridge Rd, first left: Quaker Ridge Rd, second left: Heritage La, third left: Hillsbury La, first right: Chatham Rd, second right: Dads La, Rock Rimmon Rd

# The Stamford Streets AZ

**Fara Dr**

Straight: Pepper Ridge Rd, first left: Turner Rd, second left: Ogden Rd, third left: Hirsch Rd, first right: Silver Hill La, second right: White Birch La, third right: Kensington Rd
Straight: Silver Hill La, first left: Pepper Ridge Rd, second left: Deer La, third left: Loveland Rd W, Loveland Rd, first right: Cody Dr, second right: Barrett Av, third right: Case Rd


**Farm Hill Rd**

Straight: Doral Farms Rd, first left: Roxbury Rd, second left: Alfred La, third left: Farm Hill Rd, first right: Farm Hill Rd, second right: Alfred La, third right: Roxbury Rd
Straight: Doral Farms Rd, first left: Farm Hill Rd, second left: Roxbury Rd, third left: Alfred La, first right: Alfred La, second right: Roxbury Rd, third right: Farm Hill Rd


**Farms Rd**
Pony Trail Rd

Straight: Riverbank Rd, first left: Rocky Rapids Rd, second left: Wildwood

# The Stamford Streets AZ

Rd, third left: Erskine Rd, first right: Deep Valley Rd, second right: Ridgecrest Rd, third right: Riverbank Dr
Straight: Taconic Rd, first left: N Stanwich Rd, second left: Howard Rd, third left: Crown La, first right: Stanwich Club, second right: E Middle Patent Rd, third right: Cherry Hill Rd

**Farr Ter**

Straight: Palmers Hill Rd, first left: Emery Dr, second left: Westover Rd, third left: Stillwater Rd, first right: Starin Dr, second right: Havemeyer La, third right: Hillcrest Park Rd, fourth right: Old Wagon Rd

**Faucett St**
Frisbie St

Straight: Center St, first left: Morris St, second left: Scofield Av, third left: Goodwin St, first right: Hallmark Pl, second right: Brooklawn Av
Straight: Hope St, first left: Kennedy La, second left: Frisbee St, third left: Treat Av, first right: Rock Spring Rd, second right: Plymouth Rd, third right: Pilgrim Walk, Scofield Av

# The Stamford Streets AZ

**Fawn Dr**
Denise Dr

Straight: Pepper Ridge Pl, first left: Harvest Hill La, second left: Berrian Rd, third left: Robinson Dr, first right: Pepper Ridge Pl, second right: Crestwood Dr, third right: Kensington Rd


**Fawnfield Rd**

Straight: Riverbank Rd, first left: Windward La, second left: Bangall Rd, third left: Thunder Hill Dr, first right: June Rd, second right: Riverbank Dr, third right: Ridgecrest Rd, fourth right: Deep Valley Rd


**Federal St**

Straight: Guernsey Av
Straight: Atlantic St, first left: Tresser Blvd 1, second left: Bell St, third left: Bank St, first right: N State St, E8 Governor John Davis Lodge Tpke I-95, second right: S State St, E 8 Governor John Davis Lodge Tpke I-95, third right: Manhattan St

# The Stamford Streets AZ

**Fenway St**

Straight: Arlington Rd, first left: Glenbrook Rd, Daskam Pl, first right: Valley Rd, second right: Underhill St
Straight: Hillandale Av, Wenzel Terrace, first left: Underhill St, second left: Hoyt St, Prospect St, Grove St, Strawberry Hill Av, first right: Hope St

**Fernwood Dr**

Straight: Woodbine Rd, first left: Reservoir La, second left: Ingleside Dr, third left: Laurel Rd, first right: Bittersweet La, second right: Round Lake Rd, third right: Cedar Wood Rd

**Ferris Av**
Aberdeen St

Straight: Harvard Av, first left: Grenhart Rd, E6 Governor John Davis Lodge Tpke I-95, second left: E6 Governor John Davis Lodge Tpke I-95, Baxter Av, third left: Ardmore Rd, first right: Commerce Rd, second right: Boston Post Rd 1
Straight: West Av, first left: Sylvandale Av, Leon Pl, second left: Annie Pl, third left: Boston Post Rd 1,

# The Stamford Streets AZ

first right: Piave St, second right: Grenhart Rd, E6 Governor John Davis Lodge Tpke I-95, third right: Baxter Av, E6 Governor John Davis Lodge Tpke I-95, fourth right: Ardmore Rd

**Ferro Dr**

Straight: Hale St, Martin St, first left: George St, second left: Horton St, first right: Willowbrook Pl, Willowbrook Ct, second right: Willowbrook Av
Straight: Elmwood St, straight: George St, first left: Cove Rd, first right: Martin St, second right: Robin St, third right: Charles St

**Field St**

Straight: Hamilton Av, first left: Midland Av, Hamilton Av, Courtland Hill St, first right: Courtland Av 106, second right: Maitland Rd, third right: Sutton Dr, Judy La
Straight: Tremont Av, first left: Courtland Av 106, first right: Midland Av

# The Stamford Streets AZ

**Fieldstone Circle**

Straight: Fieldstone Terrace, first left: Fieldstone La, second left: Fieldstone Rd, first right: Fieldstone Rd

**Fieldstone La**

Straight: Fieldstone Terrace, first left: Fieldstone Circle, second left: Fieldstone Rd, first right: Fieldstone Rd
Straight: Strawberry Hill Av, Upland Rd, first left: Crane Rd, Newfield Av, first right: Holbrook Dr, second right: Colonial Rd, third right: 5th St

**Fieldstone Rd**
Fieldstone Ter, Fieldstone Ter

**Fieldstone Terrace**
Fieldstone La, Fieldstone Circle

Straight: Fieldstone Rd, first left: Fieldstone Terrace
Straight: Fieldstone Rd, first right: Fieldstone Terrace

# The Stamford Streets AZ

**Finney La**
Stillwater Av, Hillhurst St

Straight: Spruce St, first left: Wright St, first right: Stillwater Av, second right: Boston Post Rd 1

**Finch St**

Straight: Dunn Av, first left: Dunn Ct, second left: Winter St, first right: Cedar Heights Rd

**First St, 1st St**

Straight: Bedford St, first left: 2nd St, second left: 3 rd St, third left: 4th St, first right: Oak St, second right: Hoyt St, third right: Dolsen Pl
Straight: Summer St, Woodside St, first left: Oak St, second left: Hoyt St, third left: North St, first right: 2nd St, second right: 3rd St, third right: 4th St

**First Stamford Pl**

Straight: Greenwich Av, first left: S State St, E 7 Governor John Davis Lodge Tpke I-95, second left: West St, first

# The Stamford Streets AZ

right: Pulaski St, Waterside Pl, second right: Davenport St
Straight: Fairfield Av, first left: Jackson St, second left: Waverly Pl, first right: Madison Pl, second right: Taylor St

**Fishing Trail**
Woody Trail, Short Trail

Straight: West Trail, first left: Mountain Trail, first right: Sunset Rd

**Fifth St, 5th St**
Bedford St, Revonah Av, Morgan St, Vincent Ct

Straight: Strawberry Hill Av, first left: Colonial Rd, second left: Holbrook Dr, third left: Fieldstone La, Upland Rd, first right: Hackett Circle, second right: Rock Spring Rd, third right: Strawberry Hill Ct
Straight: Summer St, first left: 4th St, second left: 3 rd St, third left: 2nd St, first right: 6th St, second right: Bridge St, third right: 7th St

# The Stamford Streets AZ

## Flint Rock Rd

Straight: Den Rd, first left: Hardesty Rd, second left: Constance La, Bangall Rd, third left: Barclay Dr, first right: Old Orchard La, second right: Arrow Head Dr, third right: Long Ridge Rd 104 Straight: Iron Gate Rd, Flint Rock Rd E

## Flora Pl

Straight: High Ridge Rd 137, first left: Laurel Rd, second left: Mayapple Rd, third left: Trinity Pass, first right: Russet Rd, second right: Briar Brae Rd, third right: Briar Brae Rd, fourth right: Ingleside Dr

## Florence Ct

Straight: Elaine Dr, first left: Clorinda Ct, second left: Three Lakes Dr, first right: Woodridge Dr S

## Flying Cloud Rd

Straight: Dolphin Cove Quay, first left: Half Moon Way, second left: Joshua Slocum Dock, third left: Gypsy Moth Landing

# The Stamford Streets AZ

**Forest Lawn Av**
Fowler St

Straight: Summer St, first left: Hoover Av, second left: Long Ridge Rd 104, Bedford St, High Ridge Rd 137, first right: 8th St, second right: 7th St, third right: Bridge St


**Forest St**
Prospect St, Greyrock Pl, Suburban Av, Grove St, Ridge Pl, Pleasant St

Straight: Lindale St, first left: Highland Rd, second left: Hillcrest Av, third left: Grove St, first right: Boston Post Rd 1
Straight: Bedford St, first left: Spring St, second left: Broad St, Atlantic St, third left: Luther St, first right: Walton Pl, second right: North St, third right: Dolsen Pl, fourth right: Hoyt St


**Forestwood Dr**

Straight: Dundee Rd, first right: Timber Mill Rd, second right: Sawmill Rd

# The Stamford Streets AZ

## Four Brooks Circle

Straight: Four Brooks Rd, first left: Wire Mill Rd, first right: Wake Robin La

## Four Brooks Rd
Four Brooks Circle, Wake Robin La

Straight: Wire Mill Rd, first left: Linwood La, second left: Red Fox Rd, third left: Studio Rd, fourth left: Gutzon Borglum Rd, first right: Cedar Heights Rd, second right: Cedar Tree La, Hunting La, third right: Long Ridge Rd 104

## Fourth St, 4th St
Summer St, Bedford St

Straight: Revonah Av, first left: 5th St, second left: Chester St, third left: Urban St, first right: 3rd St
Straight: Washington Blvd 137, first left: 2nd St, second left: Linden Pl, Hoyt St, third left: North St, first right: 2nd St, second right: Bridge St, third right: W Forest Lawn Av, fourth right: Paragon La

# The Stamford Streets AZ

**Fowler St**

Straight: Forest Lawn Av, first left: Summer St

**Fox Glen Dr**

Straight: Hunting Ridge Rd, first left: Fox Ridge Rd, second left: Foxwood Rd, first right: Old Long Ridge Rd

**Fox Hill Rd**
Fox Ridge Rd

Straight: Foxwood Rd, first left: Hunting Ridge Rd, first right: Fox Ridge Rd

**Fox Ridge Rd**
Tyler Dr, Foxwood Rd

Straight: Fox Hill Rd, first right: Foxwood Rd
Straight: Hunting Ridge Rd, first left: Foxwood Rd, second left: Haviland Rd, third left: Wildwood Rd, Konandreas Dr, first right: Fox Glen Dr, second right: Old Long Ridge Rd

# The Stamford Streets AZ

**Foxwood Rd**
Fox Hill Rd, Fox Ridge Rd

Straight: Hunting Ridge Rd, first left: Haviland Rd, second left: Wildwood Rd, Konandreas Dr, third left: Lawrence Hill Rd, first right: Fox Ridge Rd, second right: Fox Glen Dr, third right: Old Long Ridge Rd


**Francis Av**

Straight: Newfield Av, first left: Oaklawn Av, second left: Burdick St, third left: Crane Rd, first right: Fairland St, second right: Dorlen Rd, third right: Newfield Ct
Straight: Belltown Rd, first left: Fairland St, second left: Toms Rd, third left: Ledge La, first right: Leonard St, second right: Bellmere Av, third right: Burdick St


**Frank St**
Lockwood Av

Straight: Maple Av, first left: Gregory St, second left: William St, third left: Warren St, first right: E 8 Governor John Davis Lodge Tpke I-95, second right: Boston Post Rd 1

# The Stamford Streets AZ

Straight: Dale St
Lillian St, William St, Woodrow St, Ursula Pl, Ursula Pl, Cove Rd, St Benedict Circle

**Frankel Pl**

Straight: Glenbrook Rd, first left: Ely Pl, second left: Howes Av, third left: Hamilton Av, fourth left: Clovelly Rd, first right: Windell Pl, second right: Scofield Av, third right: Crescent St, fourth right: Church St
Straight: Culloden Rd
Ely Pl, Hamilton Av, Penzance Rd, Scott Pl
Straight: Crystal St, first left: Boston Post Rd 1, first right: Hundley Ct, Peveril Rd, second right: Quintard Terrace, third right: Lafayette St, Daskam Pl

**Franklin St**
Stanley Ct, North St, Hoyt St

Straight: Broad St, first left: Summer St, second left: Atlantic St, Bedford St, third left: Landmark Sq, fourth left: Greyrock Pl, first right: Washington Blvd, W Broad St

# The Stamford Streets AZ

Straight: Woodside St, first right: Summer St, 1st St

**Frederick St**
Wardwell St, Cove Rd, Shippan Av, Maple Av

Straight: Myrtle Av, first left: Elm St, Jefferson St, first right: Warren St, second right: William St, third right: Myrtle Av
Straight: Park St
Cummings Av
Straight: Shippan Av, first left: Seaview Av, second left: Harbor Dr, Magee Av, third left: Lindstrom Rd, fourth left: Rippowam Rd, first right: Hanover St, second right: Wardwell St, third right: Elm St, Cove Rd, fourth right: Frederick St

**Friar Tuck La**
Robinhood Rd

Straight: Nottingham Dr, first left: Hope St, first right: Little John La

# The Stamford Streets AZ

**Friars La**

Straight: Eden Rd, first left: E Cross Rd, Hope St, first right: Old Well Rd, second right: Woodbrook Dr, third right: Twin Brook Dr, fourth right: Parry Rd

**Frisbee St**

Straight: Hope St, first left: Treat Av, second left: Howes Av, third left: Wenzel Terrace, first right: Kennedy La, second right: Faucett St, third right: Rock Spring Rd
Straight: Frisbie St, Brooklawn Av, first left: Faucett St, first right: Center St, second right: Howes Av

**Frisbie St**

Straight: Frisbee St, Brooklawn Av, first left: Center St, second left: Howes Av, first right: Hope St
Straight: Faucett St, first left: Hope St, first right: Center St

**Frost Pond Rd**
Aspen La

# The Stamford Streets AZ

Straight: Cascade Rd, first left: Woodbine Rd, second left: Ponus Ridge, first right: Michael Rd, second right: Pembroke Dr, third right: Cascade Ct, fourth right: N Stamford Rd

# The Stamford Streets AZ

## G

**Garden St**

Straight: Henry St, first left: Pacific St, second left: Cedar St, third left: Canal St, first right: Atlantic St, second right: Rockland Pl, third right: W Henry, Washington Blvd
Straight: Manhattan St, first left: Atlantic St, first right: Pacific St, second right: John St


**Garland Dr**

Straight: Camp Av, first left: St John's Cemetery, second left: Greenwood Av, third left: Hoyt St 106, first right: Highview Av, second right: Ryan St, third right: Hope St
Straight: Cerretta St
Columbus Pl
Straight: Highview Av, first left: Camp Av, first right: Mead St, second right: Bouton St, third right: Columbus Pl


**Gary Rd**
Lolly La, Old Logging Rd

Straight: Scofieldtown Rd, first left: Old Logging Rd, second left: Janes La,

# The Stamford Streets AZ

third left: Middle Ridge Rd, first right: High Ridge Rd 137
Straight: Katydid La, first left: Janes La, first right: Janes La

**Gatehouse Rd**
Signal Rd

Straight: Top Gallant Rd, first left: Fairfield Av, first right: Dolphin Cove Quay, second right: Southfield Av, Davenport Dr
Straight: Cummings Point Rd, first right: Shore Rd, Fairfield Av

**Gatewood Rd**

Straight: Mill Rd, first left: Rock Rimmon Rd, first right: Dulan Dr, second right: Mill Spring La, third right: Mohawk Trail, fourth right: Old Long Ridge Rd

**Gaxton Rd**
Norvel La

Straight: Intervale Rd, first left: Joan Rd, Newfield Av, first right: Turn Of River Rd

# The Stamford Streets AZ

### Gaymoor Circle

Straight: Gaymoor Dr, first left: Sterling Pl, second left: Minivale Rd, third left: Salem Pl, first right: Bouton St W


### Gaymoor Dr
Salem Pl, Minivale Rd, Sterling Pl, Gaymoor Circle

Straight: Prudence Dr, first left: Bouton St W
Straight: Bouton St W, first left: Bouton Circle, second left: Weed Hill Av, first right: Sunset St, second right: Minivale Rd, third right: Old Colony Rd, fourth right: Prudence Dr


### General Waterbury La

Straight: Merriebrook La, first right: Westover Rd


### George St
Elmwood St, Martin St, Robin St

Straight: Cove Rd, first left: Hobbie St, second left: Duffy St, third left: Willowbrook Av, Blachley Rd, first

# The Stamford Streets AZ

right: Horton St, second right: Avery St, third right: Seaside Av
Straight: Charles St
Horton St, Avery St
Straight: Dean St
Straight: Cove Rd, first left: Seaside Av, second left: Avery St, third left: Horton St, first right: Dora St, second right: Euclid Av, third right: Albin Rd

## Georgian Ct

Straight: Scofieldtown Rd, first left: Chestnut Hill Rd, second left: Brookdale Rd, third left: Haviland Rd, first right: Campbell Dr, second right: Woodley Rd, third right: Middle Ridge Rd, fourth right: Janes La

## Gerik Rd

Straight: Turn Of River Rd, first left: Poppy La, second left: High Ridge Rd 137, Cedar Heights Rd, first right: Talmadge La, second right: Intervale Rd, third right: Sterling Lake La
Straight: Kane Av, straight: Vine Rd, first left: Vine Pl, second left: Barmore Dr, third left: Pamlynn Rd, first right: High Ridge Rd 137

# The Stamford Streets AZ

**Gilford St**

Straight: Knapp St, first left: Carroll St, second left: Hope St, Greenway St, first right: Brundage St, second right: Sleepy Hollow La, Lawton Av

**Givens Av**
Duffy St, Hobbie St

**Gleason Av**

Straight: St Marys St, first left: Halloween Blvd, first right: Magee Av
Straight: Halloween Blvd, first left: Jefferson St, first right: St Marys St

**Glen Av**
Glendale Dr, Derwin St

Straight: Hope St, first left: Toms Rd, second left: Viaduct Rd, third left: Edgewood Av, first right: Douglas Av, second right: Union St, third right: Glendale Dr
Straight: Rutz St, straight: Toms Rd, first left: Deleo Dr, second left: Overbrook Dr, third left: Dale Pl

# The Stamford Streets AZ

**Glen Terrace**

Straight: Courtland Av 106, first left: Taylor Reed Pl, Maple Tree Av, second left: Lenox Av, third left: Fairmont Av, first right: Glenbrook Rd
Straight: Oakdale Rd, Rose Rd, first left: Phillips Pl, second left: Glenbrook Rd 106, first right: Maple Tree Av

**Glenbrook Rd**
Arlington Rd, Daskam Pl, Lafayette St, Hope St, Clovelly Rd, Hamilton Av, Howes Av, Ely Pl, Frankel Pl, Windell Pl, Scofield Av, Crescent St, Church St, Cowing Pl, Arthur Pl, Courtland Av 106, Research Dr, Oakdale Rd

Straight: Middlesex Rd, Fresh Meadows La
Straight: Boston Post Rd 1, Clarks Hill Av, first left: Daly St, second left: Lafayette St, third left: Quintard Terrace, first right: Crandall St, second right: Lindale St, third right: Broad St

**Glendale Circle**
Greenfield Rd, Greenfield Rd

# The Stamford Streets AZ

Straight: Glendale Rd, first left: Tioga Pl, Elmbrook Dr, first right: Glendale Dr

**Glendale Dr**
Glendale Rd

Straight: Hope St, first left: Union St, second left: Douglas Av, third left: Glen Av, first right: Pine Hill Av, Church St, second right: Rose St, third right: Colonial Rd
Straight: Glen Av, Derwin St, first left: Rutz St, first right: Hope St

**Glendale Rd**
Glendale Circle

Straight: Glendale Dr, first left: Glen Av, Derwin St, first right: Hope St
Straight: Elmbrook Dr
Tioga Pl, Marie Pl
Straight: Pine Hill Av, first left: Hope St, Church St

**Golden Farm Rd**

Straight: Rock Rimmon Rd, first left: Breezy Hill Rd, second left: Mayapple

# The Stamford Streets AZ

Rd, first right: Ridge Brook Dr, second right: Mill Rd

**Golf View Circle**
Vuono Dr

**Goodwin St**

Straight: Center St, first left: Scofield Av, second left: Morris St, third left: Faucett St, first right: Rose St, second right: Center Terrace, third right: Church St

**Grandview Av**

Straight: Hubbard Av, first left: W North St, second left: W Broad St, first right: Vuono Dr, second right: Charles Mary La, third right: Prince Pl
Straight: Woodcliff St, first left: Hubbard Ct, Ivy St, first right: W North St, Anderson St

**Grant Av**
Sherman St

Straight: Sheridan St, first left: Lincoln Av

# The Stamford Streets AZ

Straight: Boston Post Rd 1, first left: Lawn Av, second left: Seaton Rd, Noroton Hill Pl, third left: Maher Rd, first right: Lockwood Av, second right: Lincoln Av, third right: Maple Av


**Gray Farms Rd**
Donald Rd, Mitzi Rd

Straight: Haig Av, first left: Nyselius Pl, second left: Dagmar Pl, third left: Knox Rd, Upper Haig Av, first right: Crestview Av, second right: St Charles Av, third right: Joffre Av
Straight: Newfield Av, first left: Megan La, second left: Denicola Rd, third left: Sanford La, first right: Vine Rd, second right: Club Rd, third right: Knox Rd, fourth right: Weed Hill Av


**Green St**
Hanrahan St

Straight: Adams Av, first left: Vista St, second left: W Broad St, first right: Chestnut St, second right: W North St, Powell Pl

# The Stamford Streets AZ

**Green Tree La**

Straight: W Hill Rd, first left: Carriage Dr, second left: Stony Brook Dr, third left: Greenleaf Dr, first right: Dancy Dr, second right: MacGregor Dr, third right: Drum Hill La
Straight: Skyview Dr, first left: Westwood Rd, second left: Stillwater Rd, first right: Stanton La, second right: Westwood Rd, third right: Blueberry Dr

**Greenbrier La**

Straight: Quarry Rd, first left: Blue Rock Dr, second left: New England Dr, first right: Chapin La, second right: Lakeside Dr

**Greenfield Rd**

Straight: Glendale Circle, first right: Greenfield Rd, second right: Glendale Rd
Straight: Glendale Circle, first left: Greenfield Rd, first right: Glendale Rd

**Greenleaf Dr**
Brodwood Dr

# The Stamford Streets AZ

Straight: W Hill Rd, first left: Stony Brook Dr, second left: Carriage Dr, third left: Green Tree La, first right: Blueberry Dr, second right: Wesgate Dr, third right: Wyndover La

**Greens Circle**

Straight: Fairway Dr, first right: High Ridge Rd 137

**Greenway St**

Straight: Ryan St
Camp Av
Straight: Hope St, Knapp St, first left: Hyde St, second left: Cushing St, third left: Northill St, first right: Camp Av, second right: Mulberry St, third right: Weed Hill Av

**Greenwich Av**
Milton St, Davenport St, Pulaski St, First Stamford Pl, E 7 Governor John Davis Lodge Tpke I-95, S State St, West St, Richmond Hill Av, Treglia Terrace

Straight: Boston Post Rd 1, W Main St, first left: Stillwater Av, second left:

# The Stamford Streets AZ

Rose Park, third left: Ann St, first right: Clinton Av, Tresser Blvd 1
Straight: Selleck St, Southfield Av, first left: Davenport St, first right: Orchard St, second right: Fairfield Av, third right: Fairfield Av

## Greenwood Av

Straight: Camp Av, first left: Hoyt St, second left: Spring Grove St, first right: St John's Cemetery, second right: Garland Dr
Straight: Hoyt St, first left: Woodway Rd, first right: Wakemore St

## Greenwood Hill St
Smith St

Straight: Mill River St, first left: W Broad St, first right: Main St, W Main St

## Gregory St

Straight: Myrtle Av, first left: William St, second left: Warren St, third left: Frederick St, first right: E 8 Governor John Davis Lodge Tpke I-95, second right: Boston Post Rd 1

# The Stamford Streets AZ

Straight: Maple Av, first left: Frank St, second left: E 8 Governor John Davis Lodge Tpke I-95, third left: Boston Post Rd 1, first right: William St, second right: Warren St, third right: Frederick St

**Grenhart Rd**

Roosevelt Av, Victory St, Diaz St, West Av

Straight: Harvard Av, E 6 Governor John Davis Lodge Tpke I-95, first left: Baxter Av, E6 Governor John Davis Lodge Tpke I-95, second left: Ardmore Rd, third left: Brown House Rd, Warshaw Pl, first right: Ferris Av, second right: Commerce Rd, third right: Boston Post Rd 1
Straight: Wilson St, first left: Madison Pl, second left: Hall Pl, third left: Boston Post Rd 1, Richmond Hill Av, first right: Baxter Av, second right: Pressprich St

**Grey Birch Rd**

Straight: Old Wagon Rd
Straight: Long Ridge Rd 104, first left: Erskine Rd, second left: Parsonage Rd, third left: N Lake Dr, first right: Old

# The Stamford Streets AZ

Long Ridge Rd, second right: Riverbank Rd, third right: Mountain Wood Rd

**Greyrock Pl**
Forest St, Broad St, E Main St

Straight: Grove St, first left: Highland Rd, second left: Hillcrest Av, third left: Prospect St, Hoyt St, Strawberry Hill Av, Hillandale Av, first right: Forest St, second right: Broad St, third right: E Main St
Straight: Stamford Forum, Stamford Plaza 1, Canal St, first left: Grove St, Elm St, Boston Post Rd 1, first right: Tresser Blvd, Town Center Dr

**Grove St**
Broad St, Forest St, Greyrock Pl, Highland Rd, Hillcrest Av

Straight: Prospect St, Hoyt St, Strawberry Hill Av, Hillandale Av
Straight: E Main St, first right: Suburban Av, second right: Greyrock Pl

**Guernsey Av**

Straight: Federal St, straight: Atlantic St, first left: Tresser Blvd, second

# The Stamford Streets AZ

left: Bell St, third left: Bank St, first right: N State St, E 8 Governor John Davis Lodge Tpke I-95, second right: S State St, E 8 Governor John Davis Lodge Tpke I-95, third right: Manhattan St

**Guinea Rd**
Juniper Hill Rd, Ledge Brook Rd

Straight: Stanwich Rd, first left: Rock Maple Rd, second left: Desiree Dr, third left: Barnstable La, first right: Londonderry Dr, second right: Carissa La, third right: Stag La
Straight: June Rd, first left: Tod La, Howard Rd, first right: Riverbank Rd

**Gun Club Rd**

Straight: Erskine Rd, first left: Long Ridge Rd 104, second left: Old Long Ridge Rd, first right: Jonathan Dr, second right: Bentwood Dr, third right: Riverbank Rd

**Gurley Rd**

Straight: Shippan Av, first left: Sagamore Rd, second left: Ocean Dr E,

# The Stamford Streets AZ

third left: Ocean Dr W, first right: Ralsey Rd, second right: Chesterfield Rd, third right: Lanark Rd, fourth right: Downs Av

## Gutzon Borglum Rd

Straight: Wire Mill Rd, first left: Blackwood La, second left: High Ridge Rd, first right: Studio Rd, second right: Red Fox Rd, third right: Linwood La

## Gypsy Moth Landing

Straight: Dolphin Cove Quay, first left: Top Gallant Rd, first right: Joshua Slocum Dock, second right: Half Moon Way, third right: Flying Cloud Rd

# The Stamford Streets AZ

## H

**Hackett Cir**

Straight: Hackett Circle N, Hackett Circle S
Straight: Strawberry Hill Av, first left: Rock Spring Rd, second left: Strawberry Hill Ct, first right: 5 th St, second right: Colonial Rd

**Hackett Circle N**

Straight: Hackett Circle W, first right: Hackett Circle, first left: Hackett Circle S
Straight: Mayflower Av, first left: Puritan La, second left: Plymouth Rd, third left: Colonial Rd, first right: Hackett Circle S, second right: Rock Spring Rd

**Hackett Circle S**

Straight: Hackett Circle W, Hackett Circle, first left: Strawberry Hill Av, first right: Hackett Circle N
Straight: Mayflower Av, first left: Hackett Circle N, second left: Puritan La, third left: Plymouth Rd, first right: Rock Spring Rd

# The Stamford Streets AZ

**Hackett Circle W**

Straight: Hackett Circle, Hackett Circle S, first left: Mayflower Av, first right: Strawberry Hill Av
Straight: Hackett Circle N, straight: Mayflower Av, first left: Puritan La, second left: Plymouth Rd, third left: Colonial Rd, first right: Hackett Circle S, second right: Rock Spring Rd


**Haig Av**
Joffre Av, St Charles Av, Crestview Av, Gray Farms Rd, Nyselius Pl, Dagmar Pl

Straight: Pershing Av, first left: Joffre Av, Ledge La, first right: Todd La, second right: Belltown Rd
Straight: Knox Rd, Upper Haig Av, first left: Lund Av, second left: Newfield Av, first right: Lund Av, Upper Haig Av


**Hale St**
Willowbrook Ct, Willowbrook Pl

Straight: Ferro Dr, Martin St, first left: Elmwood St, first right: George St
Straight: Willowbrook Av, first left: Wascussee La E, second left: Soundview Av, first right: Uncas Rd, second right:

# The Stamford Streets AZ

Caldwell Av, third right: Cove Rd, Blachley Rd

**Half Moon Way**

Straight: Dolphin Cove Quay, first left: Flying Cloud Rd, first right: Joshua Slocum Dock, second right: Gypsy Moth Landing, third right: Top Gallant Rd

**Hall Pl**

Straight: Fairfield Av, first left: Perry St, second left: Richmond Pl, third left: Richmond Hill Av, first right: Taylor St, second right: Madison Pl, third right: First Stamford Pl
Straight: Wilson St, first left: Madison Pl, second left: Grenhart Rd, third left: Baxter Av, first right: Boston Post Rd 1, Richmond Hill Av

**Halliwell Dr**
Bayberrie Dr, Emery Dr E, Hycliff Terrace, Sycamore Terrace

Straight: Stillwater Rd, Bridge St, first left: Bridge St, second left: Knobloch La, third left: Knoblock La, fourth left: Cold Spring Rd, first

# The Stamford Streets AZ

right: Palmers Hill Rd, E Gaynor Brennan Golf Course, second right: Connecticut Av, third right: W Broad St

**Hallmark Pl**

Straight: Center St, first left: Frisbee St, Brooklawn Av, first right: Faucett St, second right: Morris St, third right: Scofield Av

**Halloween Blvd**
St Marys St, Gleason Av

Straight: Jefferson St, first left: Magee Av, second left: Cherry St, third left: Harbor View Av, first right: Elm St, Myrtle Av

**Halpin Av**
Oaklawn Av

Straight: High Ridge Rd 137, first left: Cold Spring Rd, second left: Long Ridge Rd, Summer St, Bedford St, first right: Oaklawn Av, second right: Cross Rd, third right: Dubois St
Straight: Dubois St, first left: High Ridge Rd 137, first right: Cantwell Av

# The Stamford Streets AZ

**Hamilton Av**
Culloden Rd, Lawn Av, Sutton Dr, Judy La, Maitland Rd, Courtland Av 106, Field St, Midland Av, Courtland Hill St, King St, Hamilton Ct, Brookside Dr, De Bera La, E 9 Governor John Davis Lodge Tpke I-95, Cove View Dr

Straight: Glenbrook Rd, first left: Clovelly Rd, second left: Hope St, first right: Howes Av, second right: Ely Pl, third right: Frankel Pl
Straight: Waterbury Av, Boston Post Rd, first left: Weed Av, second left: Brookside Dr, third left: Purdy La, first right: Houston Terrace, second right: Home Ct, third right: Seaside Av, fourth right: E 9 Governor John Davis Lodge Tpke I-95

**Hamilton Ct**

Straight: Hamilton Av, first left: King St, second left: Midland Av, Courtland Hill St, first right: Brookside Dr, second right: De Bera La

# The Stamford Streets AZ

**Hampshire La**

Straight: Jay Rd, first left: Ken Ct, second left: Alpine St, first right: Duke Dr

**Hampton La**

Straight: Somerset La, first left: Perna La, first right: Dzamba Grove

**Hannahs Rd**
Larkspur Rd

Straight: Scofieldtown Rd, first left: Rock Rimmon Rd, second left: Haviland Rd, third left: Brookdale Rd, first right: Skymeadow Dr, second right: Skyline La, Sunset Rd

**Hanover St**

Straight: Shippan Av, first left: Wardwell St, second left: Elm St, Cove Rd, third left: Frederick St, first right: Park St, second right: Seaview Av, third right: Harbor Dr, Magee Av
Straight: Magee Av, first left: Pumping Station Rd, second left: Harbor Dr,

# The Stamford Streets AZ

Shippan Av, first right: St Marys St, second right: Jefferson St

**Hanrahan St**

Straight: W Broad St, first left: Mill River St, second left: Washington Blvd 137, Broad St, first right: Schuyler Av, second right: Adams Av, third right: Oak Hill St
Straight: Green St, first left: Adams Av

**Happy Hill Rd**
Blackberry Dr

Straight: Breezy Hill Rd, first right: Rock Rimmon Rd

**Harbor Dr**
Magee Av

Straight: Shippan Av, first left: Seaview Av, second left: Park St, third left: Hanover St, first right: Lindstrom Rd, second right: Rippowam Rd, third right: Mariners La

# The Stamford Streets AZ

**Harbor St**
Rugby St

Straight: Belden St, first left: Manor St, second left: Pacific St, first right: Elmcroft Rd
Straight: Dyke La, first left: Bateman Way, Elmcroft Rd, first right: Manor St, second right: Washington Blvd, Pacific St


**Harbor Plaza Dr**
Harbor Dr

Straight: Harbor Dr


**Harbor View Av**

Straight: Jefferson St, Cherry St, first left: Meadow St, second left: Canal St, Dock St, first right: Magee Av, second right: Halloween Blvd, third right: Elm St, Myrtle Av
Straight: Pumping Station Rd, straight: Magee Av, first left: Hanover St, second left: St Marys St, third left: Jefferson St, first right: Harbor Dr, Shippan Av


**Hardesty Rd**
Hartcroft Rd

# The Stamford Streets AZ

Straight: Den Rd, first left: Constance La, second left: Bangall Rd, third left: Barclay Dr, first right: Flint Rock Rd, second right: Old Orchard La, third right: Arrow Head Dr
Straight: Hartcroft Rd, straight: Hardesty Rd, first right: Den Rd

## Harding Av

Straight: Crandall St, straight: Boston Post Rd 1, first left: Lindale St, second left: Broad St, third left: Stamford Plaza 1, Elm St, first right: Clarks Hill Av, Glenbrook Rd, second right: Daly St, third right: Lafayette St

## Harpsichord Tpke

Straight: Rocky Rapids Rd, Wildwood Rd, first left: Long Ridge Rd 104, second left: Hunting Ridge Rd, Konandreas Dr, first right: High Rock Rd, second right: Indian Rock Rd, third right: Riverbank Rd
Straight: Riverbank Rd, first left: Trailing Rock Rd, second left: Erskine Rd, third left: Wildwood Rd, first right: Laurel Ledge Rd, second right:

# The Stamford Streets AZ

Hedge Brook La, third right: Long Ridge Rd 104

**Hartcroft Rd**

Straight: Hardesty Rd, first left: Hartcroft Rd, first right: Den Rd

**Hartford Av**
Bowen St

Straight: Hope St, Castle Ct
Straight: Knickerbocker Av, first left: Elizabeth Av, first right: St Charles Av, second right: Southill St, third right: Short Hill St

**Hartswood Rd**
Meadowpark Av N, Swampscott Rd, Beechwood Rd, Southwest Dr

Straight: Lewis Rd
Ayres Dr
Straight: Nichols Av, first left: Meadowpark Av N, second left: High Ridge Rd 137
Straight: High Ridge Rd 137, first left: Brandt Rd, second left: Maplewood Pl, third left: Tally Ho La, first right:

# The Stamford Streets AZ

Bel Aire Dr, second right: Swampscott Rd, third right: Emma Rd

**Harvard Av**
Brown House Rd, Warshaw Pl, Ardmore Rd, Baxter Av, E 6 Governor John Davis Lodge Tpke I-95, Grenhart Rd, E 6 Governor John Davis Lodge Tpke I-95, Ferris Av, Commerce Rd

Straight: Boston Post Rd 1, first left: Alvord La, second left: Myano La, third left: Whitmore La, fourth left: Havemeyer La, Laddin Rock Rd, first right: Aberdeen St, second right: West Av, third right: Diaz St
Straight: Selleck St, first left: Outlook St, second left: West Av, third left: Betts Av, first right: Brown House Rd

**Harvest Hill La**
Sanford La

Straight: Pepper Ridge Rd, first left: Fawn Dr, second left: Pepper Ridge Pl, third left: Crestwood Dr, first right: Berrian Rd, second right: Robinson Dr, third right: Red Bird Rd

# The Stamford Streets AZ

**Hastings La**
Swan La


**Havemeyer La**
Hassake Rd, Stuart Dr, Halsey Dr, Catoona La, MacArthur Dr, Northridge Rd

Straight: E Putnam Av 1, Boston Post Rd, Laddin Rock Rd, first left: Whitmore La, second left: Myano La, third left: Alvord La, first right: Wendle Pl, second right: Old Kings Hwy, third right: Ferris Dr
Straight: Palmer Hill Rd, first left: Hillcrest Park Rd, second left: Old Wagon Rd, third left: Cross Ridge Dr, first right: Starin Dr, second right: Emery Dr, third right: Westover Rd


**Haviland Ct**

Straight: Haviland Rd, first left: Cross Country Trail, second left: W Haviland La, third left: E Hunting Ridge Rd, first right: Deerfield Dr, second right: Hickory Farm, third right: Spinning Wheel La, fourth right: Scofield Rd

# The Stamford Streets AZ

**Haviland Dr**

Straight: Haviland Rd, first left: Wellington Dr, second left: E Hunting Ridge Rd, third left: W Haviland La, first right: Crofts La, second right: Hunting Ridge Rd

**Haviland Rd**

Spinning Wheel La, Hickory Farm, Deerfield Dr, Haviland Ct, Cross Country Trail, W Haviland La, E Hunting Ridge Rd, Wellington Dr, Haviland Dr, Crofts La

Straight: Scofieldtown Rd, first left: Rock Rimmon Rd, second left: Hannahs Rd, third left: Skymeadow Dr, first right: Brookdale Rd, second right: Chestnut Hill Rd, third right: Georgian Ct
Straight: Hunting Ridge Rd, first left: Wildwood Rd, Konandreas Dr, second left: Lawrence Hill Rd, third left: Erickson Dr, first right: Foxwood Rd, second right: Fox Ridge Rd, third right: Fox Glen Dr, fourth right: Old Long Ridge Rd

**Hawthorne St**

Straight: N State St, first left: Canal St, second left: Atlantic St, first

# The Stamford Streets AZ

right: Elm St, E8 Governor John Davis Lodge Tpke I-95
Straight: S State St, first left: Elm St E 7 Governor John Davis Lodge Tpke I-95, second left: Lafayette St, E7 Governor John Davis Lodge Tpke I-95, first right: Canal St, E7 Governor John Davis Lodge Tpke I-95, second right: Atlantic St, E 8 Governor John Davis Lodge Tpke I-95

**Hazard La**

Straight: Long Ridge Rd 104, first left: Butternut La, second left: Chestnut Hill Rd, third left: Hunting Ridge Rd, fourth left: Stone Hill Dr, first right: Den Rd, second right: Midrocks Dr, third right: Northwood La

**Hazel St**
Fairfield Av

Straight: High St, first left: Boston Post Rd 1
Straight: Boston Post Rd 1, Spruce St, first left: Spruce St, second left: Ann St, third left: Rose Park, first right: Fairfield Av, second right: High St, third right: Richmond Hill Av, Wilson St

# The Stamford Streets AZ

**Hazelwood La**

Straight: Crestwood Dr, first left: Dannell Dr, second left: Pepper Ridge Rd, first right: Hazelwood La, second right: Dannell Dr
Straight: Crestwood Dr, first left: Hazelwood La, second left: Dannell Dr, third left: Pepper Ridge Rd, first right: Dannell Dr

**Hearthstone Ct**
Bungalow Park

**Heather Dr**

Straight: Mountain Wood Rd, first right: Long Ridge Rd 104

**Hedge Brook La**

Straight: Riverbank Rd, first left: Laurel Ledge Rd, second left: Harpsichord Tpke, third left: Trailing Rock Rd, first right: Long Ridge Rd 104

# The Stamford Streets AZ

**Helen Pl**

Straight: Lawn Av, Custer St, first left: Trumbull Gate, second left: Sherman St, third left: Boston Post Rd 1, first right: Leroy Pl, second right: Hamilton Av


**Heming Way**

Straight: Stone Fence La
Straight: Old Long Ridge Rd, first left: Erskine Rd, second left: Shag Bark Rd, third left: Mill Rd, first right: Parsonage Rd, second right: Rock Rimmon Rd, third right: Long Ridge Rd 104


**Hemlock Dr**
Wyndover La

Straight: Paul Rd
Straight: Pond Rd, first left: Blueberry Dr, second left: Blueberry Dr, first right: Stillwater Rd


**Hendrie Ct**

Straight: Fairfield Av, first left: Top Gallant Rd, second left: Dee La, third

# The Stamford Streets AZ

left: Burwood Av, first right: Shore Rd, second right: Cummings Point Rd


**Henry St**
Rockland Pl, Atlantic St, Garden St, Pacific St, Cedar St

Straight: Canal St, first left: Market St, second left: Dock St, Jefferson St, third left: S State St, E 7 Governor John Davis Lodge Tpke I-95, first right: Ludlow St
Straight: W Henry St, Washington Blvd, first left: Pulaski St, second left: Atlantic St, third left: Crosby St, first right: Station Pl, second right: S State St, third right: N State St, E 8 Governor John Davis Lodge Tpke I-95


**Heritage La**

Straight: E Hunting Ridge Rd, first left: Hillsbury La, second left: Haviland Rd, first right: Quaker Ridge Rd, second right: Falmouth Rd, third right: Chatham Rd, fourth right: Dads La, Rock Rimmon Rd

# The Stamford Streets AZ

## Hickory Dr

Straight: Southfield Av, first left: Eureka Terrace, first right: Cook Rd, second right: Top Gallant Rd, Davenport Dr, third right: Burwood Av
Straight: Davenport Dr, first left: Cook Rd, second left: Top Gallant Rd, Southfield Av, first right: Eureka Terrace

## Hickory Farm

Straight: Haviland Rd, first left: Spinning Wheel La, second left: Scofieldtown Rd, first right: Deerfield Dr, second right: Haviland Ct

## Hickory Rd

Straight: High Ridge Rd 137, first left: Bracchi Dr, Hoyclo Rd, second left: Hoyclo Rd, Acre View Dr, third left: Cedar Wood Rd, first right: Hickory Rd, second right: Sunset Rd, third right: Alexandra Dr
Straight: High Ridge Rd, first left: Hickory Rd, second left: Hoyclo Rd, Bracchi Dr, third left: Hoyclo Rd, Acre View Dr, first right: Sunset Rd, second

# The Stamford Streets AZ

right: Alexandra Dr, third right: Ingleside Dr

**Hickory Way**
Muriel Dr, Muriel Dr

Straight: Weed Hill Av, first left: Elmer St, second left: Sterling Pl, third left: Hope St, first right: Ridgeway St, second right: Estwick Pl, third right: Bouton St W

**Hidden Brook Dr**
Madeline Ct

Straight: Woodway Rd, first left: Regent Ct, second left: Hoyt St 106, first right: Highview Av, second right: Hope St

**High Clear Dr**
Kijek St, Unity Rd, Dann Dr

Straight: Colony Ct, High Ridge Rd 137, first left: High Ridge Rd, second left: High Ridge Rd, third left: Terrace Av, fourth left: McClean Av, first right: Brownley Dr, second right: Unity Rd, third right: Lakeview Dr

# The Stamford Streets AZ

Straight: Turner Rd, first left: Pepper Ridge Rd, second left: Cody Dr, third left: Barrett Av, first right: Sherwood Rd, second right: Dann Dr

**High Line Trail S**

Straight: High Line Trail, first left: Windermere La, first right: Westover Rd

**High Line Trail**
Windermere La, High Line Trail S

Straight: Westover Rd, first left: Winding Brook La, second left: Old Mill La, first right: Nathan Hale Dr, second right: Canfield Dr, third right: Canfield Dr, fourth right: Long Close Rd

**High Ridge Rd 137**
Cold Spring Rd, Halpin Av, Oaklawn Av, Cross Rd, Dubois St, McClean Av, Terrace Av, High Ridge Rd, High Ridge Rd, Colony Ct, High Clear Dr, Brownley Dr, Unity Rd, Lakeview Dr, Loveland Rd W, Longview Av, Knollwood Av, Mercedes La, Dannell Dr, Yale Ct, Janice Rd, Ridge Park Av, Nichols Av, Emma Rd, Swampscott Rd, Bel Aire Dr, Hartswood Rd, Brandt Rd, Maplewood Pl, Tally Ho La, Bradley Pl,

## The Stamford Streets AZ

Donata La, Merriman Rd, Vine Rd, Cedar Heights Rd, Turn Of River Rd, Olga Dr, Square Acre Dr, Dunn Av, E 35 Merritt Pkwy 15, CT15, Buxton Farm Rd, E 35 Merritt Pkwy 15, CT15, High Ridge Rd, E 35 Merritt Pkwy 15, CT15, High Ridge Rd, E 35 Merritt Pkwy 15, CT15, Wire Mill Rd, Willard Terrace, Opper Rd, Brantwood La, Marva La, Pine Hill Terrace, Perna La, Blue Ridge Dr, Diamondcrest La, Meredith La, Scofieldtown Rd, High Ridge Rd, High Ridge Rd, Interlaken Rd, Bird Song La, Brookdale Rd, N Stamford Rd, Alma Rock Rd, N Stamford Rd, Skymeadow Dr, Bartlett La, Pinner La, Cedar Wood Rd, Hoyclo Rd, Acre View Dr, Bracchi Dr, Hoyclo Rd, Hickory Rd, Hickory Rd, Sunset Rd, Alexandra Dr, Ingleside Dr, Briar Brae Rd, Briar Brae Rd, Russet Rd, Flora Pl, Laurel Rd, Mayapple Rd, Trinity Pass, Riding Stable Trail, Fairway Dr, Craig Ct, Pound Ridge Country Club, NY

Straight: Long Ridge Rd 104, Summer St, Bedford St, first left: Locust La, second left: Marlou La, third left: Urban St, first right: Cold Spring Rd, second right: Cross Rd, third right: McClean Av
Straight: Pound Ridge, NY

# The Stamford Streets AZ

### High Rock Rd

Straight: Wildwood Rd, first left: Indian Rock Rd, second left: Riverbank Rd, first right: Rocky Rapids Rd, Harpsichord Tpke, second right: Long Ridge Rd 104, third right: Hunting Ridge Rd, Konandreas Dr

### High St
Hazel St

Straight: Boston Post Rd 1, first left: Fairfield Av, second left: Hazel St, Spruce St, third left: Spruce St, first right: Richmond Hill Av, Wilson St, second right: Roosevelt Av, third right: Liberty St

### High Valley Way

Straight: Deep Valley Rd, first left: Riverbank Rd

### Highland Rd
Lindale St, Terrace Pl

Straight: Valley Rd, straight: Arlington Rd, first left: Underhill St, first

# The Stamford Streets AZ

right: Fenway St, second right: Glenbrook Rd, Daskam Pl
Straight: Grove St, first left: Greyrock Pl, second left: Forest St, third left: Broad St, first right: Hillcrest Av, second right: Prospect St, Hoyt St, Strawberry Hill Av, Hillandale Av

**Highview Av**
Cerretta St, Mead St, Bouton St, Columbus Pl

Straight: Woodway Rd, first left: Hope St, first right: Hidden Brook Dr, second right: Regent Ct, third right: Hoyt St 106
Straight: Camp Av, first left: Garland Dr, second left: St John's Cemetery, third left: Greenwood Av, first right: Ryan St, second right: Hope St

**Hillandale Av**
Holcomb Av, Wenzel Terrace, Fenway St, Underhill St

Straight: Treat Av, first left: Cowan Av, second left: Coolidge Av, third left: Rock Spring Rd, first right: Hope St
Straight: Grove St, Prospect St, Hoyt St, Strawberry Hill Av

# The Stamford Streets AZ

**Hillcrest Av**

Straight: Grove St, first left: Highland Rd, second left: Greyrock Pl, third left: Forest St, first right: Prospect St, Hoyt St, Strawberry Hill Av, Hillandale Av
Straight: Lindale St
Highland Rd, Valley Rd, Forest St
Straight: Boston Post Rd 1, first left: Crandall St, second left: Glenbrook Rd, Clarks Hill Av, third left: Daly St, first right: Broad St, second right: Elm St, Stamford Plaza 1

**Hillhurst St**

Straight: Spruce St, first left: Finney La, second left: Wright St, first right: Stillwater Av
Straight: Finney La, first left: Stillwater Av, first right: Spruce St

**Hillsbury La**

Straight: E Hunting Ridge Rd, first left: Haviland Rd, first right: Heritage La, second right: Quaker Ridge Rd, third right: Falmouth Rd

# The Stamford Streets AZ

### Hillside Av

Straight: W North St, first left: Powell Pl, Adams Av, second left: North St, first right: Woodcliff St, Anderson St, second right: Hinckley Av, third right: Hubbard Av, fourth right: St George Av
Straight: Ivy St, first left: Woodcliff St, Hubbard Ct, first right: Powell Pl

### Hilltop Av

Straight: Weed Hill Av, first left: Barholm Av, second left: Upper Haig Av, third left: Bouton St W, first right: Newfield Av
Straight: Barholm Av, Sunset St, first right: Weed Hill Av

### Hillview La

Straight: Ridge Park Av, first left: Rosano Rd, Wood Ridge Dr, first right: Longview Av, second right: Knollwood Av, third right: Wood Ridge Dr, fourth right: High Ridge 137

# The Stamford Streets AZ

**Hinckley Av**

Straight: W Broad St, first left: Wright St, second left: Anderson St, third left: Stephen St, fourth left: Oak Hill St, first right: Shelburne Rd, second right: Hubbard Av, third right: St George Av, fourth right: Shelburne Rd
Straight: W North St, first left: Hubbard Av, second left: St George Av, third left: Rachelle Av, first right: Anderson St, Woodcliff St, second right: Hillside Av, third right: Powell Pl, Adams Av


**Hirsch Rd**

Straight: Newfield Av, first left: Ogden Rd, second left: Turner Rd, Belltown Rd, third left: Todd La, first right: Newfield Ct, second right: Dorlen Rd, third right: Fairland St, fourth right: Francis Av
Straight: Pepper Ridge Rd, first left: Marschall Pl, second left: Oaklawn Av, first right: Ogden Rd, second right: Turner Rd, third right: Fara Dr


**Hobbie St**
Givens Av

# The Stamford Streets AZ

Straight: Palmer Av, first left: Duffy St
Straight: Cove Rd, first left: George St, second left: Horton St, third left: Avery St, first right: Duffy St, second right: Blachley Rd, Willowbrook Av, third right: Ranson St, Cove Rd

**Hobson St**
Brightside Dr, Ocean Dr E, Rockledge Dr

Straight: Shippan Av, first left: Sound Av, second left: Fairview Av, third left: Westminster Rd, first right: Rockledge Dr, second right: Ocean Dr W, third right: Ocean Dr E
Straight: Sea Beach Dr, straight: Ocean Dr E, first left: Rockledge Dr, second left: Hobson St, third left: Fairview Av, first right: Rockledge Dr, second right: Ocean Dr W, third right: Ocean Dr E, fourth right: Sagamore Rd

**Holbrook Dr**
Apple Tree Dr, Boxwood Dr

Straight: Strawberry Hill Av, first left: Colonial Rd, second left: 5th St, third left: Hackett Circle, first right: Upland Rd, second right: Fieldstone La,

# The Stamford Streets AZ

Upland Rd, third right: Crane Rd, fourth right: Burdick St

**Holcomb Av**
Van Buren Circle, Ardsley Rd, Coolidge Av, Cowan Av

Straight: Hillandale Av, first left: Treat Av, first right: Wenzel Terrace, Fenway St, second right: Underhill St, third right: Grove St, Prospect St, Hoyt St, Strawberry Hill Av
Straight: Strawberry Hill Av, first left: Hidden Rd, second left: Hoyt St, third left: Hoyt St, Prospect St, Hillandale Av, Grove St, first right: Hidden Rd, second right: Strawberry Hill Ct, third right: Rock Spring Rd, fourth right: Hackett Circle

**Hollow Oak La**
Little Hill Dr

Straight: Rolling Wood Dr, first left: Little Hill Dr, second left: Bel Aire Dr, first right: Berrian Rd
Straight: Bel Aire Dr, first left: High Ridge Rd 137, first right: Rolling Wood Dr

# The Stamford Streets AZ

### Holly Cove Cir

Straight: Weed Av, first left: Birch St, second left: E Main St, first right: Mathews St, second right: Weed Cir

### Hollywood Ct

Straight: North St, first left: W North St, first right: W Washington Av, second right: Washington Ct, third right: Renwick St, fourth right: Washington Blvd 137

### Holmes Av

Intervale Rd, Rose La, Park La, Beechwood Rd, West Av

Straight: Middlesex Rd, first left: Red Barn Rd, second left: Denhurst Pl, first right: Abbey Rd, second right: Hoyt St, Christie Hill Rd
Straight: West Av, Hazel St, first left: Holmes St, second left: Park La, first right: Catherine St, second right: Robinson St

# The Stamford Streets AZ

**Holmes Ct**

Straight: Intervale Rd, first left: Abbey Rd, second left: Holmes Av, first right: Stanley Rd, second right: Forest Rd
Straight: Beechwood Rd, first right: Holmes Av


**Home Ct**
Webb Av

Straight: Boston Post Rd 1, first left: Seaside Av, second left: E 9 Governor John Davis Lodge Tpke I-95, third left: E 9 Governor John Davis Lodge Tpke I-95, fourth left: Courtland Av 106, E 9 Governor John Davis Lodge Tpke I-95, first right: Houston Terrace, second right: Hamilton Av, Waterbury Av, third right: Weed Av


**Homestead Av**
Orchard St

Straight: Southfield Av, first left: Selleck St, Greenwich Av, first right: Taff Av, second right: Sunnyside Av, third right: Burley Av, fourth right: McClurg Av

# The Stamford Streets AZ

**Honey Hill Rd**

Straight: Dogwood Ct, first right: Dogwood La

**Hoover Av**
Richards Av

Straight: Summer St, first left: Long Ridge Rd, High Ridge Rd, Bedford St, first right: Forest Lawn Av, second right: 8th St, third right: 7th St

**Hope St**
Wenzel Terrace, Howes Av, Treat Av, Frisbee St, Kennedy La, Faucett St, Rock Spring Rd, Plymouth Rd, Pilgrim Walk, Scofield Av, Colonial Rd, Rose St, Pine Hill Av, Church St, Glendale Dr, Hope St, Union St, Hope St, Douglas Av, Glen Av, Toms Rd, Viaduct Rd, Edgewood Av, Riverbend Dr S, Chatfield St, Hartford Av, Castle Ct, Barnstable La, Avon La, Short Hill St, Omega Dr, Clearview Av, Largo Dr, Bennett St, Fahey St, Northill St, Cushing St, Hyde St, Knapp St, Greenway St, Camp Av, Mulberry St, Weed Hill Av, Minivale Rd, Mead St, Bouton St W, Bouton St, Woodway Rd, Robinhood Rd, Putter Dr, Mary Violet Rd, Nottingham Dr, Deep Spring La, Camelot Ct, Slice

# The Stamford Streets AZ

Dr, Eden Rd, E Cross Rd, Broad Brook La, W Cross Rd

Straight: Glenbrook Rd, first left: Clovelly Rd, second left: Hamilton Av, third left: Howes Av, first right: Lafayette St, second right: Arlington Rd, Daskam Pl, third right: Boston Post Rd 1, Clarks Hill Av
Straight: Ponus Ridge, W Cross Rd, Broad Brook La, first right: Hawks Hill Rd


**Hornez St**

Straight: Fairland St, first left: Newfield Av, first right: Belltown Rd


**Horse Shoe La**

Straight: Thornridge Dr, first left: Rambler La, second left: Davenport Ridge Rd, first right: Rambler La, second right: Davenport Ridge Rd


**Horton St**
Charles St, Robin St, Martin St

Straight: Cove Rd, first left: George St, second left: Hobbie St, third left:

# The Stamford Streets AZ

Duffy St, first right: Avery St, second right: Seaside Av, third right: Dean St
Straight: Lewelyn Rd, first left: Lewelyn Rd


**Houston Terrace**

Straight: Boston Post Rd 1, first left: Home Ct, second left: Seaside Av, third left: E 9 Governor John Davis Lodge Tpke I-95, first right: Waterbury Av, Hamilton Av, second right: Weed Av, third right: Brookside Dr
Straight: Mathews St, first left: Waterbury Av, second left: Cambridge Rd, third left: Weed Av, first right: Webb Av, second right: Seaside Av


**Howard Rd**

Straight: Tod La, June Rd, first left: Guinea Rd, second left: Riverbank Rd, first right: Stanwich Rd
Straight: Taconic Rd, first left: Crown La, second left: Stanwich Rd, third left: S Stanwich Rd, first right: N Stanwich Rd, second right: Farms Rd, third right: Stanwich Club

# The Stamford Streets AZ

**Howes Av**
Brooklawn Av, Nash Pl, Pierce Pl

Straight: Hope St, first left: Wenzel Terrace, second left: Glenbrook Rd, third left: Lafayette St, Clovelly Rd, first right: Treat Av, second right: Frisbee St, third right: Kennedy La
Straight: Glenbrook Rd, first left: Ely Pl, second left: Frankel Pl, third left: Windell Pl, first right: Hamilton Av, second right: Clovelly Rd, third right: Hope St, Glenbrook Rd


**Hoyclo Rd**
Northwind Dr

Straight: High Ridge Rd 137, Bracchi Dr, first left: Hickory Rd, second left: Hickory Rd, third left: Sunset Rd, first right: Hoyclo Rd, Acre View Dr, second right: Cedar Wood Rd, third right: Pinner La
Straight: High Ridge Rd 137, Acre View Dr, first left: Hoyclo Rd, Bracchi Dr, second left: Hickory Rd, third left: Hickory Rd, first right: Cedar Wood Rd, second right: Pinner La, third right: Skymeadow Dr, Bartlett La

# The Stamford Streets AZ

**Hoyt St**
Franklin St, Summer St, Bedford St, Morgan St, Hoyt St

Straight: Washington Blvd 137, Linden Pl, first left: North St, second left: W Broad St, 2nd St, Broad St, third left: Whittaker Pl, first right: 2nd St, second right: 2nd St, third right: Bridge St
Straight: Prospect St, Grove St, Hillandale Av, Strawberry Hill Av


**Hubbard Av**
W North St, Grandview Av, Vuono Dr, Charles Mary La, Prince Pl, Pellom Pl, Woodmere Rd, Bridge St

Straight: W Broad St, first left: Hinckley Av, second left: Wright St, third left: Anderson St, first right: St George Av, second right: Shelburne Rd, third right: Rachelle Av
Straight: Riverside Av, first right: Woodmere Rd, straight: Bridge St, first left: Washington Blvd, first right: Woodmere Rd, second right: Hubbard Av, third right: Stillwater Rd

# The Stamford Streets AZ

## Hubbard Ct

Straight: Ivy St, Woodcliff St, first left: Hillside Av, second left: Powell Pl, first right: Grandview Av, second right: W North St, Anderson St


## Huckleberry Hollow

Straight: Webbs Hill Rd, first left: Lynam Rd, second left: Jeffrey La, third left: Dogwood La, first right: Chestnut Hill Rd


## Hundley Ct

Straight: Quintard Terrace, first left: Boston Post Rd 1, first right: Crystal St
Straight: Crystal St, Peveril Rd, first left: Quintard Terrace, second left: Lafayette St, Daskam Pl, first right: Culloden Rd, second right: Boston Post Rd 1


## Hunting La
Vineyard La

Straight: Wire Mill Rd, Cedar Tree La, first left: Long Ridge Rd 104, first

# The Stamford Streets AZ

right: Cedar Heights Rd, second right: Four Brooks Rd, third right: Linwood La

**Hunting Ridge Rd**
Boulder Brook Dr, Surrey Rd, Erickson Dr, Lawrence Hill Rd, Wildwood Rd, Konandreas Dr, Haviland Rd, Foxwood Rd, Fox Ridge Rd, Fox Glen Dr

Straight: Long Ridge Rd 104, first left: Chestnut Hill Rd, second left: Butternut La, third left: Hazard La, first right: Stone Hill Dr, second right: Partridge Rd, third right: Lakewood Dr
Straight: Old Long Ridge Rd, first left: Long Ridge Rd 104, first right: Mill Rd, second right: Shag Bark Rd, third right: Erskine Rd

**Hycliff Terrace**

Straight: Halliwell Dr, first left: Sycamore Terrace, second left: Stillwater Rd, Bridge St, first right: Emery Dr E, second right: Bayberrie Dr

**Hyde St**

Straight: Hope St, first left: Cushing St, second left: Northill St, third

# The Stamford Streets AZ

left: Fahey St, first right: Knapp St, Greenway St, second right: Camp Av, third right: Mulberry St

**High Ridge Park**

Straight: Turn of River Rd, Buxton Farm Rd

# The Stamford Streets AZ

## I

**Idlewood Dr**
Robinson Dr, Idlewood Pl

Straight: Berrian Rd, first left: Pepper Ridge Rd, first right: Woods End Rd, second right: Rolling Wood Dr, third right: Little Hill Dr
Straight: Little Hill Dr, Little Hill Dr, first left: Little Hill Dr


**Idlewood Pl**

Straight: Idlewood Dr, first left: Little Hill Dr, first right: Robinson Dr, second right: Berrian Rd


**Indian Hill Rd**
Bayberrie Dr

Straight: Westover Rd, first left: Starin Dr, second left: Bayberrie Dr, third left: Emery Dr E, first right: W Hill Rd, second right: Summit Ridge Rd, third right: Westview La
Straight: Emery Dr E, first left: Knobloch La, first right: Halliwell Dr, second right: Westover Rd, third right: Emery Dr

# The Stamford Streets AZ

**Indian Rock Rd**

Straight: Wildwood Rd, first left: Riverbank Rd, first right: High Rock Rd, second right: Harpsichord Tpke, Rocky Rapids Rd, third right: Long Ridge Rd 104

**Ingall St**

Straight: Seaview Av, first left: Shippan Av

**Ingleside Dr**
Briar Brae Rd, Shady Knoll Dr, Wynnewood La, Spring Hill La E

Straight: High Ridge Rd 137, first left: Alexandra Dr, second left: Sunset Rd, third left: Hickory Rd, first right: Briar Brae Rd, second right: Briar Brae Rd, third right: Russet Rd
Straight: Laurel Rd, first left: Spring Hill La N, second left: High Ridge Rd 137, first right: Reservoir La, second right: Fernwood Dr, third right: Bittersweet La

# The Stamford Streets AZ

## Interlaken Rd

Straight: High Ridge Rd 137, first left: High Ridge Rd, second left: High Ridge Rd, Scofieldtown Rd, third left: Meredith La, first right: Bird Song La, second right: Brookdale Rd, third right: N Stamford Rd
Straight: Lakeside Dr, first left: Quarry Rd, second left: N Stamford Rd, first right: Davenport Ridge Rd, Newfield Av

## Interstate Hwy Connecticut Turnpike I-95

### South
E6: Harvard Av, Baxter Av, West Av, E7: Greenwich Av, S State St, E7: S State St, Canal St, E8: S State St, Guernsey Av, S State St, Atlantic St, Elm St, Lafayette St, E9: Seaside Av, E9: Boston Post Rd 1, Seaside Av

### North
E9: Hamilton Av, Boston Post Rd 1, E8: Courtland Av 106, Boston Post Rd 1, Blachley Rd, E8: Maple Av, Myrtle Av, N State St, Lafayette St, Elm St, N State St, E8: Washington Blvd, N State St, E7: Canal St, E8: Atlantic St, N State St, Guernsey Av, E6: Grenhart Rd, West Av, Harvard Av

# The Stamford Streets AZ

**Intervale Rd E**

Straight: Newfield Av, Sweet Briar Rd, first left: Emerald La, second left: White Oak La, third left: Wedgemere Rd, first right: Newfield Dr, second right: Sterling Farms Golf Club, third right: Weed Hill Av
Straight: Eastover Rd, Shadow La, first left: Newfield Dr


**Intervale Rd**
Gaxton Rd

Straight: Newfield Dr, Joan Rd, first left: Shadow La, second left: Newfield Av, first right: Arnold Dr
Straight: Turn Of River Rd, first left: Talmadge La, second left: Gerik Rd, third left: Poppy La, first right: Sterling Lake La, second right: Buxton Farm Rd, third right: High Ridge Park


**Iron Gate Rd**

Straight: Flint Rock Rd, Flint Rock Rd E, first left: Valley View Dr, first right: Den Rd

# The Stamford Streets AZ

**Iroquois Rd**
Mohegan Av, Ponus Av, Algonquin Av

Straight: Shippan Av, first left: Wallace St, second left: Mitchell St, third left: Lanell Dr, first right: Mariners La, second right: Rippowam Rd, third right: Lindstrom Rd
Straight: Wampanaw Rd, straight: Rippowam Rd
Mohegan Av, Ponus Av, Algonquin Av
Straight: Shippan Av, first left: Mariners La, second left: Iroquois Rd, third left: Wallace St, first right: Lindstrom Rd, second right: Harbor Dr, Magee Av, third right: Seaview Av

**Irving Av**

Straight: Selleck St, Bonner St, first left: Vassar Av, second left: Fairfield Av, third left: Fairfield Av, first right: Durant St, Montauk Dr, second right: Betts Av, third right: West Av
Straight: Pressprich St, first left: Wilson St, first right: Vassar Av, second right: Fairfield Av

# The Stamford Streets AZ

## Island Heights Circle

Straight: Island Heights Dr, first left: Aquila Rd, second left: Cove Rd, first right: Neponsit St

## Island Heights Dr
Aquila Rd, Island Heights Circle

Straight: Neponsit St, first left: Andover Rd, second left: Webster Rd, Albin Rd, third left: Dora St, first right: Cambridge Rd
Straight: Cove Rd, first left: Weed Av, first right: Albin Rd, second right: Euclid Av, third right: Dora St

## Ivy St
Hillside Av, Powell Pl

Straight: Hubbard Ct, Woodcliff St, first left: Grandview Av, second left: W North St, Anderson St

# The Stamford Streets AZ

## J

**Jackson St**

Straight: Fairfield Av, first left: First Stamford Pl, second left: Madison Pl, third left: Taylor St, first right: Baxter Av, second right: Pressprich St, third right: Selleck St

**James St**
Owen St

Straight: McMullen Av, first left: Soundview Av, first right: Soundview Av Straight: Soundview Av, first left: East Av, second left: McMullen Av, third left: Limerick St, first right: McMullen Av, second right: Tupper Dr, third right: Wascussee La

**Jamroga La**

Straight: Oaklawn Av, first left: Clifford Av, second left: Lindsey Av, third left: Dorlen Rd, first right: Pepper Ridge Rd, second right: Vanech Dr, third right: Sherwood Rd, fourth right: Dann Dr

# The Stamford Streets AZ

**Janes La**
Katydid La

Straight: Scofieldtown Rd, first left: Middle Ridge Rd, second left: Woodley Rd, third left: Campbell Dr, first right: Old Logging Rd, second right: Gary Rd, third right: High Ridge Rd 137
Straight: Katydid La, first left: Old Logging Rd, second left: Janes La


**Janice Rd**
Little Hill Dr

Straight: High Ridge Rd 137, first left: Yale Ct, second left: Mercedes La, Dannell Dr, third left: Knollwood Av, first right: Ridge Park Av, second right: Nichols Av, third right: Emma Rd
Straight: Woods End Rd, first left: Berrian Rd, first right: Dannell Dr


**Jay Rd**
Hampshire La, Ken Ct

Straight: Duke Dr, first left: Cedar Heights Rd
Straight: Alpine St, first left: Rushmore Circle, second left: Ken Ct, third left: Dunn Av, first right: Cedar Heights Rd

# The Stamford Streets AZ

**Jeanne Ct**

Straight: Davenport Ridge Rd, first left: Davenport Ridge La, Zora La, second left: Lakeside Dr, Newfield Av, first right: Davenport Farm La W, second right: Thornridge Dr, third right: Davenport Farm La E


**Jefferson St**
Meadow St, Harbor View Av, Cherry St, Magee Av, Halloween Blvd

Straight: Dock St, Canal St, first left: Market St, second left: Henry St, third left: Ludlow St, first right: S State St, E 7 Governor John Davis Lodge Tpke I-95, second right: N State St, E 7 Governor John Davis Lodge Tpke I-95, third right: Greyrock Pl, Stamford forum 1, Stamford Plaza 1
Straight: Elm St, Myrtle Av, first left: Cherry St, second left: Elm Ct, third left: S State St, E 8 Governor John Davis Lodge Tpke I-95, first right: Wardwell St, second right: Shippan Av, Cove Rd

# The Stamford Streets AZ

### Jeffrey La

Straight: Webbs Hill Rd, first left: Dogwood La, second left: Dogwood La, third left: Pheasant La, first right: Lynam Rd, second right: Huckleberry Hollow, third right: Chestnut Hill Rd


### Jessup St

Straight: Terrace Av, first left: High Ridge Rd 137, first right: Long Ridge Rd 104
Straight: Stark Pl, straight: Long Ridge Rd 104, first left: Terrace Av, second left: McClean Av, third left: Cross Rd, first right: River Ridge Ct, second right: Brook Run La, third right: Wishing Well La, fourth right: Woodridge Dr S


### Joan Rd

Straight: Arnold Dr
Straight: Newfield Dr, Intervale Rd, first left: Gaxton Rd, second left: Turn Of River Rd, first right: Shadow La, second right: Newfield Av

# The Stamford Streets AZ

**Joffre Av**
Joffre Ct, Sussex Pl

Straight: Ledge La, Pershing Av, first left: Ledge Terrace, second left: Belltown Rd, first right: Haig Av, second right: Todd La, third right: Belltown Rd
Straight: Haig Av, first left: Pershing Av, first right: St Charles Av, second right: Crestview Av, third right: Gray Farms Rd

**Joffre Ct**

Straight: Joffre Av, first left: Pershing Av, Ledge La, first right: Sussex Pl, second right: Haig Av

**John St**
Manhattan St

Straight: Dock St, straight: Canal St, Jefferson St, first left: S State St, E 7 Governor John Davis Lodge Tpke I-95, second left: N State St, E 7 Governor John Davis Lodge Tpke I-95, third left: Stamford Forum 1, Stamford Plaza 1, Greyrock Pl, first right: Market St, second right: Henry St, third right: Ludlow St

# The Stamford Streets AZ

Straight: Market St, first left: Canal St, first right: Pacific St

**Jonathan Dr**
Deer Meadow La

Straight: Erskine Rd, first left: Gun Club Rd, second left: Long Ridge Rd 104, third left: Old Long Ridge Rd, first right: Bentwood Dr, second right: Riverbank Rd
Straight: S Brook Dr

**Jordan La**

Straight: Chestnut Hill Rd, first left: Chestnut Hill La, second left: Webbs Hill Rd, third left: Long Ridge Rd 104, Butternut La, first right: W Haviland La, second right: Eagle Dr, third right: Ethan Allen La, fourth right: Scofieldtown Rd

**Joshua Slocum Dock**

Straight: Dolphin Cove Quay, first left: Gypsy Moth Landing, second left: Top Gallant Rd, first right: Half Moon Way, second right: Flying Cloud Rd

# The Stamford Streets AZ

**Judy La**
Maitland Rd

Straight: Hamilton Av, Sutton Dr, first left: Lawn Av, second left: Culloden Rd, third left: Glenbrook Rd, first right: Maitland Rd, second right: Courtland Av 106, third right: Field St

**Judy Rd**

Straight: S Brook Dr, first left: Jonathan Dr

**June Rd**
Guinea Rd

Straight: Howard Rd, Tod La, first left: Stanwich Rd, first right: Taconic Rd
Straight: Riverbank Rd, first left: Riverbank Dr, second left: Ridgecrest Rd, third left: Deep Valley Rd, first right: Fawnfield Rd, second right: Windward La, third right: Bangall Rd

# The Stamford Streets AZ

### K

**Kane Av**

Straight: Vine Rd, first left: Vine Pl, second left: Barmore Dr, third left: Pamlynn Rd, first right: High Ridge Rd 137
Straight: Gerik Rd, straight: Turn Of River Rd, first left: Poppy La, second left: High Ridge Rd 137, first right: Talmadge La, second right: Intervale Rd, third right: Sterling Lake La


**Katydid La**
Janes La, Old Logging Rd

Straight: Janes La, first left: Katydid La, first right: Scofieldtown Rd


**Keith St**

Straight: Burwood Av, first left: Silver St, second left: Southfield Av, first right: Noble St, second right: Beal St, third right: Claremont St
Straight: Congress St, first left: Noble St, second left: Beal St, third left: Fairfield Av, first right: Carlisle Pl,

# The Stamford Streets AZ

second right: Silver St, third right: Southfield Av

**Ken Ct**

Straight: Jay Rd, first left: Alpine St, first right: Hampshire La, second right: Duke Dr
Straight: Alpine St, first left: Dunn Av, first right: Rushmore Circle, second right: Jay Rd, third right: Cedar Heights Rd

**Kenilworth Dr E**
Allison Rd

Straight: Soundview Av, first left: Kenilworth Dr W, second left: Soundview Dr, third left: Soundview Ct, first right: Wallacks Dr, second right: Wallacks La
Straight: Beach View Dr, Kenilworth Dr W, first left: Allison Rd, second left: Soundview Av, first right: Allison Rd

**Kenilworth Dr W**
Allison Rd

Straight: Soundview Av, first left: Soundview Dr, second left: Soundview Ct,

# The Stamford Streets AZ

third left: Willowbrook Av, first right: Kenilworth Dr E, second right: Wallacks Dr, third right: Wallacks La
Straight: Beach View Dr, Kenilworth Dr E, first left: Allison Rd, first right: Allison Rd, second right: Soundview Av

## Kennedy La

Straight: Hope St, first left: Faucett St, second left: Rock Spring Rd, third left: Plymouth Rd, first right: Frisbee St, second right: Treat Av, third right: Howes Av
Straight: Abel Av, first left: Coolidge Av, second left: Treat Av, third left: Holcomb Av, first right: Rock Spring Rd, Puritan La

## Kensington Rd

Straight: Sanford La, first left: Harvest Hill La, first right: Newfield Av
Straight: Pepper Ridge Rd, first left: White Birch La, second left: Silver Hill La, third left: Fara Dr, first right: Crestwood Dr, second right: Pepper Ridge Pl, third right: Fawn Dr

# The Stamford Streets AZ

**Kerr Rd**

Straight: Vine Rd, first left: Simsbury Rd, second left: Newfield Av, first right: Pepper Ridge Rd, second right: Malvern Rd, third right: Brandywine Rd
Straight: Club Rd, first left: Sandy La, second left: Malvern Rd, third left: Club Circle, first right: Bertmor Dr, second right: Newfield Av

**Kijek St**
Unity Rd

Straight: High Clear Dr, first left: Unity Rd, second left: Dann Dr, third left: Turner Rd, first right: Colony Ct, High Ridge Rd 137, Colony Ct

**King St**
River View Dr

Straight: Hamilton Av, first left: Hamilton Ct, second left: Brookside Dr, third left: De Bera La, fourth left: E 9 Governor John Davis Lodge Tpke I-95, first right: Hamilton Av, Courtland Hill St, Midland Av

# The Stamford Streets AZ

**Kirkham Pl**

Straight: Church St, first left: Glenbrook Rd, second left: Cowing Pl, third left: Arthur Pl, first right: Parker Av, second right: Parker Av, third right: Elm Tree Pl, fourth right: Church St
Straight: Union St
Elm Tree Pl
Straight: Hope St, first left: Glendale Dr, second left: Pine Hill Av, Church St, third left: Rose St, first right: Glen Av, second right: Toms Rd, third right: Viaduct Rd


**Klondike Av**
Crestview Av

Straight: St Charles Av, first left: Marian St, Woodbury Av, second left: Knickerbocker Av, first right: Haig Av


**Knapp St**
Brundage St, Gilford St, Carroll St

Straight: Sleepy Hollow La, Lawton Av, first left: Woodbury Av, second left: Birchwood Rd, third left: Woodledge Rd, Lawton Av

# The Stamford Streets AZ

Straight: Hope St, Greenway St, first left: Camp Av, second left: Mulberry St, third left: Weed Hill Av, first right: Hyde St, second right: Cushing St, third right: Northill St

**Knickerbocker Av**
Bennett St, Clearview Av, Short Hill St, Southill St, St Charles Av, Hartford Av, Elizabeth Av

Straight: Northill St, first left: Carroll St, second left: Palmer St, third left: Woodledge Rd, first right: Hope St

**Knobloch La**
W Rock Trl, Emery Dr E

**Knobloch La**
Knoblock La

Straight: Stillwater Rd, first left: Knoblock La, second left: Cold Spring Rd, third left: Pond Rd, first right: Bridge St, second right: Halliwell Dr, third right: Palmers Hill Rd, E Gaynor Brennan Golf Course

# The Stamford Streets AZ

**Knoblock La**

Straight: Knobloch La, first left: Stillwater Rd
Straight: Stillwater Rd, first left: Cold Spring Rd, second left: Pond Rd, third left: Stillview Rd, first right: Knobloch La, second right: Bridge St

**Knollwood Av**

Straight: High Ridge Rd 137, first left: Mercedes La, Dannell Dr, second left: Yale Ct, third left: Janice Rd, first right: Longview Av, second right: Loveland Rd W, third right: Lakeview Dr
Straight: Ridge Park Av, first left: Longview Av, second left: Hillview La, third left: Rosano Rd, Wood Ridge Dr, first right: Wood Ridge Dr, second right: High Ridge Rd 137

**Knox Rd**
Lund Av, Upper Haig Av, Haig Av

Straight: Newfield Av, first left: Club Rd, second left: Vine Rd, third left: Gray Farms Rd, first right: Weed Hill Av, second right: Sterling Farms Golf Club, third right: Newfield Dr

# The Stamford Streets AZ

Straight: Upper Haig Av, Lund Av, first left: Knox Rd, Haig Av, first right: Weed Hill Av

**Konandreas Dr**

Straight: Hunting Ridge Rd, Wildwood Rd, first left: Lawrence Hill Rd, second left: Erickson Dr, first right: Haviland Rd, second right: Foxwood Rd

# The Stamford Streets AZ

## L

**Laddin Rock Rd**
Harding Rd, Chasmar Rd, Deepwoods La, Ferris Dr, Midbrook La

Straight: Sound Beach Av, first left: Forest Av, second left: Wesskum Wood Rd, third left: Webb Av, fourth left: Potter Dr, first right: Arch St, second right: Lockwood Rd, third right: Center Dr
Straight: Boston Post Rd 1, East Putnam Av 1, Havemeyer La, first left: Wendle Pl, second left: Old Kings Hwy, third left: Ferris Dr, first right: Whitmore La, second right: Myano La, third right: Alvord La


**Lafayette St**
E 8 Governor John Davis Lodge Tpke I-95, N State St, Boston Post Rd 1, Daskam Pl, Crystal St, Clovelly Rd

Straight: Glenbrook Rd, first left: Arlington Rd, Daskam Pl, second left: Boston Post Rd 1, Clarks Hill Av, first right: Hope St, second right: Clovelly Rd, third right: Hamilton Av
Straight: S State St, E 8 Governor John Davis Lodge Tpke I-95, first left: N State St, E 8 Governor John Davis Lodge Tpke I-95, first right: Elm St, second

# The Stamford Streets AZ

right: Canal St, E 7 Governor John Davis Lodge Tpke I-95, third right: Atlantic St, E 8 Governor John Davis Lodge Tpke I-95

**Lakeside Dr**
Interlaken Rd, Quarry Rd

Straight: Davenport Ridge Rd, Newfield Av, first left: Zora La, Davenport Ridge La, second left: Jeanne Ct, third left: Davenport Farm La W, first right: N Meadows La, second right: Eden Rd, third right: Wedgemere Rd
Straight: N Stamford Rd, first left: High Ridge Rd 137, first right: Cascade Rd, second right: High Ridge Rd 137

**Lakeview Dr**
Stone Wall Dr, Coopers Pond Rd

Straight: High Ridge Rd 137, first left: Loveland Rd W, second left: Longview Av, third left: Knollwood Av, first right: Unity Rd, second right: Brownley Dr, third right: Colony Ct, High Clear Dr
Straight: Brook Run La, first left: Baker Pl, second left: Long Ridge Rd 104

# The Stamford Streets AZ

**Lakewood Dr**

Straight: Long Ridge Rd 104, first left: Sawmill Rd, second left: Wildwood Rd, third left: Mountain Wood Rd, first right: Partridge Rd, second right: Stone Hill Dr, third right: Hunting Ridge Rd


**Lanark Rd**

Straight: Ocean Dr N, first left: Auldwood Rd, first right: Chesterfield Rd
Straight: Shippan Av, first left: Chesterfield Rd, second left: Ralsey Rd, third left: Gurley Rd, first right: Downs Av, second right: Auldwood Rd, third right: Lanell Dr


**Landmark Sq**

Straight: Broad St, first left: Bedford St, Atlantic St, second left: Palace Theater, third left: Summer St, first right: Greyrock Pl, second right: Suburban Av

# The Stamford Streets AZ

**Lancaster Pl**

Straight: Shadow Ridge Rd, first left: Cedar Heights Rd, first right: Wild Horse Rd, second right: Sun Dance Rd

**Lancer La**

Straight: Archer La, first right: Clay Hill Rd

**Lanell Dr**

Straight: Shippan Av, first left: Auldwood Rd, second left: Downs Av, third left: Lanark Rd, first right: Mitchell St, second right: Wallace St, third right: Iroquois Rd

**Lantern Circle**

Straight: Loveland Rd, first left: Dannell Dr, first right: White Birch La, second right: Silver Hill La, Loveland Rd W

# The Stamford Streets AZ

**Largo Dr S**

Straight: Omega Dr, Riverbend Dr, first left: Riverbend Dr S, first right: Hope St
Straight: Largo Dr, first left: Hope St

**Largo Dr**
Largo Dr S

Straight: Hope St, first left: Clearview Av, second left: Omega Dr, third left: Short Hill St, first right: Bennett St, second right: Fahey St, third right: Northill St

**Larkin St**

Straight: Poplar St, first left: Viaduct Rd
Straight: Viaduct Rd, Research Dr, first left: Glenbrook Rd 106, first right: Poplar St, second right: Hope St

**Larkspur Rd**
Cousins Rd, Very Merry Rd

Straight: Hannahs Rd, first right: Scofieldtown Rd

# The Stamford Streets AZ

Straight: Skymeadow Dr, first left: Scofieldtown Rd, first right: Skyline La, second right: Mary Joy La, third right: High Ridge Rd 137, Bartlett La

**Laurel Ledge Ct**

Straight: Laurel Ledge Rd, first left: Tall Oaks Rd, second left: Round Hill Dr, third left: Riverbank Rd

**Laurel Ledge Rd**
Laurel Ledge Ct, Tall Oaks Rd, Round Hill Dr

Straight: Riverbank Rd, first left: Hedge Brook La, second left: Long Ridge Rd 104, first right: Harpsichord Tpke, second right: Trailing Rock Rd, third right: Erskine Rd, fourth right: Wildwood Rd

**Laurel Rd**
Ingleside Dr, Spring Hill La N

Straight: High Ridge Rd 137, first left: Flora Pl, second left: Russet Rd, third left: Briar Brae Rd, first right: Mayapple Rd, second right: Trinity Pass, third right: Riding Stable Trail

# The Stamford Streets AZ

Straight: Reservoir La, Woodbine Rd, first left: Ponus Ridge, first right: Fernwood Dr, second right: Bittersweet La, third right: Round Lake Rd

**Lawn Av**
Sherman St, Trumbull Gate, Custer St, Helen Pl, Leroy Pl

Straight: Hamilton Av, first left: Culloden Rd, second left: Glenbrook Rd, first right: Sutton Dr, Judy La, second right: Maitland Rd, third right: Courtland Av 106
Straight: Boston Post Rd 1, first left: Seaton Rd, Noroton Hill Pl, second left: Maher Rd, third left: Blachley Rd, first right: Grant Av, second right: Lockwood Av, third right: Lincoln Av

**Lawrence Hill Rd**

Straight: Hunting Ridge Rd, first left: Erickson Dr, second left: Surrey Rd, third left: Boulder Brook Dr, first right: Wildwood Rd, Konandreas Dr, second right: Haviland Rd, third right: Foxwood Rd

# The Stamford Streets AZ

**Lawton Av**
Bennett St, Woodledge Rd, Birchwood Rd, Woodbury Av

Straight: Tower Av, first left: Bon Air Av, second left: Palmer St, third left: Clearview Av, first right: Birchwood Rd, second right: Woodbury Av
Straight: Sleepy Hollow La, Knapp St, first right: Brundage St, second right: Gilford St, third right: Carroll St

**Ledge La**
Ledge Terrace

Straight: Pershing Av, Joffre Av, first left: Haig Av, second left: Todd La, third left: Belltown Rd, first right: Joffre Ct, second right: Sussex Pl, third right: Haig Av
Straight: Belltown Rd, first left: Toms Rd, second left: Fairland St, third left: Francis Av, first right: Pershing Av, second right: Newfield Av, Turner Rd

**Ledge Brook Rd**

Straight: Guinea Rd, first left: Juniper Hill Rd, second left: Stanwich Rd, first right: June Rd

# The Stamford Streets AZ

## Ledge Terrace

Straight: Ledge La, first left: Belltown Rd, first right: Pershing Av, Joffre Av

## Lee St

Straight: William St, first left: Maple Av, second left: Myrtle Av, first right: Lockwood Av, second right: Dale St
Straight: Warren St, first left: Shippan Av, second left: Lockwood Av, first right: Maple Av, second right: Myrtle Av

## Leeds La

Straight: Hoyt St, first left: Woodway Country Club, second left: Woodway Rd, first right: Country Club Rd, second right: Barringer Rd

## Leeds St

Straight: Woodrow St, first left: Lockwood Av, first right: Dale St
Straight: Cove Rd, first left: St Benedict Circle, second left: Raymond St, third left: Dale St, first right:

# The Stamford Streets AZ

Soundview Av, second right: Lockwood Av, third right: Frederick St

**Lenox Av**
Midland Av, Courtland Hill St

Straight: Courtland Av 106, first left: Fairmont Av, second left: Tremont Av, third left: Hamilton Av, first right: Taylor Reed Pl, Maple Tree Av, second right: Glen Terrace, third right: Glenbrook Rd 106

**Leon Pl**

Straight: West Av, Sylvandale Av, first left: Ferris Av, second left: Piave St, third left: Grenhart Rd, E 6 Governor John Davis Lodge Tpke I-95, first right: Annie Pl, second right: Boston Post Rd 1, third right: Nurney St

**Leona Dr**

Straight: Mary Violet Rd, first left: Hope St

**Leonard St**
Summit Pl, Central St, Dale Pl

# The Stamford Streets AZ

Straight: Belltown Rd, first left: Bellmere Av, second left: Burdick St, third left: Upland Rd, Alton Rd, first right: Francis Av, second right: Hornez St, third right: Toms Rd

**Leroy Pl**

Straight: Lawn Av, first left: Custer St, Helen Pl, second left: Trumbull Gate, third left: Sherman St, first right: Hamilton Av

**Leslie St**

Straight: West Av, first left: Nobile St, Moore St, second left: Minor Pl. third left: Nurney St, first right: Tuttle St, second right: Acosta St, Burr St, third right: Stillwater Av

**Lewelyn Rd**
Horton St, Lewelyn Rd

**Lewis Rd**
Ayres Dr

# The Stamford Streets AZ

Straight: Nichols Av, first left: Meadowpark Av N, second left: High Ridge Rd 137
Straight: Hartswood Rd
Meadowpark Av N, Beechwood Rd, Southwest Dr
Straight: High Ridge Rd 137, first left: Brandt Rd, second left: Maplewood Pl, third left: Tally Ho La, first right: Bel Aire Dr, second right: Swampscott Rd, third right: Emma Rd


**Liberty Pl**
Noble St

Straight: McClurg Av, Carlisle Pl, first left: Burley Av, first right: Wells Av, second right: Congress St
Straight: Fairfield Av, first left: Melrose Pl, second left: Congress St, third left: Claremont St, first right: Sunnyside Av, second right: Selleck St


**Liberty St**
Anthony St


Straight: W Main St, Roosevelt Av, first left: Wilson St, second left: Richmond Hill Av, third left: High St, first

# The Stamford Streets AZ

right: Victory St, second right: Virgil St
Straight: Stillwater Av, first left: Colahan St, second left: Virgil St, first right: Stillwater Pl, second right: Finney La, third right: Fairfield Av

**Lighthouse Way**

Straight: Ocean Dr W, first left: Fairview Av, second left: Ralsey Rd S, third left: Van Rensselaer Av, first right: Rogers Rd, second right: Verplank Av, third right: Saddle Rock Rd

**Lillian St**

Straight: Lockwood Av, first left: William St, second left: Woodrow St, third left: Warren St, first right: Frank St, second right: Orange St, third right: Boston Post Rd, Lincoln Av
Straight: Dale St, first left: Frank St, first right: William St, second right: Woodrow St, third right: Ursula Pl

# The Stamford Streets AZ

**Limerick St**

Straight: Soundview Av, first left: McMullen Av, second left: East Av, third left: James St, first right: Wardwell St, second right: Cove Rd


**Lincoln Av**
Sherman St, Sheridan St

Straight: Boston Post Rd, first left: Lockwood Av, second left: Grant Av, third left: Lawn Av, first right: Maple Av, second right: Myrtle Av, third right: Crystal St
Straight: Custer St, straight: Helen Pl, Lawn Av, first left: Leroy Pl, second left: Hamilton Av, first right: Trumbull Gate, second right: Sherman St, third right: Boston Post Rd 1


**Lindale St**
Forest St, Highland Rd, Valley Rd

Straight: Boston Post Rd 1, first left: Crandall St, second left: Clarks Hill Av, Glenbrook Rd, third left: Daly St, first right: Broad St, second right: Elm St, Stamford Plaza 1
Straight: Hillcrest Av, straight: Grove St, first left: Highland Rd, second

# The Stamford Streets AZ

left: Greyrock Pl, third left: Forest St, first right: Prospect St, Hoyt St, Strawberry Hill Av, Hillandale Av


**Linden Pl**

Straight: W Washington Av, first left: North St, first right: Court St
Straight: Hoyt St, Washington Blvd 137, first left: 2nd St, second left: 2nd St, third left: Bridge St, first right: North St, second right: W Broad St, Broad St, third right: Whittaker Pl


**Lindsey Av**
Rome Pl, Brighton Pl

Straight: Oaklawn Av, first left: Clifford Av, second left: Jamroga La, third left: Pepper Ridge Rd, first right: Dorlen Rd, second right: Newfield Av
Straight: Rome Pl, S Lindsey Av, first left: Brighton Pl, second left: Crane Rd N, first right: Clifford Av, second right: Vanech Dr

# The Stamford Streets AZ

### Lindstrom Rd

Straight: Shippan Av, first left: Harbor Dr, Magee Av, second left: Seaview Av, third left: Park St, first right: Rippowam Rd, second right: Mariners La, third right: Iroquois Rd

### Linwood La

Straight: Wire Mill Rd, first left: Four Brooks Rd, second left: Cedar Heights Rd, third left: Cedar Tree La, Hunting La, first right: Red Fox Rd, second right: Studio Rd, third right: Gutzon Borglum Rd

### Lipton Pl

Straight: Atlantic St, first left: Henry St, second left: Rockland Pl, third left: Station Pl, first right: Woodland Av, second right: Lipton Pl, third right: Walter Wheeler Dr
Straight: Atlantic St, first left: Woodland Av, second left: Lipton Pl, third left: Henry St, first right: Walter Wheeler Dr, second right: Washington Blvd

# The Stamford Streets AZ

**Lisa La**

Straight: S Lake Dr, first right: Wallenberg Dr
Straight: N Lake Dr, first right: Long Ridge Rd 104


**Little Hill Dr**
Berrian Rd, Hollow Oak La, Rolling Wood Dr, Idlewood Dr

Straight: Janice Rd, first left: Woods End Rd, first right: High Ridge Rd 137


**Little John La**
Nottingham Dr


**Lockwood Av**
Warren St, Woodrow St, William St, Lillian St, Frank St, Orange St

Straight: Cove Rd, first left: Soundview Av, second left: Leeds St, third left: St Benedict Circle, first right: Frederick St, second right: Shippan Av, Elm St
Straight: Boston Post Rd 1, first left: Lincoln Av, second left: Maple Av, third left: Myrtle Av, first right: Grant Av,

# The Stamford Streets AZ

second right: Lawn Av, third right: Seaton Rd, Noroton Hill Pl

**Locust La**

Straight: Bedford St, first left: Marlou La, second left: Urban St, third left: Chester St, 6th St, first right: Summer St, Long Ridge Rd, High Ridge Rd 137

**Logan's Run**

Straight: Stillwater Rd, first left: Westwood Rd, second left: Long Hill Dr, first right: Skyview Dr, second right: Clover Hill Dr

**Lolly La**
Straight: Gary Rd, first left: Old Logging Rd, first right: Scofieldtown Rd

**London La**

Straight: Stillwater Rd, first left: Stillview Rd, second left: Pond Rd, third left: Cold Spring Rd, first right: River Hill Dr, second right: Clover Hill Dr, third right: Skyview Dr, fourth right: Logan's Run

# The Stamford Streets AZ

## Long Close Rd

Straight: Westover Rd, first left: Merriebrook La, second left: Long Close Rd, third left: W Glen Dr, fourth left: Mianus Rd, first right: Canfield Dr, second right: Canfield Dr, third right: Nathan Hale Dr
Straight: Westover Rd, first left: W Glen Dr, second left: Mianus Rd, third left: Westover Av, first right: Merriebrook La, second right: Long Close Rd, third right: Canfield Dr

## Long Hill Dr
Long Hill Dr, Long Hill Dr, Long Hill Dr, Long Hill Dr, Tree Top Ct

Straight: Stillwater Rd, first left: Westwood Rd, second left: Logan's Run, third left: Skyview Dr, first right: Long Ridge Rd 104, second right: Roxbury Rd
Straight: Clover Hill Dr, first left: Evergreen Ct, second left: Long Ridge Rd 104, first right: Stillwater Rd

## Long Ridge Rd 104
Cold Spring Rd 137, Cross Rd, McClean Av, Terrace Av, Stark Pl, River Ridge Ct, Brook Run La, Wishing Well La,

# The Stamford Streets AZ

Woodridge Dr S, Three Lakes Dr, Clover Hill Dr, Stillwater Rd, Roxbury Rd, Buckingham Dr, Barnes Rd, Loughran Av, Maltbie Av, Vineyard La, Wire Mill Rd, E 34 Merritt Pkwy 15, CT15, E 34 Merritt Pkwy 15, CT15, Webbs Hill Rd, Northwood La, Midrocks Dr, Den Rd, Hazard La, Chestnut Hill Rd, Butternut La, Chestnut Hill Rd, Hunting Ridge Rd, Stone Hill Dr, Partridge Rd, Lakewood Dr, Sawmill Rd, Wildwood Rd, Mountain Wood Rd, Riverbank Rd, Old Long Ridge Rd, Grey Birch Rd, Erskine Rd, Parsonage Rd, N Lake Dr, Echo Hill Dr, Old Long Ridge Rd, NY Rockrimmon Country Club, NY Rockrimmon Country Club, NY

Straight: Summer St, High Ridge Rd, Bedford St, first left: Cold Spring Rd, second left: Halpin Av, third left: Oaklawn Av, first right: Hoover Av, second right: Forest Lawn Av, third right: 8th St

**Longview Av**

Straight: High Ridge Rd 104, first left: Knollwood Av, second left: Mercedes La, Dannell Dr, third left: Yale Ct, first right: Loveland Rd W, second right: Lakeview Dr, third right: Unity Rd, fourth right: Brownley Dr

# The Stamford Streets AZ

Straight: Ridge Park Av, first left: Hillview La, second left: Rosano Rd, Wood Ridge Dr, first right: Knollwood Av, second right: Wood Ridge Dr, third right: High Ridge Rd 137

**Loughran Av**

Straight: Long Ridge Rd 104, first left: Barnes Rd, second left: Roxbury Rd, Stillwater Rd, Buckingham Dr, third left: Clover Hill Dr, first right: Maltbie Av, second right: Vineyard La, third right: Wire Mill Rd
Straight: Maltbie Av, first left: Long Ridge Rd 104, first right: Mid River Run

**Loveland Rd W**

Straight: High Ridge Rd 137, first left: Lakeview Dr, second left: Unity Rd, third left: Brownley Dr, first right: Longview Av, second right: Knollwood Av, third right: Mercedes La, Dannell Dr
Straight: Loveland Rd, Silver Hill La, first left: White Birch La, second left: Lantern Circle, third left: Dannell Dr, first right: Deer La, second right: Pepper Ridge Rd, third right: Fara Dr

# The Stamford Streets AZ

**Loveland Rd**

Straight: White Birch La, first left: Lantern Circle, second left: Dannell Dr, first right: Deer La, second right: Pepper Ridge Rd
Straight: Loveland Rd W, Silver Hill La, first left: Deer La, second left: Pepper Ridge Rd, third left: Fara Dr, first right: High Ridge Rd 137

**Ludlow Pl**

Straight: Ludlow St, first left: Canal St, first right: Cedar St, second right: Pacific St, Woodland Av

**Ludlow St**
Canal St, Ludlow Pl, Cedar St

Straight: Woodland Av, Pacific St, first left: Woodland Pl, second left: Walter Wheeler Dr, E Walnut St, third left: Remington St, first right: Henry St, second right: Market St, third right: Manhattan St

# The Stamford Streets AZ

**Lumanor Dr**

Straight: New England Dr, first left: Quarry Rd, first right: Cypress Dr

**Lund Av**

Straight: Knox Rd, Upper Haig Av, Haig Av, first left: Weed Hill Av, first right: Knox Rd, second right: Dagmar Pl, third right: Nyselius Pl
Straight: Knox Rd, first left: Upper Haig Av, Haig Av, second left: Upper Haig Av, Lund Av, first right: Newfield Av

**Luther St**

Straight: Atlantic St, first left: Main St, second left: Town Center Dr, third left: Bank St, first right: Broad St, Bedford St

**Lynam Ct**

Straight: Lynam Rd, first left: Nob Hill La, second left: Webbs Hill Rd

# The Stamford Streets AZ

**Lynam Rd**
Lynam Ct, Nob Hill La

Straight: Webbs Hill Rd, first left: Jeffrey La, second left: Dogwood La, third left: Dogwood La, fourth left: Pheasant La, first right: Huckleberry Hollow, second right: Chestnut Hill Rd

# The Stamford Streets AZ

## M

### MacArthur La

Straight: Doolittle Rd, first left: Pakenmer Rd, first right: Den Rd

### MacGregor Dr
Akbar Rd, Akbar Rd

Straight: W Hill Rd, first left: Drum Hill La, second left: W Hill La, third left: Roxbury Rd, first right: Dancy Dr, second right: Green Tree La, third right: Carriage Dr

### Madeline Ct

Straight: Hidden Brook Dr, first right: Woodway Rd

### Madison Pl

Straight: Wilson St, first left: Grenhart Rd, second left: Baxter Av, third left: Pressprich St, first right: Hall Pl, second right: Boston Post Rd 1, Richmond Hill Av
Straight: Fairfield Av, first left: Taylor St, second left: Hall Pl, third

# The Stamford Streets AZ

left: Perry St, first right: First Stamford Pl, second right: Jackson St, third right: Baxter Av

**Magee Av**
Pumping Station Rd, Hanover St, St Marys St

Straight: Shippan Av, Harbor Dr, first left: Seaview Av, second left: Park St, third left: Hanover St
Straight: Jefferson St, first left: Cherry St, second left: Harbor View Av, third left: Meadow St, first right: Halloween Blvd, second right: Elm St, Myrtle Av

**Maher Rd**
Ursula Pl, Orange St

Straight: E Main St, first left: Seaton Rd, Noroton Hill Pl, second left: Lawn Av, first right: Blachley Rd, second right: Standish Rd, third right: E9 Governor John Davis Lodge Tpke I-95

**Main St**
Bank St, Clark St, W Park Pl, Summer St, Washington Blvd 137, Rippowam Pl, Clinton Av

# The Stamford Streets AZ

Straight: Mill River St, W Main St, first left: Boston Post Rd 1, Greenwich Av, first right: Greenwood Hill St, Smith St, second right: W Broad St
Straight: Atlantic St, first left: Luther St, second left: Broad St, Bedford St, first right: Town Center Dr, second right: Bank St, third right: Bell St, fourth right: Tresser Blvd 1

**Maitland Rd**

Straight: Judy La, first right: Hamilton Av, Sutton Dr
Straight: Hamilton Av, first left: Sutton Dr, Judy La, second left: Lawn Av, third left: Culloden Rd, first right: Courtland Av 106, second right: Field St, third right: Midland Av, Courtland Hill St

**Malibu Rd**
Butternut La

**Maltbie Av**
Loughran Av, Mid River Run

Straight: Long Ridge Rd 104, first left: Loughran Av, second left: Barnes Rd, third left: Roxbury Rd, Buckingham Dr,

# The Stamford Streets AZ

fourth left: Stillwater Rd, first right: Vineyard La, second right: Wire Mill Rd, third right: E 34 Merritt Pkwy 15, CT15

**Malvern Rd**

Straight: Vine Rd, first left: Pepper Ridge Rd, second left: Kerr Rd, third left: Simsbury Rd, first right: Brandywine Rd, second right: Pamlynn Rd, third right: Barmore Dr, fourth right: Vine Pl
Straight: Club Rd, first left: Club Circle, first right: Sandy La, second right: Kerr Rd, third right: Bertmor Dr

**Manhattan St**
Garden St, Pacific St

Straight: John St, first left: Dock St, first right: Market St
Straight: Atlantic St, first left: Station Pl, second left: Rockland Pl, third left: Henry St, first right: S State St, E 8 Governor John Davis Lodge Tpke I-95, second right: N State St, E 8 Governor John Davis Lodge Tpke I-95, third right: Federal St, fourth right: Tresser Blvd 1

# The Stamford Streets AZ

**Manor St**

Straight: Dyke La, first left: Harbor St, second left: Elmcroft Rd, first right: Pacific St
Straight: Belden St, first left: Pacific St, first right: Harbor St, second right: Elmcroft Rd

**Maple Av**
Warren St, William St, Gregory St, Frank St, E 8 Governor John Davis Lodge Tpke I-95

Straight: Boston Post Rd 1, first left: Myrtle Av, second left: Crystal St, third left: N State St, first right: Lincoln Av, second right: Lockwood Av, third right: Grant Av
Straight: Frederick St, first left: Shippan Av, second left: Cove Rd, third left: Wardwell St, first right: Myrtle Av

**Maple Tree Av**
Oakdale Rd, Radio Pl

Straight: Courtland Av 106, Taylor Reed Pl, first left: Lenox Av, second left: Fairmont Av, third left: Tremont Av,

# The Stamford Streets AZ

first right: Glen Terrace, second right: Glenbrook Rd
Straight: West Av

**Maplewood Pl**

Straight: High Ridge Rd 137, first left: Tally Ho La, second left: Bradley Pl, third left: Donata La, first right: Brandt Rd, second right: Hartswood Rd, third right: Bel Aire Dr

**Marian St**
Elizabeth Av, St Charles Av, Cady St, Buena Vista St, Crestview Av, Tower Av

Straight: Lawton Av, first left: Knapp St, Sleepy Hollow La, first right: Birchwood Rd, second right: Woodledge Rd, third right: Bennett St

**Marie Pl**

Straight: Elmbrook Dr, first left: Tioga Pl, second left: Glendale Rd, first right: Pine Hill Av
Straight: Alton Rd, first left: Pine Tree Dr, first right: Tioga Pl, second right: Norman Rd, third right: Upland Rd

# The Stamford Streets AZ

**Mariners La**
Nelson St

Straight: Shippan Av, first left: Rippowam Rd, second left: Lindstrom Rd, third left: Harbor Dr, Magee Av, first right: Iroquois Rd, second right: Wallace St, third right: Mitchell St

**Market St**
John St

Straight: Canal St, first left: Dock St, Jefferson St, second left: S State St, E 7 Governor John Davis Lodge Tpke I-95, third left: N State St, E 7 Governor Dakms Lodge Tpke I-95, fourth left: Stamford Forum 1, Stamford Plaza 1, Greyrock Pl, first right: Henry St, second right: Ludlow St
Straight: Pacific St, first left: Henry St, second left: Woodland Av, Ludlow St, third left: Woodland Pl, first right: Manhattan St

**Marlou La**

Straight: Bedford St, first left: Locust La, second left: Summer St, Long Ridge Rd 104, High Ridge Rd 137, first right:

# The Stamford Streets AZ

Urban St, second right: 6th St, Chester St, third right: 5th St

**Marschall Pl**

Straight: Pepper Ridge Rd, first left: Hirsch Rd, second left: Ogden Rd, third left: Turner Rd, first right: Oaklawn Av, Jamroga La

**Martin St**
George St

Straight: Horton St, first left: Cove Rd, first right: Robin St, second right: Charles St, third right: Lewelyn Rd
Straight: Ferro Dr, Hale St, first right: Elmwood St

**Marva La**

Straight: High Ridge Rd, first left: Pine Hill Terrace, second left: Perna La, third left: Blue Ridge Dr, first right: Brantwood La, second right: Opper Rd, third right: Willard Terrace, fourth right: Wire Mill Rd

# The Stamford Streets AZ

**Mary Joy La**

Straight: Skymeadow Dr, first left: Skyline La, second left: Larkspur Rd, third left: Scofieldtown Rd, first right: High Ridge Rd 137, Bartlett La

**Mary Violet Rd**
Leona Dr

Straight: Hope St, first left: Nottingham Dr, second left: Deep Spring La, third left: Camelot Ct, first right: Putter Dr, second right: Robinhood Rd, third right: Woodway Rd

**Maryanne La**

Straight: Todd La, first left: Pershing Av, Haig Av, first right: Edward Pl, second right: Newfield Av

**Mather Rd**

Straight: Woodbine Rd, first left: Woodbine Way, second left: Cascade Rd, first right: Pinewood Rd, second right: Brushwood Rd, third right: Cedar Wood Rd

# The Stamford Streets AZ

**Mathews St**
Cambridge Rd, Waterbury Av, Houston Terrace, Webb Av

Straight: Seaside Av, first left: Sylvan Knoll Rd, second left: Cove Rd, first right: Bungalow Park, second right: Webb Av, third right: E9 Governor John Davis Lodge Tpke I-95
Straight: Weed Av, first left: Holly Cove Circle, second left: Birch St, third left: Boston Post Rd 1, first right: Weed Circle, second right: Cove Rd


**Mayapple Rd**
Russet Rd, Country Club Rd, Boulderol Rd, Tanglewood La, Apple Valley Rd

Straight: High Ridge Rd 137, first left: Trinity Pass, second left: Riding Stable Trail, third left: Fairway Dr, fourth left: Craig Ct, first right: Laurel Rd, second right: Flora Pl, third right: Russet Rd
Straight: Rock Rimmon Rd, first left: Breezy Hill Rd, second left: Golden Farm Rd, third left: Ridge Brook Dr, first right: Rock Meadow La, second right: Pond View La, third right: Winslow Dr, fourth right: Old Long Ridge Rd

# The Stamford Streets AZ

**Mayflower Av**
Hackett Circle S, Hackett Circle N, Puritan La, Plymouth Rd

Straight: Rock Spring Rd, first left: Treat Av, second left: Puritan La, Coolidge Av, third left: Hope St, first right: Ardsley Rd, second right: Strawberry Hill Av
Straight: Colonial Rd, first left: Strawberry Hill Av, first right: Pilgrim Walk, second right: Hope St


**McClean Av**

Straight: Long Ridge Rd 104, first left: Cross Rd, second left: Cold Spring Rd 137, third left: Summer St, High Ridge Rd 137, Bedford St, first right: Terrace Av, second right: Stark Pl, third right: River Ridge Ct
Straight: High Ridge Rd 137, first left: Terrace Av, second left: High Ridge Rd, third left: High Ridge Rd, fourth left: Colony Ct, High Clear Dr, first right: Dubois St, second right: Cross Rd, third right: Oaklawn Av

# The Stamford Streets AZ

**McClurg Av**

Straight: Southfield Av, first left: Burley Av, second left: Sunnyside Av, third left: Taff Av, first right: Wells Av, second right: Congress St, third right: Burwood Av
Straight: Carlisle Pl, Liberty Pl, first left: Wells Av, second left: Congress St, first right: Burley Av


**McIntosh Ct**

Straight: McIntosh Rd, first left: Black Twig Pl, second left: Russet Rd, third left: Mayapple Rd, first right: Winesap Rd


**McIntosh Rd**
McIntosh Ct, Black Twig Pl

Straight: Russet Rd, first left: Mayapple Rd, first right: Winesap Rd, second right: High Ridge Rd 137
Straight: Winesap Rd, first left: Crab Apple Pl, second left: Russet Rd, first right: Shady La, Merriland Rd


**McMullen Av**
James St, Owen St

# The Stamford Streets AZ

Straight: Soundview Av, first left: James St, second left: East Av, third left: McMullen Av, first right: Tupper Dr, second right: Carter Dr
Straight: Soundview Av, first left: Limerick St, second left: Wardwell St, third left: Cove Rd, first right: East Av, second right: James St, third right: McMullen Av

**Mead St**
Oenoke Pl

Straight: Highview Av, first left: Columbus Pl, second left: Woodway Rd, first right: Mead St, second right: Cerretta St, third right: Camp Av
Straight: Hope St, first left: Minivale Rd, second left: Weed Hill Av, third left: Mulberry St, first right: Bouton St W, Bouton St, second right: Woodway Rd, third right: Robinhood Rd

**Meadowpark Av E**
Brookvale Pl

Straight: Meadowpark Av S, Meadowpark Av W, first right: Meadowpark Av E, Meadowpark Av N
Straight: Meadowpark Av W, Meadowpark Av N, first left: Meadowpark Av S, first

# The Stamford Streets AZ

right: Meadowpark Av N, second right: Nichols Av, third right: Ayres Dr


**Meadow St**

Straight: Jefferson St, first left: Canal St, Dock St, first right: Harbor View Av, second right: Cherry St, third right: Magee Av


**Meadowpark Av N**
Nichols Av, Ayres Dr, Swampscott Rd

Straight: Hartswood Rd, first left: Ayres Dr, Lewis Rd, first right: Beechwood Rd, second right: Southwest Dr, third right: High Ridge Rd 137 Straight: Meadowpark Av E, Meadowpark Av W, first left: Brookvale Pl, second left: Meadowpark Av S, Meadowpark Av W, first right: Meadowpark Av S, Meadowpark Av E


**Meadowpark Av S**

Straight: Meadowpark Av W, Meadowpark Av E, first left: Meadowpark Av N, Nichols Av, second left: Ayres Dr, first right: Brookvale Pl, second right: Meadowpark Av N, Nichols Av, third right: Ayres Dr

# The Stamford Streets AZ

## Meadowpark Av W

Straight: Meadowpark Av S, Meadowpark Av E, first left: Brookvale Pl, second left: Meadowpark Av N
Straight: Meadowpark Av E, Meadowpark Av N, first left: Nichols Av, second left: Ayres Dr, third left: Swampscott Rd, first right: Brookvale Pl, second right: Meadowpark Av S

## Medical Center

Straight: Morgan St, first left: Hoyt St, first right: 3 Rd St, Strawberry Hill Ct
Straight: Strawberry Hill Av first left: Holcomb Av, first right: Hoyt St, Hillandale Av, Prospect St

## Megan La

Straight: Newfield Av, first left: Denicola Rd, second left: Sanford La, third left: Case Rd, Swan La, first right: Gray Farms Rd, second right: Vine Rd, third right: Club Rd, fourth right: Knox Rd

# The Stamford Streets AZ

**Melrose Pl**

Straight: Fairfield Av, first left: Liberty Pl, second left: Sunnyside Av, third left: Selleck St, first right: Congress St, second right: Claremont St, third right: Barry Pl
Straight: Barry Pl, straight: Fairfield Av, first left: Claremont St, second left: Congress St, third left: Melrose Pl, first right: Burwood Av, second right: Dee La, third right: Top Gallant Rd

**Mercedes La**

Straight: High Ridge Rd 137, Dannell Dr, first left: Yale Ct, second left: Janice Rd, third left: Ridge Park Av, fourth left: Nichols Av, first right: Knollwood Av, second right: Longview Av, third right: Loveland Rd W

**Meredith La**

Straight: High Ridge Rd 137, first left: Diamondcrest La, second left: Blue Ridge Dr, third left: Perna La, first right: Scofieldtown Rd, second right: High Ridge Rd, third right: High Ridge Rd, fourth right: Interlaken Rd

# The Stamford Streets AZ

**Merrell Av**
Edison Rd, Carolina Rd

Straight: W Broad St, first left: Delaware Av, second left: Stillwater Av, third left: Connecticut Av, first right: Rachelle Av, second right: Shelburne Rd, third right: St George Av
Straight: Stillwater Av, first left: Virgil St, second left: Colahan St, third right: Liberty St, first right: Corbo Terrace, second right: West Av, third right: Progress Dr

**Merriebrook La**
General Waterbury La

Straight: Westover Rd, first left: Long Close Rd, second left: Canfield Dr, third left: Canfield Dr, first right: Long Close Rd, second right: W Glen Dr, third right: Mianus Rd

**Merriland Rd**

Straight: Shady La, Winesap Rd, first left: Briar Brae Rd, first right: McIntosh Rd, second right: Crab Apple Pl, third right: Russet Rd

# The Stamford Streets AZ

**Merriman Rd**

Straight: Vine Pl, straight: Vine Rd, first left: Kane Av, second left: High Ridge Rd 137, first right: Barmore Dr, second right: Pamlynn Rd, third right: Brandywine Rd
Straight: High Ridge Rd 137, first left: Donata La, second left: Bradley Pl, third left: Tally Ho La, first right: Vine Rd, second right: Cedar Heights Rd, Turn Of River Rd, third right: Olga Dr, fourth right: Square Acre Dr


**Merritt Pkwy 15, CT15**
E35: High Ridge Rd, E34: Long Ridge Rd 104, E33: Den Rd

Straight: New Canaan, CT
Straight: Greenwich, CT


**Mianus Rd**

Straight: Westover Rd, first left: W Glen Dr, second left: Long Close Rd, third left: Merriebrook La, first right: Westover Av, second right: Westover La, third right: Bartina La
Straight: Valley Rd

# The Stamford Streets AZ

**Michael Rd**

Straight: Cascade Rd, first left: Frost Pond Rd, second left: Woodbine Rd, third left: Ponus Ridge Rd, first right: Pembroke Dr, second right: Cascade Ct, third right: N Stamford Rd

**Middle Ridge Rd**

Straight: Scofieldtown Rd, first left: Janes La, second left: Old Logging Rd, third left: Gary Rd, first right: Woodley Rd, second right: Campbell Dr, third right: Georgian Ct, fourth right: Chestnut Hill Rd

**Middlebury St**
Webster Rd, Andover Rd

Straight: Cambridge Rd, first left: Mathews St, first right: Neponsit St

**Midland Av**
Tremont Av, Fairmont Av

Straight: Hamilton Av, Courtland Hill St, Hamilton Av, first left: Fairmont Av, second left: Lenox Av, first right:

# The Stamford Streets AZ

Courtland Av 106, second right: Maitland Rd, third right: Sutton Dr, Judy La
Straight: Lenox Av, first left: Courtland Av 106, first right: Courtland Hill St


**Midrocks Dr**

Straight: E Ridge Rd
Straight: Long Ridge Rd 104, first left: Den Rd, second left: Hazard La, third left: Butternut La, Chestnut Hill Rd, first right: Northwood La, second right: Webbs Hill Rd, third right: E 34 Merritt Pkwy 15, CT15


**Mill Brook Rd W**

Straight: Mill Brook Rd, first left: Old Mill La


**Mill Brook Rd**
Mill Brook Rd W

Straight: Old Mill La, first right: Brookhollow La, second right: Westover Rd

# The Stamford Streets AZ

**Mill Rd**
Mohawk Trail, Mill Spring La, Dulan Dr, Gatewood Rd

Straight: Old Long Ridge Rd, first left: Hunting Ridge Rd, second left: Long Ridge Rd, first right: Shag Bark Rd, second right: Erskine Rd, third right: Heming Way
Straight: Rock Rimmon Rd, first left: Ridge Brook Dr, second left: Golden Farm Rd, third left: Breezy Hill Rd, first right: Briar Brae Rd, second right: Saddle Hill Rd, third right: Dads La, E Hunting Ridge Rd

**Mill River St**
Greenwood Hill St, Smith St

Straight: W Main St, Main St, first left: Clinton Av, second left: Rippowam Pl, third left: Washington Blvd 137, first right: Boston Post Rd 1, Greenwich Av
Straight: W Broad St, first left: Hanrahan St, second left: Schuyler Av, third left: Adams Av, first right: Washington Blvd 137

**Mill Spring La**
Mill Valley La

# The Stamford Streets AZ

Straight: Mill Rd, first left: Dulan Dr, second left: Gatewood Rd, third left: Rock Rimmon Rd, first right: Mohawk Trail, second right: Old Long Ridge Rd

**Mill Stone Circle**

Straight: Sawmill Rd, first left: Dundee Rd, second left: Mill Stream Rd, first right: Wind Mill Circle, second right: Cider Mill Rd, third right: Long Ridge Rd 104

**Mill Stream Rd**

Straight: Sawmill Rd, first left: Dundee Rd, second left: Mill Stone Circle, third left: Wind Mill Circle, fourth left: Cider Mill Rd

**Mill Valley La**

Straight: Mill Spring La, first right: Mill Rd
Straight: Blackberry Dr, first right: Blackberry Dr E, second right: Happy Hill Rd

# The Stamford Streets AZ

## Milton St

Straight: Greenwich Av, first left: Davenport St, second left: Pulaski St, third left: First Stamford Pl, first right: Selleck St, second right: Homestead Av, third right: Taff Av, fourth right: Sunnyside Av
Straight: Orchard St

## Minivale Rd
Prudence Dr, Salem Pl, Gaymoor Dr, Bouton St W

Straight: Hope St, first left: Mead St, second left: Bouton St W, Bouton St, third left: Woodway Rd, first right: Weed Hill Av, second right: Mulberry St, third right: Camp Av

## Minor Pl

Straight: Virgil St, first left: Stillwater Av, first right: Dryden St, second right: Boston Post Rd 1
Straight: West Av, first left: Nurney St, second left: Boston Post Rd 1, first right: Nobile St, Moore St, second right: Leslie St, third right: Tuttle St, fourth right: Acosta St, Burr St

# The Stamford Streets AZ

**Miramar La**

Straight: Ocean Dr E, first left: Fairview Av, second left: Hobson St, third left: Rockledge Dr, first right: Ocean Dr W, Shippan Av


**Mission St**
West St

Straight: Richmond Hill Av, first left: Rose Park, second left: Taylor St, Ann St, third left: Spruce St, first right: Greenwich Av, second right: Clinton Av, third right: Washington Blvd


**Mitchell St**

Straight: Shippan Av, first left: Wallace St, second left: Iroquois Rd, third left: Mariners La, first right: Lanell Dr, second right: Auldwood Rd, third right: Downs Av, fourth right: Lanark Rd


**Mitzi Rd**

Straight: Donald Rd, straight: Gray Farms Rd, first left: Newfield Av, first right: Mitzi Rd, second right: Haig Av

# The Stamford Streets AZ

Straight: Gray Farms Rd, first left: Donald Rd, second left: Newfield Av, first right: Haig Av

## Mohawk Ct

Straight: Montauk Dr, first left: Southwood Dr, second left: Pequot Dr, third left: Selleck St, first right: Orlando Av, Pequot Dr

## Mohawk Trail

Straight: Mill Rd, first left: Old Long Ridge Rd, first right: Mill Spring La, second right: Dulan Dr, third right: Gatewood Rd

## Mohegan Av

Straight: Rippowam Rd, first left: Shippan Av, first right: Ponus Av, second right: Algonquin Av, third right: Wampanaw Rd
Straight: Iroquois Rd, first left: Ponus Av, second left: Algonquin Av, third left: Wampanaw Rd, first right: Shippan Av

# The Stamford Streets AZ

**Montauk Dr**
Mohawk Ct, Southwood Dr, Pequot Dr

Straight: Selleck St, Durant St, first left: Bonner St, Irving Av, first right: Betts Av
Straight: Orlando Av, Pequot Dr, first left: Southwood Dr, second left: Montauk Dr, first right: West Av


**Moore St**

Straight: Nobile St, West Av, first left: Minor Pl, second left: Nurney St, third left: Boston Post Rd 1, first right: Leslie St, second right: Tuttle St, third right: Acosta St, Burr St


**Morgan St**
Medical Center, Strawberry Patch La, Strawberry Hill Ct, 3rd St

Straight: Hoyt St, first left: Hoyt St, second left: Prospect St, Grove St, Strawberry Hill Av, Hillandale Av, first right: Bedford St, second right: Summer St, third right: Franklin St, fourth right: Linden Pl, Washington Blvd 137
Straight: 5th St, first left: Revonah Av, second left: Bedford St, third left:

# The Stamford Streets AZ

Summer St, first right: Vincent Ct, second right: Strawberry Hill Av

**Morris St**
Center St

Straight: Oscar St, first left: Scofield Av

**Mountain Trail**

Straight: West Trail, first right: Fishing Trail, second right: Settlers Trail, third right: Sunset Rd

**Mountain Wood Rd**
Heather Dr

Straight: Long Ridge Rd 104, first left: Wildwood Rd, second left: Sawmill Rd, third left: Lakewood Dr, first right: Riverbank Rd, second right: Old Long Ridge Rd, third right: Grey Birch Rd, fourth right: Erskine Rd

**Mulberry St**
Carroll St, Elmer St, Brundage St, Ridgeway St

# The Stamford Streets AZ

Straight: Hope St, first left: Weed Hill Av, second left: Minivale Rd, third left: Mead St, first right: Camp Av, second right: Knapp St, Greenway St, third right: Hyde St

**Munko Dr**

Straight: Roxbury Rd, first left: Barncroft Rd, second left: Doral Farms Rd, third left: Overhill Rd, first right: Den Rd, second right: Roxbury Terrace, third right: Riverbank Rd, Cow Path Dr, Westover Rd

**Muriel Dr**

Straight: Hickory Way, first right: Muriel Dr, second right: Weed Hill Av
Straight: Hickory Way, first left: Muriel Dr, first right: Weed Hill Av

**Myano Ct**

Straight: Myano La, first left: Oakwood Pl, second left: Catoona La, third left: Boston Post Rd, first right: Connecticut Av

# The Stamford Streets AZ

**Myano La**
Myano Ct, Oakwood Pl, Catoona La

Straight: Connecticut Av, first right: Stillwater Rd
Straight: Boston Post Rd 1, first left: Alvord La, second left: Harvard Av, third left: Aberdeen St, first right: Whitmore La, second right: Havemeyer La, Laddin Rock Rd, E Putnam Av


**Myrtle Av**
Frederick St, Warren St, William St, Gregory St, E 8 Governor John Davis Lodge Tpke I-95

Straight: Boston Post Rd 1, first left: Crystal St, second left: N State St, third left: Quintard Terrace, first right: Maple Av, second right: Lincoln Av, third right: Lockwood Av, fourth right: Grant Av
Straight: Elm St, Jefferson St, first left: Wardwell St, second left: Shippan Av, Cove Rd, first right: Cherry St, second right: Elm Ct, third right: S State St, E 8 Governor John Davis Lodge Tpke I-95

# The Stamford Streets AZ

## N

### N Briar Brae Rd

Straight: Briar Brae Rd, first left: High Ridge Rd, first right: Shady La, second right: Briar Wood Trail, third right: Rock Rimmon Rd

### N Lake Dr
Lisa La

Straight: Long Ridge Rd 104, first left: Echo Hill Dr, second left: Old Long Ridge Rd, third left: Rockrimmon Country Club, first right: Parsonage Rd, second right: Erskine Rd, third right: Grey Birch Rd

### N Meadows La

Straight: Newfield Av, first left: Eden Rd, second left: Wedgemere Rd, first right: Lakeside Dr, Davenport Ridge Rd

### N Stamford Rd
Cascade Rd, Lakeside Dr

Straight: High Ridge Rd 137, first left: Brookdale Rd, second left: Bird Song La,

# The Stamford Streets AZ

third left: Interlaken Rd, first right: Alma Rock Rd, second right: N Stamford Rd, third right: Skymeadow Dr, Bartlett La
Straight: High Ridge Rd 137, first left: Alma Rock Rd, second left: N Stamford Rd, third left: Brookdale Rd, first right: Skymeadow Dr, Bartlett La, second right: Pinner La, third right: Cedar Wood Rd

**N State St**
Daly St, Lafayette St, S State St

Straight: Clarks Hill Av, straight: Boston Post Rd 1, Glenbrook Rd, first left: Crandall St, second left: Lindale St, third left: Broad St, first right: Daly St, second right: Lafayette St, third right: Quintard Terrace
Straight: Boston Post Rd 1, first left: Quintard Terrace, second left: Lafayette St, third left: Daly St, first right: Crystal St, second right: Myrtle Av, third right: Maple Av

**Nash Pl**

Straight: Howes Av, first left: Brooklawn Av, second left: Hope St,

# The Stamford Streets AZ

first right: Pierce Pl, second right: Glenbrook Rd

**Nathan Hale Dr**

Straight: Westover Rd, first left: Canfield Dr, second left: Canfield Dr, third left: Long Close Rd, first right: High Line Trail, second right: Winding Brook La

**Nelson St**

Straight: Wallace St, first right: Shippan Av
Straight: Mariners La, first right: Shippan Av

**Neponsit St**
Dora St, Webster Rd, Albin Rd, Andover Rd, Island Heights Dr

Straight: Cambridge Rd
Middlebury St
Straight: Mathews St, first left: Waterbury Av, second left: Houston Terrace, third left: Webb Av, first right: Weed Av

# The Stamford Streets AZ

**New England Dr**
Lumanor Dr

Straight: Quarry Rd, first right: Blue Rock Dr, second right: Greenbrier La, third right: Chapin La, fourth right: Lakeside Dr
Straight: Cypress Dr


**Newfield Av**
N Meadows La, Eden Rd, Wedgemere Rd, White Oak La, Emerald La, Intervale Rd E, Sweet Briar Rd, Newfield Dr, Sterling Farms Golf Club, Weed Hill Av, Knox Rd, Club Rd, Vine Rd, Gray Farms Rd, Megan La, Denicola Rd, Sanford La, Case Rd, Swan La, Todd La, Turner Rd, Belltown Rd, Ogden Rd, Hirsch Rd, Newfield Ct, Dorlen Rd, Fairland St, Francis Av, Oaklawn Av, Burdick St, Crane Rd

Straight: Strawberry Hill Av
Straight: Lakeside Dr, Davenport Ridge Rd, first left: Interlaken Rd, second left: Quarry Rd, third left: N Stamford Rd, first right: Zora La, Davenport Ridge La, second right: Jeanne Ct, third right: Davenport Farm La W, fourth right: Thornridge Dr

# The Stamford Streets AZ

**Newfield Ct**

Straight: Newfield Av, first left: Hirsch Rd, second left: Ogden Rd, third left: Turner Rd, Belltown Rd, first right: Dorlen Rd, second right: Fairland St, third right: Francis Av

**Newfield Dr**
Shadow La

Straight: Intervale Rd, Joan Rd, first left: Arnold Dr, first right: Gaxton Rd, second right: Turn Of River Rd
Straight: Newfield Av, first left: Sweet Briar Rd, Intervale Rd E, second left: Emerald La, third left: White Oak La, first right: Sterling Farms Golf Club, second right: Weed Hill Av, third right: Knox Rd

**Nichols Av**
Lewis Rd, Meadowpark Av N

Straight: High Ridge Rd 137, first left: Emma Rd, second left: Swampscott Rd, third left: Bel Aire Dr, first right: Ridge Park Av, second right: Janice Rd, third right: Yale Ct

# The Stamford Streets AZ

**Nob Hill La**

Straight: Lynam Rd, first left: Webbs Hill Rd, first right: Lynam Ct

**Nobile St**
Depinedo Av

Straight: West Av, Moore St, first left: Leslie St, second left: Tuttle St, third left: Acosta St, Burr St, first right: Minor Pl, second right: Nurney St, third right: Boston Post Rd 1

**Noble St**
Congress St

Straight: Burwood Av, first left: Keith St, second left: Silver St, third left: Southfield Av, first right: Beal St, second right: Claremont St, third right: Fairfield Av
Straight: Liberty Pl, first left: Fairfield Av, first right: Carlisle Pl, McClurg Av

**Norman Rd**

Straight: Upland Rd, first left: Pine Tree Dr, second left: Strawberry Hill

# The Stamford Streets AZ

Av, Fieldstone La, first right: Alton Rd, second right: Burdick St, third right: Bellmere Av, Belltown Rd
Straight: Bellmere Av, first left: Belltown Rd, Upland Rd

**Noroton Hill Pl**

Straight: E Main St, Seaton Rd, first left: Lawn Av, second left: Grant Av, first right: Maher Rd, second right: Blachley Rd

**North St**
Hollywood Ct, W Washington Av, Washington Ct, Renwick St, Washington Blvd 137, Franklin St, Summer St, Dolsen Pl, Bedford St

Straight: Prospect St, first left: Hoyt St, Strawberry Hill Av, Hillandale Av, first right: Walton Pl, second right: Forest St, third right: Bedford St, Spring St
Straight: W North St

**Northerly Woods Rd**

Straight: Southerly Woods Rd

# The Stamford Streets AZ

Straight: Barn Hill Rd, straight: E Middle Patent Rd, first left: Cherry Hill Rd, second left: Taconic Rd, first right: Ledge Rd

**Northill St**
Knickerbocker Av, Carroll St, Palmer St

Straight: Woodledge Rd, first left: Lawton Av, second left: Bennett St, third left: Tower Av
Straight: Hope St, first left: Cushing St, second left: Hyde St, third left: Knapp St, Greenway St, first right: Fahey St, second right: Bennett St, third right: Largo Dr

**Northwind Dr**
Skyline La, Hoyclo Rd

Straight: Skyline La, first left: Sunset Rd, Scofieldtown Rd, first right: Northwind Dr, second right: Skymeadow Dr
Straight: High Ridge Rd 137, Bracchi Dr, first left: Hickory Rd, second left: Hickory Rd, third left: Sunset Rd, first right: Hoyclo Rd, Acre View Dr, second right: Cedar Wood Rd, third right: Pinner La

# The Stamford Streets AZ

**Northwood La**
Rockridge La

Straight: Long Ridge Rd 104, first left: Midrocks Dr, second left: Den Rd, third left: Hazard La, first right: Webbs Hill Rd, second right: E 34 Merritt Pkwy 15, CT15

**Northwood Rd**

Straight: Bon Air Av, first left: Buena Vista St, Clearview Av, first right: Crestview Av, second right: Northwood Rd, third right: Tower Av
Straight: Bon Air Av, first left Crestview Av, second left: Northwood Rd, third left: Buena Vista St, Clearview Av, first right: Tower Av

**Northwoods Rd**

Straight: West La, first left: East La, first right: Toilsome Brook Rd, second right: East La
Straight: Oaklawn Av, first left: Old Stamford Rd, Cantwell Av, second left: Halpin Av, third left: High Ridge Rd 137, first right: Benstone St, second

# The Stamford Streets AZ

right: Stanwick Pl, third right: Camore St

**Norvel La**

Straight: Gaxton Rd, first left: Intervale Rd

**Nottingham Dr**
Friar Tuck La

Straight: Hope St, first left: Mary Violet Rd, second left: Putter Dr, third left: Robinhood Rd, first right: Deep Spring La, second right: Camelot Ct, third right: Slice Dr
Straight: Little John La

**Nurney St**

Straight: West Av, first left: Minor Pl, second left: Nobile St, Moore St, third left: Leslie St, first right: Boston Post Rd 1, second right: Annie Pl, third right: Sylvandale Av, Leon Pl

**Nutmeg La**

Straight: Simsbury Rd, first left: Vine Rd

# The Stamford Streets AZ

Straight: Pepper Ridge Rd, first left: Red Bird Rd, second left: Robinson Dr, third left: Berrian Rd, first right: Vine Rd

**Nyselius Pl**
Dagmar Rd

Straight: Haig Av, first left: Dagmar Pl, second left: Knox Rd, Upper Haig Av, first right: Gray Farms Rd, second right: Crestview Av, third right: St Charles Av, fourth right: Joffre Av

# The Stamford Streets AZ

## O

**Oak Hill St**

Straight: W Broad St, first left: Stephen St, second left: Anderson St, third left: Wright St, first right: Adams Av, second right: Schuyler Av, third right: Hanrahan St, fourth right: Mill River St
Straight: Pine Av, straight: Schuyler Av, first left: W Broad St, first right: Smith St


**Oak St**

Straight: Summer St, first left: Hoyt St, second left: North St, third left: Spring St, first right: Woodside St, 1st St, second right: 2nd St, third right: 3rd St
Straight: Bedford St, first left: 1st St, second left: 2nd St, third left: 3rd St, first right: Hoyt St, second right: Dolsen Pl, third right: North St


**Oakdale Rd**
Glen Terrace, Phillips Pl, Rose Rd

# The Stamford Streets AZ

Straight: Glenbrook Rd 106, first left: Research Dr, second left: Courtland Av 106, third left: Arthur Pl, first right: Fresh Meadows La, Middlesex Rd


**Oaklawn Av**
Halpin Av, Cantwell Av, Old North Stamford Rd, Northwoods Rd, Benstone St, Stanwick Pl, Camore St, Dartley St, Fairfield Memorial Park Cemetery, Dann Dr, Sherwood Rd, Vanech Dr, Pepper Ridge Rd, Jamroga La, Clifford Av, Lindsey Av, Dorlen Rd

Straight: Newfield Av, first left: Francis Av, second left: Fairland St, third left: Dorlen Rd, first right: Burdick St, second right: Crane Rd N, Strawberry Hill Av
Straight: High Ridge Rd 137, first left: Halpin Av, second left: Cold Spring Rd, third left: Long Ridge Rd, Summer St, Bedford St, first right: Cross Rd, second right: Dubois St, third right: McClean Av


**Oakwood Pl**

Straight: Myano La, first left: Catoona La, second left: W Main St, first right: Myano Ct, second right: Connecticut Av

# The Stamford Streets AZ

**Ocean Dr E**
Westcott Rd, Sea Beach Dr, Rockledge Dr, Hobson St, Fairview Av, Miramar La

Straight: Shippan Av, Ocean Dr W, first right: Verplank Av, second right: Westminster Rd, third right: Fairview Av Straight: Shippan Av, first left: Ocean Dr W, second left: Rockledge Dr, third left: Hobson St, first right: Sagamore Rd, second right: Gurley Rd, third right: Ralsey Rd


**Ocean Dr N**
Lanark Rd, Auldwood Rd

Straight: Chesterfield Rd, straight: Shippan Av, first left: Ralsey Rd, second left: Gurley Rd, third left: Sagamore Rd, first right: Lanark Rd, second right: Downs Av, third right: Auldwood Rd

**Ocean Dr W**
Stamford Av, Saddle Rock Rd, Verplank Av, Rogers Rd, Lighthouse Way, Fairview Av, Ralsey Rd S, Van Rensselaer Av, Stamford Av, Woolsey Rd

Straight: Shippan Av, Ocean Dr E, first left: Verplank Av, second left: Westminster Rd, third left: Fairview Av

# The Stamford Streets AZ

Straight: Shippan Av, first left: Ocean Dr E, second left: Sagamore Rd, third left: Gurley Rd, first right: Rockledge Dr, second right: Hobson St, third right: Sound Av

**Ocean View Dr**

Straight: Fairview Av
Ocean Dr E, Brightside Dr, Shippan Av, Cresthill Pl, Stamford Av, Van Rensselaer Av, Ocean Dr W

**Oenoke Pl**

Straight: Mead St, first left: Hope St, first right: Highview Av

**Ogden Rd**

Straight: Pepper Ridge Rd, first left: Hirsch Rd, second left: Marschall Pl, third left: Oaklawn Av, first right: Turner Rd, second right: Fara Dr, third right: Silver Hill La
Straight: Newfield Av, first left: Turner Rd, Belltown Rd, second left: Todd La, third left: Case Rd, Swan La, first right: Hirsch Rd, second right: Newfield Ct, third right: Dorlen Rd

## The Stamford Streets AZ

**Old Barn Rd N**

Straight: Old Barn Rd W, straight: Old Barn Rd S
Old Barn Rd N, Old Barn Rd
Straight: Cold Spring Rd 137, first left: Randall Av, second left: Long Ridge Rd, third left: High Ridge Rd, first right, Travis Av, second right: Washington Blvd, third right: Windsor Rd
Straight: Old Barn Rd S, first left: Old Barn Rd, second left: Cold Spring Rd 137, first right: Old Barn Rd W

**Old Barn Rd S**
Old Barn Rd N, Old Barn Rd

Straight: Cold Spring Rd 137, first left: Randall Av, second left: Long Ridge Rd 104, third left: High Ridge Rd 137, first right: Travis Av, second right: Washington Blvd, third right: Windsor Rd
Straight: Old Barn Rd, straight: Old Barn Rd W, straight: Old Barn Rd N, straight: Old Barn Rd S

**Old Barn Rd W**

Straight: Old Barn Rd N, straight: Old Barn Rd S, first left: Old Barn Rd S,

## The Stamford Streets AZ

second left: Old Barn Rd S, third left: Cold Spring Rd 137, first right: Old Barn Rd
Straight: Old Barn Rd, straight: Old Barn Rd S
Old Barn Rd N, Old Barn Rd S, Old Barn Rd S
Straight: Cold Spring Rd 137, first left: Randall Av, second left: Long Ridge Rd 104, third left: High Ridge Rd first right: Travis Av, second right: Washington Blvd 137, third right: Windsor Rd

**Old Barn Rd**

Straight: Old Barn Rd S, Old Barn Rd N, Old Barn Rd S, Old Barn Rd S, straight: Cold Spring Rd 137, first left: Randall Av, second left: Long Ridge Rd, first right: Travis Av,
second right: Washington Blvd
Straight: Old Barn Rd W, straight: Old Barn Rd N, straight: Old Barn S, first left: Old Barn Rd S, second left: Old Barn Rd S, third left: Cold Spring Rd 137, first right: Old Barn Rd, second right: Old Barn Rd W

# The Stamford Streets AZ

### Old Colony Ct

Straight: Bouton St W, first left: Prudence Dr, second left: Hope St, Bouton St, first right: Minivale Rd, second right: Sunset St, third right: Gaymoor Dr

### Old Colony Rd
Putter Dr

Straight: Bouton St W, first left: Prudence Dr, second left: Hope St, Bouton St, first right: Minivale Rd, second right: Sunset St, third right: Gaymoor Dr

### Old Logging Rd
Gary Rd

Straight: Scofieldtown Rd, first left: Janes La, second left: Middle Ridge Rd, third left: Woodley Rd, first right: Gary Rd, second right: High Ridge Rd 137 Straight: Katydid La, first left: Janes La, first right: Janes La

# The Stamford Streets AZ

**Old Long Ridge Rd**
Hunting Ridge Rd, Mill Rd, Shag Bark Rd, Erskine Rd, Heming Way, Parsonage Rd, Rock Rimmon Rd

Straight: Long Ridge Rd 104, first left: Echo Hill Dr, second left: N Lake Dr, third left: Parsonage Rd, first right: Rockrimmon Country Club, second right: White Birch Rd
Straight: Long Ridge Rd 104, first left: Riverbank Rd, second left: Mountain Wood Rd, third left: Wildwood Rd, first right: Grey Birch Rd, second right: Erskine Rd, third right: Parsonage Rd


**Old Mill La**
Mill Brook Rd, Brookhollow La

Straight: Westover Rd, first left: Cow Path Dr, second left: Roxbury Rd, Riverbank Rd, first right: Winding Brook La, second right: High Line Trail


**Old North Stamford Rd**

Straight: Oaklawn Av, Cantwell Av, first left: Halpin Av, second left: High Ridge Rd 137, first right: Northwoods Rd, second right: Benstone St, third right: Stanwick Pl

# The Stamford Streets AZ

**Old Orchard La**

Straight: Den Rd, first left: Arrow Head Dr, second left: Long Ridge Rd 104, first right: Flint Rock Rd, second right: Hardesty Rd, third right: Constance La, Bangall Rd

**Old Stamford Rd 106**
Talmadge Hill Rd, E36 Merritt Pky 15, E36 Merritt Pky 15, Jelliff Mill Rd, Weed St, Lapham Rd

Straight: Hoyt St, Barringer Rd

**Old Wagon Rd**

Straight: Grey Birch Rd, straight: Long Ridge Rd 104, first left: Erskine Rd, second left: Parsonage Rd, third left: N Lake Dr, first right: Riverbank Rd, second right: Mountain Wood Rd, third right: Wildwood Rd

**Old Well Rd**

Straight: Eden Rd, first left: Woodbrook Dr, second left: Twin Brook Dr, third left: Parry Rd, first right: Friars La, second right: Hope St, E Cross Rd

# The Stamford Streets AZ

Straight: Deep Spring La, first left: Hope St


**Olga Dr**

Straight: Square Acre Dr, first right: High Ridge Rd
Straight: High Ridge Rd 137, first left: Square Acre Dr, second left: Dunn Av, third left: E 35 Merritt Pkwy 15, CT15, Buxton Farm Rd, fourth left: E 35 Merritt Pkwy 15, CT15, first right: Turn Of River Rd, Cedar Heights Rd, second right: Vine Rd, third right: Merriman Rd


**Omega Dr**

Straight: Largo Dr S, Riverbend Dr, first left: Largo Dr, first right: Riverbend Dr S, straight: Hope St
Straight: Hope St, first left: Short Hill St, second left: Avon La, third left: Barnstable La, first right: Clearview Av, second right: Largo Dr, third right: Bennett St


**Opper Rd**
Redmont Rd

# The Stamford Streets AZ

Straight: High Ridge Rd 137, first left: Brantwood La, second left: Marva La, third left: Pine Hill Terrace, fourth left: Perna La, first right: Willard Terrace, second right: Wire Mill Rd, third right: E 35 Merritt Pkwy 15, CT15
Straight: Blackwood La, first left: Wire Mill Rd, first right: Deming La

**Orange St**
Ursula Pl, Stafford Rd

Straight: Lockwood Av, first left: Frank St, second left: Lillian St, third left: William St, first right: Boston Post Rd
Straight: Maher Rd, first left: Ursula Pl, second left: Boston Post Rd 1

**Orchard St**
Selleck St, Homestead Av, Taff Av

Straight: Milton St, straight: Greenwich Av, first left: Davenport St, second left: Pulaski St, third left: First Stamford Pl, first right: Selleck St, Southfield Av
Straight: Sunnyside Av, first left: Southfield Av, first right: Fairfield Av

# The Stamford Streets AZ

**Orlando Av**

Straight: Pequot Dr, Montauk Dr, first left: Mohawk Ct, second left: Southwood Dr, first right: Southwood Dr, second right: Montauk Dr
Straight: West Av, first left: Selleck St, second left: Winsted St, first right: Warshaw Pl, second right: Ardmore Rd, third right: Baxter Av, E 6 Governor John Davis Lodge Tpke I-95


**Oscar St**
Morris St

Straight: Scofield Av, first left: Center St, second left: Pilgrim Walk, Hope St, first right: Parker Av, second right: Glenbrook Rd


**Outlook St**

Straight: Winsted St, straight: West Av, first left: Selleck St, second left: Orlando Av, third left: Warshaw Pl
Straight: Selleck St, first left: Harvard Av, second left: Brown House Rd, first right: West Av, second right: Betts Av, third right: Durant St, Montauk Dr

# The Stamford Streets AZ

**Overbrook Dr**

Overbrook Dr

Straight: Toms Rd, first left: Deleo Dr, second left: Rutz St, third left: Derwin St, first right: Dale Pl, second right: Autumn La, third right: Central St

**Overhill Rd**

Barncroft Rd

Straight: Barncroft Rd, first left: Barncroft Rd, second left: Roxbury Rd, first right: Overhill Rd, second right: Barncroft Rd
Straight: Roxbury Rd, first left: W Hill Rd, second left: Stillwater Rd, third left: Long Ridge Rd 104, Buckingham Dr, first right: Doral Farms Rd, second right: Barncroft Rd, third right: Munko Dr

**Overlook Pl**

Straight: Columbus Pl, first left: Cerretta St, first right: River Pl, second right: Highview Av

# The Stamford Streets AZ

**Owen St**

Straight: James St, first left: Soundview Av, first right: McMullen Av
Straight: McMullen Av, first left: James St, second left: Soundview Av, first right: Soundview Av

**Oxford Ct**

Straight: Stillwater Av, first left: W Broad St, second left: Connecticut Av: third left: Palmers Hill Rd, first right: Progress Dr, second right: West Av, third right: Corbo Terrace

# The Stamford Streets AZ

## P

**Pacific St**
Washington Blvd, Dyke La, Belden St, Crosby St, Remington St, Walter Wheeler Dr, E Walnut St, Woodland Pl, Woodland Av, Ludlow St, Henry St, Market St, Manhattan St

**Pakenmer Rd**

Straight: Doolittle Rd, first right: MacArthur La, second right: Den Rd

**Palmer Av**
Duffy St, Hobbie St

**Palmer St**

Straight: Northill St, first left: Woodledge Rd, first right: Carroll St, second right: Knickerbocker Av, third right: Hope St

**Palmers Hill Rd**
Westover Rd, Emery Dr, Starin Dr, Hillcrest Park Rd, Old Wagon Rd, Palmer Hill Rd

# The Stamford Streets AZ

Straight: Stillwater Rd, E Gaynor Brennan Golf Course, first left: Halliwell Dr, Bridge St, second left: Knoblock La, first right: Connecticut Av, second right: W Broad St
Straight: Palmer Hill Rd

**Pamlynn Rd**

Straight: Vine Rd, first left: Brandywine Rd, second left: Malvern Rd, third left: Pepper Ridge Rd, first right: Barmore Dr, second right: Vine Pl, third right: Kane Av
Straight: Barmore Dr E, first left: Barmore Dr, Barmore Dr W, first right: Barmore Dr W

**Paragon La**

Straight: Cold Spring Rd, Washington Blvd 137, first left: W Forest Lawn Av, second left: Bridge St, third left: 2nd St, first right: Cold Spring Rd, second right: Travis Av, third right: Old Barn Rd S

**Park St**
Cummings Av

# The Stamford Streets AZ

Straight: Shippan Av, first left: Seaview Av, second left: Magee Av, Harbor Dr, third left: Lindstrom Rd, first right: Hanover St, second right: Wardwell St, third right: Elm St, Cove Rd
Straight: Frederick St


**Parker Av**

Straight: Scofield Av, first left: Glenbrook Rd, first right: Oscar St, second right: Center St, third right: Hope St, Pilgrim Walk
Straight: Church St, first left: Elm Tree Pl, second left: Center St, third left: Hope St, Pine Hill Av, first right: Kirkham Pl, second right: Glenbrook Rd


**Parry Ct**

Straight: Parry Rd, first right: Woodbrook Dr, second right: Eden Rd


**Parry Rd**
Parry Ct

Straight: Eden Rd, first left: Twin Brook Dr, second left: Woodbrook Dr,

# The Stamford Streets AZ

third left: Old Well Rd, first right: Eden La, second right: Newfield Av

**Parsonage Rd**
Long Ridge Rd 104

Straight: Old Long Ridge Rd, first left: Rock Rimmon Rd, second left: Long Ridge Rd 104, first right: Heming Way, second right: Erskine Rd, third right: Shag Bark Rd

**Partridge Rd**
Wild Duck Rd

Straight: Long Ridge Rd 104, first left: Lakewood Dr, second left: Sawmill Rd, third left: Wildwood Rd, first right: Stone Hill Dr, second right: Hunting Ridge Rd, third right: Chestnut Hill Rd

**Patricia La**

Straight: Sandy La, first right: Club Rd

**Paul Rd**
Hemlock Dr

# The Stamford Streets AZ

**Peak St**

Straight: Dunn Av, first left: Alpine St, second left: Dunn Av Ext, third left: High Ridge Rd, first right: Derry St, second right: Winter St, third right: Dunn Ct

**Pell Pl**

Straight: Pellom Pl, first right: Hubbard Av

**Pellom Pl**
Pell Pl

Straight: Hubbard Av, first left: Prince Pl, second left: Charles Mary La, third left: Vuono Dr, fourth left: Grandview Av, first right: Woodmere Rd, second right: Bridge St, third right: Riverside Av

**Pembroke Dr**

Straight: Cascade Rd, first left: Michael Rd, second left: Frost Pond Rd, third left: Woodbine Rd, first right: Cascade Ct, second right: N Stamford Rd

# The Stamford Streets AZ

**Penzance Rd**

Straight: Clovelly Rd, first left: Scott Pl, second left: Lafayette St, first right: Glenbrook Rd
Straight: Culloden Rd, first left: Hamilton Av, second left: Ely Pl, third left: Frankel Pl, first right: Scott Pl, second right: Crystal St

**Pepper Ridge Cir**

Straight: Pepper Ridge Rd, first left: Nutmeg La, second left: Vine Rd, first right: Red Bird Rd, second right: Robinson Dr, third right: Berrian Rd

**Pepper Ridge Pl**

Straight: Pepper Ridge Rd, first left: Crestwood Dr, second left: Kensington Rd, third left: White Birch La, first right: Fawn Dr, second right: Harvest Hill La, third right: Berrian Rd

**Pepper Ridge Rd**
Marschall Pl, Hirsch Rd, Ogden Rd, Turner Rd, Fara Dr, Silver Hill La, White Birch La, Kensington Rd, Crestwood Dr, Pepper Ridge Pl, Fawn Dr, Harvest

# The Stamford Streets AZ

Hill La, Berrian Rd, Robinson Dr, Red Bird Rd, Nutmeg La

Straight: Oaklawn Av, first left: Jamroga La, second left: Clifford Av, third left: Lindsey Av, first right: Vanech Dr, second right: Sherwood Rd, third right: Dann Dr
Straight: Vine Rd, first left: Malvern Rd, second left: Brandywine Rd, third left: Pamlynn Rd, first right: Kerr Rd, second right: Simsbury Rd, third right: Newfield Av


**Pequot Dr**
Southwood Dr

Straight: Montauk Dr, first left: Southwood Dr, second left: Mohawk Ct, third left: Orlando Av, first right: Selleck St, Durant St
Straight: Orlando Av, Montauk Dr, straight: West Av


**Perna La**
Somerset La

Straight: High Ridge Rd 137, first left: Pine Hill Terrace, second left: Marva La, third left: Brantwood La, first right: Blue Ridge Dr, second right:

# The Stamford Streets AZ

Diamondcrest La, third right: Meredith La

**Perry St**

Straight: Taylor St, first left: Richmond Hill Av, Ann St, first right: Fairfield Av
Straight: Fairfield Av, first left: Hall Pl, second left: Taylor St, third left: Madison Pl, fourth left: First Stamford Pl, first right: Richmond Pl, second right: Richmond Hill Av, third right: Boston Post Rd 1 (W Main St)

**Pershing Av**
Haig Av, Todd La

Straight: Joffre Av, Ledge La, first left: Joffre Ct, second left: Sussex Pl, third left: Haig Av, first right: Ledge Terrace, second right: Belltown Rd
Straight: Belltown Rd, first left: Ledge La, second left: Toms Rd, third left: Fairland St, first right: Newfield Av, Turner Rd

# The Stamford Streets AZ

**Peveril Rd**

Straight: Crystal St, Hundley Ct, first left: Quintard Terrace, second left: Lafayette St, Daskam Pl, first right: Culloden Rd, second right: Boston Post Rd 1
Straight: Scott Pl, first left: Clovelly Rd, first right: Culloden Rd

**Phaiban La**

Straight: Wyndover La, first left: N Wyndover La, second left: Hemlock Dr, first right: W Hill Rd

**Pheasant La**

Straight: Webbs Hill Rd, first left: Long Ridge Rd, first right: Dogwood La, second right: Dogwood La, third right: Jeffrey La, fourth right: Lynam Rd

**Phillips Pl**

Straight: Oakdale Rd, first left: Glen Terrace, Rose Rd, second left: Maple Tree Av, first right: Glenbrook Rd, Middlesex Rd

# The Stamford Streets AZ

**Piave St**
Diaz St

Straight: Victory St, first left: Boston Post Rd 1, first right: Grenhart Rd
Straight: West Av, first left: Grenhart Rd, second left: Baxter Av, third left: Ardmore Rd, first right: Ferris Av, second right: Leon Pl, Sylvandale Av, third right: Annie Pl


**Pierce Pl**

Straight: Howes Av, first left: Glenbrook Rd, first right: Nash Pl, second right: Brooklawn Av, third right: Hope St


**Pilgrim Walk**

Straight: Colonial Rd, first left: Mayflower Av, second left: Strawberry Hill Av, first right: Hope St
Straight: Scofield Av, first left: Colonial Rd, second left: Rose St, third left: Pine Hill Av, Church St, first right: Plymouth Rd, second right: Rock Spring Rd, third right: Faucett St

# The Stamford Streets AZ

**Pin Oak Circle**

Straight: Rock Rimmon Rd, first left: Rock Rimmon Dr, second left: Rock Rimmon La, third left: Queen of Peace Cemetery, Scofield Town Park, first right: Ridge Tree La, second right: Dads La, E Hunting Ridge Rd

**Pine Av**

Straight: Oak Hill St, straight: W Broad St, first left: Stephen St, second left: Anderson St, third left: Wright St, first right: Adams Av, second right: Schuyler Av, third right: Hanrahan St Straight: Schuyler Av, first left: W Broad St, first right: Smith St

**Pine Hill Av**
Elmbrook Dr

Straight: Hope St, Church St, first left: Glendale Dr, second left: Union St, third left: Douglas Av, first right: Rose St, second right: Colonial Rd, third right: Pilgrim Walk, Scofield Av

# The Stamford Streets AZ

**Pine Hill Terrace**

Straight: High Ridge Rd 137, first left: Perna La, second left: Blue Ridge Dr, third left: Diamondcrest La, first right: Marva La, second right: Brantwood La, third right: Opper Rd


**Pine Tree Dr**
Alton Rd, Apple Tree Dr, Boxwood Dr

Straight: Upland Rd, first left: Fieldstone La, Strawberry Hill Av, first right: Norman Rd, second right: Alton Rd, third right: Burdick St, fourth right: Bellmere Av


**Pinewood Rd**

Straight: Cedar Wood Rd, first left: High Ridge Rd, first right: Woodbine Rd
Straight: Woodbine Rd, first left: Brushwood Rd, second left: Cedar Wood Rd, third left: Round Lake Rd, first right: Mather Rd, second right: Woodbine Way, third right: Cascade Rd

# The Stamford Streets AZ

## Pinnacle Rock Rd

Straight: Rocky Rapids Rd, first left: Shelter Rock Rd, second left: Wildwood Rd, Harpsichord Tpke, first right: Ridgecrest Rd, second right: Riverbank Rd

## Pinner La

Straight: High Ridge Rd 137, first left: Skymeadow Dr, second left: Bartlett La, third left: N Stamford Rd, fourth left: Alma Rock Rd, first right: Cedar Wood Rd, second right: Hoyclo Rd, Acre View Dr, third right: Hoyclo Rd, Bracchi Dr

## Pleasant St

Straight: Forest St, first left: Ridge Pl, second left: Grove St, third left: Suburban Av, first right: Lindale St

## Plymouth Rd

Straight: Mayflower Av, first left: Puritan La, second left: Hackett Circle N, third left: Hackett Circle S, first right: Colonial Rd

# The Stamford Streets AZ

Straight: Hope St, first left: Pilgrim Walk, Scofield Av, second left: Colonial Rd, third left: Rose St, first right: Rock Spring Rd, second right: Faucett St, third right: Kennedy La, fourth right: Frisbee St

**Pond Rd**
Hemlock Dr, Blueberry Dr

Straight: Blueberry Dr, first left: Skyview Dr, second left: W Hill Rd, first right: Pond Rd
Straight: Stillwater Rd, first left: Stillview Rd, second left: London La, third left: River Hill Dr, first right: Cold Spring Rd, second right: Knoblock La, third right: Knobloch La, fourth right: Bridge St

**Pond View La**

Straight: Rock Rimmon Rd, first left: Winslow Dr, second left: Old Long Ridge Rd, first right: Rock Meadow La, second right: Mayapple Rd, third right: Breezy Hill Rd

# The Stamford Streets AZ

**Ponus Av**

Straight: Rippowam Rd, first left: Mohegan Av, second left: Shippan Av, first right: Algonquin Av, second right: Wampanaw Rd
Straight: Iroquois Rd, first left: Algonquin Av, second left: Wampanaw Rd, first right: Mohegan Av, second right: Shippan Av


**Pony Trail Rd**

Straight: Farms Rd, first left: Riverbank Rd, first right: Taconic Rd


**Poplar St**
Larkin St

Straight: Viaduct Rd, first left: Larkin St, Research Dr, first right: Viaduct Rd, second right: Hope St


**Poppy La**

Straight: Turn Of River Rd, first left: High Ridge Rd 137, Cedar Heights Rd, first right: Gerik Rd, second right: Talmadge La, third right: Intervale Rd

# The Stamford Streets AZ

**Powell Pl**

Straight: Ivy St, first left: Hillside Av, second left: Hubbard Ct, Woodcliff St
Straight: W North St, Adams Av, first left: North St, first right: Hillside Av, second right: Woodcliff St, Anderson St, third right: Hinckley Av

**Pressprich St**
Vassar Av, Irving Av

Straight: Fairfield Av, first left: Baxter Av, second left: Jackson St, third left: First Stamford Pl, first right: Selleck St
Straight: Wilson St
Hall Pl, Madison Pl, Grenhart Rd, Baxter Av
Straight: Boston Post Rd, Richmond Hill Av

**Prince Pl**

Straight: Hubbard Av, first left: Charles Mary La, second left: Vuono Dr, third left: Grandview Av, first right: Pellom Pl, second right: Woodmere Rd, third right: Bridge St

# The Stamford Streets AZ

### Princess Ct

Straight: Sunset Rd, first left: Skyline La, second left: Skymeadow Dr, first right: Sunset Ct, second right: West Trl

### Progress Dr

Straight: Stillwater Av, first left: Oxford Ct, second left: W Broad St, third left: Connecticut Av, first right: West Av, second right: Corbo Terrace, third right: Merrell Av, fourth right: Virgil St

### Prospect St
Forest St, Walton Pl, North St

Straight: Grove St, Hillandale Av, Strawberry Hill Av, Hoyt St
Straight: Bedford St, Spring St, first left: Broad St, Atlantic St, first right: Forest St, second right: Walton Pl, third right: North St

### Prudence Dr
Gaymoor Dr, Bouton St W

# The Stamford Streets AZ

Straight: Minivale Rd, first left: Hope St, first right: Salem Pl, second right: Gaymoor Dr, third right: Bouton St W


**Pulaski St**
Water St, Berkeley St

Straight: Washington Blvd, first left: w Henry St, Henry St, second left: Station Pl, third left: S State St, first right: Atlantic St, second right: Crosby St, third right: Pacific St
Straight: Greenwich Av, first left: Davenport St, second left: Milton St, third left: Selleck St, first right: First Stamford Pl, second right: S State St, E 7 Governor John Davis Lodge Tpke I-95, third right: West St


**Pumping Station Rd**

Straight: Harbor View Av, straight: Jefferson St, first left: Meadow St, second left: Canal St, Dock St, first right: Cherry St, second right: Magee Av, third right: Halloween Blvd
Straight: Magee Av, first left: St Marys St, second left: Jefferson St, first right: Harbor Dr, Shippan Av

# The Stamford Streets AZ

**Puritan La**

Straight: Rock Spring Rd, Coolidge Av, first left: Hope St, first right: Treat Av, second right: Mayflower Av, third right: Ardsley Rd
Straight: Mayflower Av, first left: Hackett Circle N, second left: Hackett Circle S, third left: Rock Spring Rd, first right: Plymouth Rd, second right: Colonial Rd

**Putter Dr**
Tree La

Straight: Hope St, first left: Mary Violet Rd, second left: Nottingham Dr, third left: Deep Spring La, first right: Robinhood Rd, second right: Woodway Rd, third right: Bouton St W, Bouton St, fourth right: Mead St

# The Stamford Streets AZ

## Q

**Quails Trail**

Straight: Bittersweet La, first left: Woodbine Rd, first right: Thornwood Rd

**Quaker Ridge Rd**

Straight: E Hunting Ridge Rd, first left: Heritage La, second left: Hillsbury La, third left: Haviland Rd, first right: Falmouth Rd, second right: Chatham Rd, third right: Dads La, Rock Rimmon Rd

**Quarry Rd**
Chapin La, Greenbrier La, Blue Rock Dr, New England Dr

Straight: Lakeside Dr, first left: Interlaken Rd, second left: Davenport Ridge Rd, Newfield Av, first right: N Stamford Rd, second right: High Ridge Rd
137

# The Stamford Streets AZ

## Queen of Peace Cemetery

Straight: Rock Rimmon Rd, first left: Scofieldtown Rd, first right: Rock Rimmon La, second right: Rock Rimmon Dr

## Quintard Terrace

Straight: Town Center Dr, first left: Atlantic St, first right: Tresser Blvd 1, Stamford Forum 1

# The Stamford Streets AZ

## R

**Rachelle Av**
W North St

Straight: W Broad St, Shelburne Rd, first left: St George Av, second left: Hubbard Av, third left: Hinckley Av, first right: Merrell Av, second right: Delaware Av, third right: Stillwater Av

**Radio Pl**

Straight: West Av, Maple Tree Av, first left: Oakdale Rd, second left: Courtland Av 106, Crescent St, first right: Park La, second right: Holmes Av, third right: Holmes Av, Hazel St

**Ralph St**
Whittaker St

Straight: Downs Av, first right: Whittaker St, second right: Shippan Av, Lanark Rd

**Ralsey Rd S**
Sagamore Rd, S Sagamore La

# The Stamford Streets AZ

Straight: Ralsey Rd, first right: Stamford Av, second right: Shippan Av
Straight: Ocean Dr W, first left: Van Rensselaer Av, second left: Stamford Av, third left: Woolsey Rd, fourth left: Shippan Av, first right: Ocean Dr W, second right: Lighthouse Way, third right: Rogers Rd

**Ralsey Rd**
Ralsey Rd S, Stamford Av

Straight: Shippan Av, first left: Chesterfield Rd, second left: Lanark Rd, third left: Downs Av, first right: Gurley Rd, second right: Sagamore Rd, third right: Ocean Dr E

**Rambler La**

Straight: Thornridge Dr, first left: Horse Shoe La, second left: Rambler La, first right: Davenport Ridge Rd
Straight: Thornridge Dr, first left: Davenport Ridge Rd, first right: Horse Shoe La, second right: Rambler La, third right: Davenport Ridge Rd

**Randall Av**
Richards Av

# The Stamford Streets AZ

Straight: Cold Spring Rd 137, first left: Old Barn Rd S, second left: Travis Av, third left: Washington Blvd 137, first right: Long Ridge Rd 104, second right: High Ridge Rd

**Ranson St**
Robert Ct

Straight: Caldwell Av, first left: Willowbrook Av, first right: Van Buskirk Av
Straight: Cove Rd, first left: Cove Rd, second left: Van Buskirk Av, third left: Dale St, first right: Willowbrook Av, Blachley Rd, second right: Duffy St, third right: Hobbie St, fourth right: George St

**Rapids Rd**

Straight: Cedar Heights Rd, first left: Clay Hill Rd, second left: Duke Dr, third left: Apple Tree La, first right: Wire Mill Rd

**Raymond St**

Straight: Cove Rd, first left: Dale St, second left: Van Buskirk Av, third left:

# The Stamford Streets AZ

Cove Rd, fourth left: Cove Rd, Ranson St, first right: St Benedict Circle, second right: Leeds St, third right: Soundview Av

**Red Bird Rd**

Straight: Pepper Ridge Rd, first left: Robinson Dr, second left: Berrian Rd, third left: Harvest Hill La, first right: Nutmeg La, second right: Vine Rd

**Red Fox Rd**
Wake Robin La, Big Oak Rd, White Fox Rd

Straight: Wire Mill Rd, first left: Studio Rd, second left: Gutzon Borglum Rd, third left: Blackwood La, first right: Linwood La, second right: Four Brooks Rd, third right: Cedar Heights Rd

**Redmont Rd**

Straight: Opper Rd, first left: High Ridge Rd, first right: Blackwood La
Straight: Diamondcrest La, straight: High Ridge Rd 137, first left: Meredith La, second left: Scofieldtown Rd, High Ridge Rd, third left: High Ridge Rd, fourth left: Interlaken Rd, first right:

# The Stamford Streets AZ

Blue Ridge Dr, second right: Perna La, third right: Pine Hill Terrace

**Reed Pl**

Straight: Cantwell Av, first left: Oaklawn Av, Old North Stamford Rd, first right: Dubois St

**Regent Ct**
Dorset La

Straight: Woodway Rd, first left: Hidden Brook Dr, second left: Highview Av, third left: Hope St, first right: Hoyt St 106

**Relay Pl**

Straight: Rippowam Pl, first left: Main St, first right: Washington Blvd 137

**Remington St**

Straight: Elmcroft Rd, first left: E Walnut St, second left: Woodland Pl, first right: Belden St, second right: Rugby St, third right: Dyke La

# The Stamford Streets AZ

Straight: Pacific St, first left: Crosby St, second left: Belden St, third left: Dyke La, first right: Walter Wheeler Dr, E Walnut St, second right: Woodland Pl, third right: Woodland Av, Ludlow St

**Renwick St**

Straight: Vernon Pl
Straight: North St, first left: Washington Ct, second left: W Washington Av, third left: Hollywood Ct, first right: Washington Blvd 137, second right: Franklin St, third right: Summer St

**Research Dr**

Straight: Viaduct Rd, Larkin St, first left: Poplar St, second left: Viaduct Rd, third left: Hope St, first right: Poplar St
Straight: Glenbrook Rd 106, first left: Oakdale Rd, second left: Fresh Meadows La, Middlesex Rd, first right: Courtland Av 106, second right: Arthur Pl, third right: Cowing Pl

# The Stamford Streets AZ

**Reservoir La**

Straight: Woodbine Rd, Laurel Rd, first left: Fernwood Dr, second left: Bittersweet La, third left: Round Lake Rd, first right: Ingleside Dr, second right: Spring Hill La N, third right: High Ridge Rd 137
Straight: Ponus Ridge, first left: Lake Wind Rd, second left: Lake Wind Rd, third left: Dan's Hwy, first right: Toby's La, second right: Rippowam Rd, third right: Clearview La


**Revere Dr**

Straight: Standish Rd, first left: Boston Post Rd 1, first right: Seaton Rd
Straight: Seaton Rd, first left: Trumbull Gate, second left: Standish Rd, third left: Boston Post Rd 1, Noroton Hill Pl, first right: Courtland Av 106


**Revonah Av**
4th St, 5th St, Chester St, Urban St, Revonah Circle

Straight: 3rd St, first left: Morgan St, second left: Morgan St, third left: Strawberry Patch La, Strawberry Hill Ct, first right: Bedford St

# The Stamford Streets AZ

Straight: East La
West La
Straight: West La

**Revonah Circle**

Straight: Revonah Circle, first left: Revonah Av

**Reynolds Av**
Austin Av, Berges Av

Straight: Travis Av, first left: Duncanson St, first right: Cold Spring Rd 137

**Robinhood Rd**
Friar Tuck La

Straight: Hope St, first left: Woodway Rd, second left: Bouton St W, Bouton St, third left: Mead St, first right: Putter Dr, second right: Mary Violet Rd, third right: Nottingham Dr

**Richards Av**

Straight: Randall Av, first right: Cold Spring Rd 137

# The Stamford Streets AZ

Straight: Hoover Av, first right: Summer St


**Richmond Hill Av**
Clinton Av, Greenwich Av, Mission St, Rose Park, Ann St, Taylor St, Spruce St, Fairfield Av, Wilson St

Straight: Washington Blvd 137, first left: Division St, second left: Tresser Blvd 1, third left: Bell St, first right: N State St, E 8 Governor John Davis Lodge Tpke I-95, second right: S State St, third right: Station Pl
Straight: Boston Post Rd 1, first left: Roosevelt Av, second left: Liberty St, third left: Victory St, first right: High St, second right: Fairfield Av, third right: Hazel St, Spruce St


**Richmond Pl**

Straight: Fairfield Av, first left: Richmond Hill Av, second left: Boston Post Rd 1, third left: Hazel St, first right: Perry St, second right: Hall Pl, third right: Taylor St

# The Stamford Streets AZ

**Ridge Brook La**

Straight: Ridge Brook Dr, first left: Rock Rimmon Rd

**Ridge Brook Dr**
Ridge Brook La

Straight: Rock Rimmon Rd, first left: Golden Farm Rd, second left: Breezy Hill Rd, third left: Mayapple Rd, first right: Mill Rd, second right: Briar Brae Rd, third right: Saddle Hill Rd

**Ridge Park Av**
Hillview La, Longview Av, Knollwood Av, Wood Ridge Dr

Straight: High Ridge Rd 137, first left: Nichols Av, second left: Emma Rd, third left: Swampscott Rd, first right: Janice Rd, second right: Yale Ct, third right: Mercedes La, Dannell Dr
Straight: Rosano Rd, Wood Ridge Dr, first right: Brookvale Pl, second right: Ridge Park Av

# The Stamford Streets AZ

**Ridge Pl**

Straight: Forest St, first left: Grove St, second left: Suburban Av, third left: Greyrock Pl, fourth left: Prospect St, first right: Pleasant St, second right: Lindale St


**Ridge Tree La**

Straight: Rock Rimmon Rd, first left: Pin Oak Circle, second left: Rock Rimmon Dr, third left: Rock Rimmon La, fourth left: Queen of Peace Cemetery, first right: Dads La, E Hunting Ridge Rd, second right: Saddle Hill Rd, third right: Briar Brae Rd


**Ridgecrest Rd**
Easthill Rd

Straight: Rocky Rapids Rd, first left: Riverbank Rd, first right: Pinnacle Rock Rd, second right: Shelter Rock Rd, third right: Wildwood Rd, Harpsichord Tpke
Straight: Riverbank Rd, first left: Riverbank Dr, second left: June Rd, third left: Fawnfield Rd, first right: Deep Valley Rd, second right: Farms Rd, third right: Rocky Rapids Rd

# The Stamford Streets AZ

**Ridgeway Plaza**

Straight: 6th St, first left: Bedford St, Chester St, first right: Summer St

**Ridgeway St**

Straight: Mulberry St, first left: Brundage St, second left: Elmer St, third left: Carroll St, fourth left: Hope St
Straight: Weed Hill Av, first left: Estwick Pl, second left: Bouton St W, third left: Upper Haig Av, first right: Hickory Way, second right: Elmer St, third right: Sterling Pl, fourth right: Hope St

**Ridgewood Av**
Cleveland St, Chatfield St

Straight: Elizabeth Av, first left: Selby Pl, second left: Marian St, first right: Knickerbocker Av

**Riding Stable Trail**

Straight: High Ridge Rd 137, first left: Trinity Pass, second left: Mayapple Rd, third left: Laurel Rd, first right:

# The Stamford Streets AZ

Fairway Dr, second right: Craig Ct, third right: Pound Ridge Country Club


**Rippowam Pl**
Relay Pl


Straight: Main St, first left: Clinton Av, second left: W Main St, Mill River St, first right: Washington Blvd 137, second right: W Park Pl, Summer St, Bank St, Clark St, third right: Atlantic St
Straight: Washington Blvd 137, first left: Main St, second left: W Park Pl, third left: Whittaker Pl, first right: Bell St, second right: Tresser Blvd 1, third right: Division St


**Rippowam Rd**
Mohegan Av, Ponus Av, Algonquin Av

Straight: Shippan Av, first left: Mariners La, second left: Iroquois Rd, third left: Wallace St, first right: Lindstrom Rd, second right: Harbor Dr, Magee Av, third right: Seaview Av
Straight: Wampanaw Rd, straight: Iroquois Rd
Algonquin Av, Ponus Av, Mohegan Av
Straight: Shippan Av, first left: Wallace St, second left: Mitchell St,

# The Stamford Streets AZ

first right: Mariners La, second right: Rippowam Rd

**River Ridge Ct**

Straight: Long Ridge Rd, first left: Brook Run La, second left: Wishing Well La, first right: Stark Pl, second right: Terrace Av

**Rising Rock Rd**

Straight: Shelter Rock Rd, first left: Riverbank Dr, second left: Rocky Rapids Rd

**River Hill Dr**

Straight: Stillwater Rd, first left: London La, second left: Stillview Rd, third left: Pond Rd, first right: Clover Hill Dr, second right: Skyview Dr, third right: Logan's Run

**River View Dr**

Straight: King St, first left: Hamilton Av

# The Stamford Streets AZ

Straight: Brookside Dr, first right: Hamilton Av, second right: De Bera La

**River Pl**

Straight: Columbus Pl, first left: Overlook Pl, second left: Cerretta St, first right: Highview Av

**Riverview Dr**

Straight: Brookside Dr, first right: Hamilton Av, De Bera La
Straight: King St, first left: Hamilton Av

**Riverbank Dr**
Branch La

Straight: Shelter Rock Rd, first left: Rocky Rapids Rd, first right: Rising Rock Rd
Straight: Riverbank Rd, first left: June Rd, second left: Fawnfield Rd, third left: Windward La, first right: Ridgecrest Rd, second right: Deep Valley Rd, third right: Farms Rd

# The Stamford Streets AZ

**Riverbank Rd**

Hedge Brook La, Laurel Ledge Rd, Harpsichord Tpke, Trailing Rock Rd, Erskine Rd, Wildwood Rd, Rocky Rapids Rd, Farms Rd, Deep Valley Rd, Ridgecrest Rd, Riverbank Dr, June Rd, Fawnfield Rd, Windward La, Bangall Rd, Thunder Hill Dr, Cow Path Dr

Straight: Long Ridge Rd, first left: Old Long Ridge Rd, second left: Grey Birch Rd, third left: Erskine Rd, first right: Mountain Wood Rd, second right: Wildwood Rd, third right: Sawmill Rd
Straight: Roxbury Rd, Westover Rd, first left: Roxbury Ter, second left: Den Rd, first right: Old Mill La, second right: Winding Brook La


**Riverbend Dr**

Straight: Omega Dr, Largo Dr S, first left: Hope St, first right: Largo Dr
Straight: Riverbend Dr S


**Riverbend Dr S**

Straight: Hope St, first left: Edgewood Av, second left: Viaduct Rd, first right: Chatfield St, second right: Hartford Av, Castle Ct

# The Stamford Streets AZ

Straight: Riverbend Dr, straight: Omega Dr, Largo Dr S

**Riverside Av**
Woodmere Rd

Straight: Bridge St, first left: Washington Blvd 137, second left: Woodside Green, third left: Summer St, first right: Woodmere Rd, second right: Hubbard Av, third right: Stillwater Rd
Straight: Hubbard Av
Bridge St, Woodmere Rd, Pellom Pl, Prince Pl, Charles Mary La, Vuono Dr, Grandview Av, W North St
Straight: W Broad St, first left: Hinckley Av, second left: Wright St, third left: Anderson St, first right: St George Av, second right: Shelburne Rd, third right: Rachelle Av

**Robert Ct**

Straight: Ranson St, first left: Cove Rd, first right: Caldwell Av

# The Stamford Streets AZ

**Robin St**

Straight: Horton St, first left: Martin St, second left: Cove Rd, first right: Charles St, second right: Lewelyn Rd
Straight: George St, first left: Charles St, first right: Martin St, second right: Elmwood St, third right: Cove Rd

**Robinson Dr**
Pepper Ridge Rd

Straight: Idlewood Dr, first left: Berrian Rd, first right: Idlewood Pl, second right: Little Hill Dr

**Rock Meadow La**

Straight: Rock Rimmon Rd, first left: Pond View La, second left: Winslow Dr, third left: Old Long Ridge Rd, first right: Mayapple Rd, second right: Breezy Hill Rd, third right: Golden Farm Rd

**Rock Rimmon Dr**

Straight: Rock Rimmon Rd, first left: Pin Oak Circle, second left: Ridge Tree La, third left: Dads La, E Hunting Ridge Rd, first right: Rock Rimmon La, second

# The Stamford Streets AZ

right: Queen of Peace Cemetery, third right: Scofieldtown Rd

**Rock Rimmon La**

Straight: Rock Rimmon Rd, first left: Rock Rimmon Dr, second left: Pin Oak Circle, third left: Ridge Tree La, first right: Queen of Peace Cemetery, second right: Scofieldtown Rd

**Rock Rimmon Rd**
Queen Of Peace Cemetery, Rock Rimmon La, Rock Rimmon Dr, Pin Oak Circle, Ridge Tree La, Dads La, E Hunting Ridge Rd, Saddle Hill Rd, Briar Brae Rd, Mill Rd, Ridge Brook Dr, Golden Farm Rd, Breezy Hill Rd, Mayapple Rd, Rock Meadow La, Pond View La, Winslow Dr

Straight: Scofieldtown Rd, first left: Hannahs Rd, second left: Skymeadow Dr, third left: Skyline La, first right: Haviland Rd, second right: Brookdale Rd, third right: Chestnut Hill Rd
Straight: Old Long Ridge Rd, first left: Parsonage Rd, second left: Heming Way, third left: Erskine Rd, first right: Long Ridge Rd 104, second right: Rockrimmon Country Club, third right: White Birch Rd, NY

# The Stamford Streets AZ

**Rock Spring Rd**
Ardsley Rd, Mayflower Av, Treat Av, Puritan La, Coolidge Av

Straight: Hope St, first left: Plymouth Rd, second left: Scofield Av, Pilgrim Walk, third left: Colonial Rd, first right: Faucett St, second right: Kennedy La, third right: Frisbee St
Straight: Strawberry Hill Av, first left Strawberry Hill Ct, second left: Medical Center, third left: Holcomb Av, fourth left: Medical Center, first right: Hackett Circle, second right: 5th St, third right: Colonial Rd

**Rockland Pl**

Straight: Henry St, first left: Atlantic St, second left: Garden St, third left: Pacific St, first right: Washington Blvd, W Henry St
Straight: Atlantic St, first left: Station Pl, second left: Manhattan St, third left: S State St, E 8 Governor John Davis Lodge Tpke I-95, first right: Henry St, second right: Lipton Pl, third right: Woodland Av

**Rockledge Dr**
Westcott Rd, Ocean Dr E

# The Stamford Streets AZ

Straight: Hobson St, first left: Sea Beach Dr, first right: Ocean Dr E, second right: Brightside Dr, third right: Shippan Av
Straight: Shippan Av, first left: Hobson St, second left: Sound Av, third left: Fairview Av, first right: Ocean Dr W, second right: Ocean Dr E, third right: Sagamore Rd


**Rockridge La**

Straight: Northwood La, first right: Long Ridge Rd 104


**Rocky Rapids Rd**
Ridgecrest Rd, Pinnacle Rock Rd, Shelter Rock Rd

Straight: Riverbank Rd, first left: Farms Rd, second left: Deep Valley Rd, third left: Ridgecrest Rd, first right: Wildwood Rd, second right: Erskine Rd, third right: Trailing Rock Rd
Straight: Wildwood Rd, Harpsichord Tpke, first left: High Rock Rd, second left: Indian Rock Rd, third left: Riverbank Rd, first right: Long Ridge Rd 104, second right: Konandreas Dr, Hunting Ridge Rd

# The Stamford Streets AZ

**Rogers Rd**

Straight: Saddle Rock Rd, first left: Ocean Dr W
Straight: Ocean Dr W, first left: Lighthouse Way, second left: Fairview Av, third left: Ralsey Rd S, first right: Verplank Av, second right: Saddle Rock Rd, third right: Stamford Av

**Rolling Ridge Rd**

Straight: Coventry Rd, first right: Country Club Rd
Straight: Country Club Rd, first left: Coventry Rd, first right: Mayapple Rd

**Rolling Wood Dr**
Bel Aire Dr, Little Hill Dr, Hollow Oak La

Straight: Berrian Rd, first left: Woods End Rd, second left: Idlewood Dr, third left: Pepper Ridge Rd, first right: Little Hill Dr

**Rome Pl**
Clifford Av

# The Stamford Streets AZ

Straight: Lindsey Av, S Lindsey Av, first left: Oaklawn Av, first right: Brighton Pl, second right: Crane Rd N Straight: Vanech Dr, straight: Oaklawn Av, first left: Sherwood Rd, second left: Dann Dr, third left: Fairfield Memorial Park Cemetery, first right: Pepper Ridge Rd, second right: Jamroga La, third right: Clifford Av

**Roosevelt Av**

Straight: Grenhart Rd, first left: Wilson St, first right: Victory St, second right: Diaz St, third right: E 6 Governor John Davis Lodge Tpke I-95 Straight: Boston Post Rd 1, first left: Liberty St, second left: Victory St, third left: Virgil St, first right: Wilson St, second right: Richmond Hill Av, third right: High St

**Rosa Hartman Park**
Brown House Rd

**Rosano Rd**

Straight: Wood Ridge Dr, Ridge Park Av, first left: Brookvale Pl, second left: Ridge Park Av, first right: Hillview La,

# The Stamford Streets AZ

second right: Longview Av, third right: Knollwood Av

**Rose Park**

Straight: Boston Post Rd 1, first left: Ann St, second left: Spruce St, third left: Spruce St, Hazel St, first right: Stillwater Av, second right: W Main St, Greenwich Av, third right: Clinton Av, Tresser Blvd 1
Straight: Richmond Hill Av, first left: Mission St, second left: Greenwich Av, third left: Clinton Av, first right: Taylor St, Ann St, second right: Spruce St, third right: Fairfield Av

**Rose St**

Straight: Center St, first left: Center Terrace, second left: Church St, first right: Goodwin St, second right: Scofield Av, third right: Morris St
Straight: Hope St, first left: Colonial Rd, second left: Pilgrim Walk, Scofield Av, third left: Plymouth Rd, first right: Pine Hill Av, Church St, second right: Glendale Dr, third right: Union St

# The Stamford Streets AZ

**Round Hill Dr**

Straight: Tall Oaks Rd, first left: Tall Oaks Ct, first right: Laurel Ledge Rd
Straight: Laurel Ledge Rd, first left: Tall Oaks Rd, second left: Laurel Ledge Ct, first right: Riverbank Rd

**Round Lake Rd**

Straight: Woodbine Rd, first left: Bittersweet La, second left: Fernwood Dr, third left: Reservoir La, first right: Cedar Wood Rd, second right: Brushwood Rd, third right: Pinewood Rd

**Roxbury Rd**
Stillwater Rd, W Hill Rd, Overhill Rd, Doral Farms Rd, Barncroft Rd, Munko Dr, Den Rd, Roxbury Terrace

Straight: Westover Rd, Cow Path Dr, Riverbank Rd, first left: Old Mill La, second left: Winding Brook La, first right: Thunder Hill Dr, second right: Bangall Rd, third right: Windward La
Straight: Long Ridge Rd 104, Buckingham Dr, first left: Barnes Rd, second left: Loughran Av, third left: Maltbie Av, first right: Stillwater Rd, second

# The Stamford Streets AZ

right: Clover Hill Dr, third right: Three Lakes Dr

**Roxbury Ter**
Straight: Roxbury Rd, first left: Westover Rd, Cow Path Dr, Riverbank Rd, second left: Thunder Hill Dr, first right: Den Rd, second right: Munko Dr, third right: Barncroft Rd

**Rugby St**

Straight: Elmcroft Rd, first left: Belden St, second left: Remington St, third left: E Walnut St, first right: Dyke La
Straight: Harbor St, first left: Dyke La, first right: Belden St

**Rushmore Circle**

Straight: Alpine St, first left: Jay Rd, second left: Cedar Heights Rd, first right: Ken Ct, second right: Dunn Av

**Russet Rd**
Winesap Rd, McIntosh Rd

# The Stamford Streets AZ

Straight: High Ridge Rd 137, first left: Flora Pl, second left: Laurel Rd, third left: Mayapple Rd, first right: Briar Brae Rd, second right: Briar Brae Rd, third right: Ingleside Dr
Straight: Mayapple Rd, first left: Country Club Rd, second left: Boulderol Rd, third left: Tanglewood La, first right: High Ridge Rd 137

**Rutz St**

Straight: Toms Rd, first left: Deleo Dr, second left: Overbrook Dr, third left: Dale Pl, first right: Derwin St, second right: Hope St
Straight: Glen Av
Derwin St
Straight: Hope St, first left: Toms Rd, second left: Viaduct Rd, third left: Edgewood Av, first right: Douglas Av, second right: Union St, third right: Glendale Dr

**Ryan St**
Camp Av

Straight: Greenway St, straight: Hope St, Knapp St, first left: Hyde St, second left: Cushing St, third left: Northill St, fourth left: Fahey St,

# The Stamford Streets AZ

first right: Camp Av, second right: Mulberry St, third right: Weed Hill Av

**Rose Rd**

Straight: Oakdale Rd, first left: Glen Ter, first right: Glenbrook Rd

**Revonah Cir S**

Straight: Revonah Cir, first left: Revonah Av, East La

# The Stamford Streets AZ

## S

**S Brook Dr**
Jonathan Dr


**S Lake Dr**
Lisa La, Wallenberg Dr


**S Lindsey Av**
Brighton Pl, Rome Pl

Straight: Crane Rd N, first left: Crane Rd, second left: Newfield Av, Strawberry Hill Av, first right: Crane Rd
Straight: Oaklawn Av, first left: Clifford Av, second left: Jamroga La, third left: Pepper Ridge Rd, first right: Dorlen Rd, second right: Newfield Av


**S Sagamore La**

Straight: Ralsey Rd S, first left: Ocean Dr W, first right: Sagamore Rd, Ralsey Rd S
Straight: Sagamore Rd, first left: Ralsey Rd S, first right: Stamford Av, second right: Woolsey Rd, third right: Shippan Av

# The Stamford Streets AZ

**S State St**
Washington Blvd, Guernsey Av, Atlantic St, E 8 Governor John Davis Lodge Tpke I-95, Canal St, E 7 Governor John Davis Lodge Tpke I-95, Elm St, E 8 Governor John Davis Lodge Tpke I-95, Lafayette St, E 8 Governor John Davis Lodge Tpke I-95

Straight: E 7 Governor John Davis Lodge Tpke I-95, Greenwich Av, first left: First Stamford Pl, second left: Pulaski St, third left: Davenport St, first right: West St, second right: Richmond Hill Av, third right: Treglia Terrace
Straight: N State St, first left: Lafayette St, second left: Daly St, third left: Clarks Hill Av, first right: Boston Post Rd 1


**St John's Cemetery**
Camp Av, Hoyt St

Straight: Camp Av, first left: Garland Dr, first right: Greenwood Av, second right: Hoyt St
Straight: Hoyt St, first left: Camp Av, first right: Lynn Ct, second right: Heather La

# The Stamford Streets AZ

**Sachem Pl**
Uncas Rd

Straight: Van Buskirk Av, first left: East Av, first right: Caldwell Av, second right: Cove Rd
Straight: Wascussee La, first left: Uncas Rd, first right: Wascussee La E, second right: Soundview Av

**Saddle Hill La**

Straight: Saddle Hill Rd, first left: Rock Rimmon Rd

**Saddle Hill Rd**
Saddle Hill La

Straight: Rock Rimmon Rd, first left: Briar Brae Rd, second left: Mill Rd, third left: Ridge Brook Dr, first right: Dads La, Rock Rimmon Rd, second right: Chatham Rd, third right: Falmouth Rd

**Saddle Rock Rd**
Rogers Rd

Straight: Ocean Dr W, first left: Verplank Av, second left: Rogers Rd,

# The Stamford Streets AZ

first right: Stamford Av, second right: Shippan Av

**Sagamore Rd**
S Sagamore La, Stamford Av, Woolsey Rd

Straight: Shippan Av, first left: Gurley Rd, second left: Ralsey Rd, third left: Chesterfield Rd, first right: Ocean Dr E, second right: Ocean Dr W, third right: Rockledge Dr
Straight: Ralsey Rd S, first left: S Sagamore La, second left: Ocean Dr W, first right: Ralsey Rd

**Salem Pl**

Straight: Gaymoor Dr, first left: Minivale Rd, second left: Sterling Pl, third left: Gaymoor Circle, first right: Prudence Dr
Straight: Minivale Rd, first left: Prudence Dr, second left: Hope St, first right: Gaymoor Dr, second right: Bouton St W

**Sandy La**
Patricia La

# The Stamford Streets AZ

Straight: Club Rd, first left: Kerr Rd, second left: Bertmor Dr, third right: Newfield Av, first right: Malvern Rd, second right: Club Circle

**Sanford La**
Kensington Rd, Harvest Hill La

Straight: Newfield Av, first left: Denicola Rd, second left: Megan La, third left: Gray Farms Rd, first right: Case Rd, Swan La, second right: Todd La, third right: Turner Rd, Belltown Rd

**Sawmill Rd**
Mill Stream Rd, Dundee Rd, Mill Stone Circle, Wind Mill Circle, Cider Mill Rd

Straight: Long Ridge Rd 104, first left: Wildwood Rd, second left: Mountain Wood Rd, third left: Riverbank Rd, first right: Lakewood Dr, second right: Partridge Rd, third right: Stone Hill Dr

**Saxon Ct**

Straight: Vine Pl, first left: Donata La

# The Stamford Streets AZ

**Schuyler Av**
Pine Av

Straight: Smith St, first left: Greenwood Hill St, second left: Mill River St, W Main St, first right: Stephen St, second right: Stillwater Av, third right: Alden St
Straight: W Broad St, first left: Adams Av, second left: Oak Hill St, third left: Stephen St, first right: Hanrahan St, second right: Mill River St, third right: Washington Blvd 137, Broad St


**Scofield Av**
Parker Av, Oscar St, Center St

Straight: Pilgrim Walk, Hope St, first left: Plymouth Rd, second left: Rock Spring Rd, third left: Faucett St, first right: Colonial Rd, second right: Rose St, third right: Pine Hill Av, Church St
Straight: Glenbrook Rd, first left: Crescent St, second left: Church St, third left: Cowing Pl, first right: Windell Pl, second right: Frankel Pl, third right: Ely Pl

# The Stamford Streets AZ

## Scofield Town Park

Straight: Scofieldtown Rd, Hannahs Rd, first left: Skymeadow Dr, second left: Skyline La, Sunset Rd, first right: Rock Rimmon Rd, second right: Haviland Rd


## Scofieldtown Rd
Gary Rd, Old Logging Rd, Janes La, Middle Ridge Rd, Woodley Rd, Campbell Dr, Georgian Ct, Chestnut Hill Rd, Brookdale Rd, Haviland Rd, Rock Rimmon Rd, Hannahs Rd, Skymeadow Dr, Skyline La

Straight: High Ridge Rd 137, first left: High Ridge Rd, second left: High Ridge Rd, third left: Interlaken Rd, fourth left: Bird Song La, first right: Meredith La, second right: Diamondcrest La, third right: Blue Ridge Dr
Straight: Sunset Rd
West Trail, Princess Ct, Skyline La
Straight: High Ridge Rd 137, first left: Alexandra Dr, second left: Ingleside Dr, third left: Briar Brae Rd, first right: Hickory Rd, second right: Hickory Rd, third right: Bracchi Dr, Hoyclo Rd, fourth right: Hoyclo Rd, Acre View Dr


## Scott Pl
Culloden Rd, Peveril Rd

# The Stamford Streets AZ

Straight: Clovelly Rd, first left: Lafayette St, first right: Penzance Rd, second right: Glenbrook Rd

**Sea Beach Dr**

Straight: Ocean Dr E, first left: Rockledge Dr, second left: Hobson St, third left: Fairview Av, first right: Westcott Rd, second right: Shippan Av
Straight: Hobson St
Rockledge Dr, Ocean Dr E, Brightside Dr
Straight: Shippan Av, first left: Sound Av, second left: Fairview Av, third left: Westminster Rd, first right: Rockledge Dr, second right: Ocean Dr W, third right: Ocean Dr E

**Seaside Av**
Sylvan Knoll Rd, Mathews St, Bungalow Park, Webb Av, E 9 Governor John Davis Lodge Tpke I-95, E 9 Governor John Davis Lodge Tpke I-95

Straight: Boston Post Rd 1, first left: E 9 Governor John Davis Lodge Tpke I-95, second left: E 9 Governor John Davis Lodge Tpke I-95, third left: Courtland Av 106, E 9 Governor John Davis Lodge Tpke I-95, first right: Home Ct, second

# The Stamford Streets AZ

right: Houston Terrace, third right: Hamilton Av, Waterbury Av
Straight: Cove Rd, first left: Dean St, second left: Dora St, third left: Euclid Av, first right: Avery St, second right: Horton St, third right: George St

**Seaton Rd**
Standish Rd, Trumbull Gate, Revere Dr

Straight: Courtland Av 106, first left: Hamilton Av, second left: Tremont Av, third left: Fairmont Av, first right: Boston Post Rd 1, E 9 Governor John Davis Lodge Tpke I-95
Straight: Boston Post Rd 1, Noroton Hill Pl, first left: Maher Rd, second left: Blachley Rd, third left: Standish Rd, first right: Lawn Av, second right: Grant Av, third right: Lockwood Av

**Seaview Av**
Ingall St

Straight: Shippan Av, first left: Harbor Dr, Magee Av, second left: Lindstrom Rd, third left: Rippowam Rd, first right: Park St, second right: Hanover St, third right: Wardwell St

# The Stamford Streets AZ

**Second St, 2nd St**
Summer St

Straight: Bedford St, first left: 3rd St, second left: 4th St, third left: 5th St, first right: 1st St, second right: Oak St, third right: Hoyt St
Straight: Washington Blvd 137, first left: Linden Pl, Hoyt St, second left: North St, third left: W Broad St, Broad St, first right: Bridge St, second right: W Forest Lawn Av, third right: Paragon La, Cold Spring Rd


**Selby Pl**

Straight: Elizabeth Av, first left: Marian St, first right: Ridgewood Av, second right: Knickerbocker Av


**Selleck St**
Greenwich Av, Southfield Av, Orchard St, Fairfield Av, Vassar Av, Bonner St, Irving Av, Durant St, Montauk Dr, Betts Av, West Av, Outlook St, Harvard Av

Straight: Davenport St, straight: Greenwich Av, first left: Milton St, second left: Selleck St, Southfield Av, first right: Pulaski St, second right: First Stamford Pl, third right: E 7

# The Stamford Streets AZ

Governor John Davis Lodge Tpke I-95, S State St
Straight: Brown House Rd, first left: Harding Rd, second left: Kensington Ct, third left: Forest Av, first right: Harvard Av, Warshaw Pl

**Serenity La**

Straight: Benenson Dr, first left: Daffodil La, first right: Shelter Dr, second right: W Glen Dr

**Settlers Trail**

Straight: West Trail, first left: Fishing Trail, second left: Mountain Trail, first right: Sunset Rd

**Seventh St, 7th St**
Weil St

Straight: first left: 8th St, second left: Forest Lawn Av, third left: Hoover Av, first right: Bridge St, second right: 6th St, third right: 5th St
Straight: Waterford La, first right: 8th St

# The Stamford Streets AZ

### Severance Dr

Straight: Cold Spring Rd, first left: Stillwater Rd, first right: Windsor Rd, second right: Severance Dr, third right: Windsor Rd, fourth right: Cold Spring Rd 137

### Shad Rd W

Straight: White Birch Rd, first left: White Birch Rd S, second left: Long Ridge Rd, first right: White Birch La

### Shadow La
Eastover Rd

Straight: Newfield Dr, first left: Newfield Av, first right: Joan Rd, Intervale Rd
Straight: Intervale Rd E, straight: Newfield Av, Sweet Briar Rd, first left: Emerald La, second left: White Oak La, third left: Wedgemere Rd, first right: Newfield Dr, second right: Sterling Farms Golf Club, third right: Weed Hill Av

### Shadow Ridge Rd
Wild Horse Rd, Lancaster Pl

# The Stamford Streets AZ

Straight: Cedar Heights Rd, first left: Cedar Circle, second left: Alpine St, third left: Apple Tree La, first right: Dunn Av, second right: High Ridge Rd 137, Turn Of River Rd
Straight: Sun Dance Rd, first left: Snow Crystal La


**Shady Knoll Dr**

Straight: Ingleside Dr, first left: Wynnewood La, second left: Spring Hill La E, third left: Laurel Rd, Woodbine Rd, first right: Briar Brae Rd, High Ridge Rd 137, second right: High Ridge Rd 137


**Shady La**

Straight: Merriland Rd, Winesap Rd, first left: McIntosh Rd, second left: Crab Apple Pl, third left: Russet Rd
Straight: Briar Brae Rd, first left: High Ridge Rd 137, first right: Briar Wood Trail, second right: Rock Rimmon Rd


**Shag Bark Rd**

Straight: Old Long Ridge Rd, first left: Mill Rd, second left: Hunting Ridge Rd,

# The Stamford Streets AZ

third left: Long Ridge Rd 104, first right: Erskine Rd, second right: Heming Way, third right: Parsonage Rd

**Shelburne Rd**
Edison Rd

Straight: W Broad St, first left: Rachelle Av, second left: Merrell Av, third left: Delaware Av, first right: St George Av, second right: Hubbard Av, third right: Hinckley Av

**Shelter Rock Rd**
Riverbank Dr, Rising Rock Rd

Straight: Rocky Rapids Rd, first left: Pinnacle Rock Rd, second left: Ridgecrest Rd, third left: Riverbank Rd, first right: Wildwood Rd, Harpsichord Tpke

**Sheridan St**
Grant Av

Straight: Lincoln Av, first left: Sherman St, second left: Boston Post Rd, Lockwood Av, first right: Custer St

# The Stamford Streets AZ

**Sherman St**
Lincoln Av, Grant Av

Straight: Lawn Av, first left: Trumbull Gate, second left: Custer St, Helen Pl, third left: Leroy Pl, first right: Boston Post Rd 1
Straight: Lincoln Av, first left: Boston Post Rd 1, Lockwood Av, first right: Sheridan St, second right: Custer St


**Sherwood Rd**

Straight: Turner Rd, first left: Dann Dr, first right: High Clear Dr, second right: Pepper Ridge Rd, third right: Cody Dr
Straight: Oaklawn Av, first left: Vanech Dr, second left: Pepper Ridge Rd, third left: Jamroga La, first right: Dann Dr, second right: Fairfield Memorial Park Cemetery, third right: Dartley St


**Shippan Av**
Ocean Dr W, Ocean Dr E, Verplank Av, Westminster Rd, Fairview Av, Sound Av, Hobson St, Rockledge Dr, Ocean Dr W, Ocean Dr E, Sagamore Rd, Gurley Rd, Ralsey Rd, Chesterfield Rd, Lanark Rd, Downs Av, Auldwood Rd, Mitchell St, Wallace St, Iroquois Rd, Mariners La,

# The Stamford Streets AZ

Rippowam Rd, Lindstrom Rd, Harbor Dr, Magee Av, Seaview Av, Park St, Hanover St, Wardwell St, Wardwell St, Elm St, Cove Rd, Frederick St

Straight: Warren St, first left: Lee St, second left: Maple Av, third left: Myrtle Av, first right: Lockwood Av

### Shore Rd
Tomac Av, Tait Rd, Ford La, Random Rd, Tower La, Sylvan La, Binney La, Grant Av, Ballwood Rd, Ledge Rd, Sound Beach Av, Meadowbank Rd, Rocky Pt Rd, Wahneta Rd, Nawthorne Rd, Shoreham Club Rd, E Point La, N Crossway, S Crossway, Cove Rd, Tods Driftway

Straight: Fairfield Av, Cummings Point Rd, first left: Hendrie Ct, second left: Top Gallant Rd, third left: Dee La, first right: Gatehouse Rd

### Short Hill St

Straight: Knickerbocker Av, first left: St Charles Av, second left: Hartford Av, third left: Elizabeth Av, first right: Clearview Av, second right: Bennett St, third right: Northill St

# The Stamford Streets AZ

Straight: Hope St, first left: Omega Dr, second left: Clearview Av, third left: Largo Dr, first right: Avon La, second right: Barnstable La, third right: Hartford Av, Castle Ct


**Short Trail**

Straight: Fishing Trail, first left: Woody Trail, second left: West Trail


**Signal Rd**
Thread Needle La

Straight: Gatehouse Rd, first left: Cummings Point Rd, first right: Top Gallant Rd


**Silver Hill La**
Barrett Av, Cody Dr, Fara Dr, Pepper Ridge Rd, Deer La

Straight: Case Rd, Brinkerhoff Av, first left: Newfield Av, Swan La, first right: Turner Rd
Straight: Loveland Rd, Loveland Rd W, first left: High Ridge Rd 137, first right: White Birch La, second right: Lantern Circle, third right: Dannell Dr

# The Stamford Streets AZ

**Silver St**

Straight: Burwood Av, first left: Southfield Av, first right: Keith St, second right: Noble St, third right: Beal St
Straight: Congress St, first left: Carlisle Pl, second left: Keith St, third left: Noble St, fourth left: Beal St, first right: Southfield Av


**Simsbury Rd**
Nutmeg La

Straight: Vine Rd, first left: Kerr Rd, second left: Pepper Ridge Rd, third left: Malvern Rd, first right: Newfield Av


**Sixth St, 6th St**
Ridgeway Plaza

Straight: Bedford St, Chester St, first left: Urban St, second left: Marlou La, third left: Locust La, first right: 5th St, second right: 4th St, third right: 3rd St
Straight: Summer St, first left: 5th St, second left: 4th St, third left: 3rd St, first right: Bridge St, second right: 7th St, third right: 8th St

# The Stamford Streets AZ

**Skyline La**
Northwind Dr, Northwind Dr

Straight: Skymeadow Dr, first left: Mary Joy La, second left: High Ridge Rd 137, Bartlett La, first right: Larkspur Rd, second right: Scofieldtown Rd
Straight: Scofieldtown Rd, Sunset Rd, first left: Skymeadow Dr, second left: Hannahs Rd, third left: Rock Rimmon Rd, first right: Princess Ct, second right: West Trail, third right: High Ridge Rd 137


**Skymeadow Dr**
Larkspur Rd, Skyline La, Mary Joy La

Straight: Bartlett La, High Ridge Rd 137, first left: Pinner La, second left: Cedar Wood Rd, third left: Hoyclo Rd, Acre View Dr, first right: N Stamford Rd, second right: Alma Rock Rd, third right: N Stamford Rd
Straight: Scofieldtown Rd, first left: Hannahs Rd, second left: Rock Rimmon Rd, third left: Haviland Rd, first right: Skyline La, Sunset Rd

# The Stamford Streets AZ

**Skyview Ct**

Straight: Stillwater Rd, first left: Westwood Rd, second left: Long Hill Dr, first right: Skyview Dr, second right: Clover Hill Dr

**Skyview Dr E**

Straight: Westwood Rd, Skyview Dr, first left: Westwood Ct, second left: Stanton La, first right: Westwood Pl, second right: Stillwater Rd
Straight: Stillwater Rd, first left: Skyview Ct, second left: Logan's Run, first right: Clover Hill Dr, second right: River Hill Dr

**Skyview Dr**
Westwood Rd, Green Tree La, Stanton La, Westwood Rd

Straight: Stillwater Rd, first left: Logan's Run, second left: Westwood Rd, third left: Long Hill Dr, first right: Clover Hill Dr, second right: River Hill Dr, third right: London La
Straight: Blueberry Dr, first left: Pond Rd, second left: Pond Rd, first right: W Hill Rd

# The Stamford Streets AZ

**Sleepy Hollow La**

Straight: Knapp St, Lawton Av, first left: Brundage St, second left: Gilford St, third left: Carroll St, first right: Woodbury Av, second right: Birchwood Rd, third right: Woodledge Rd, Lawton Av


**Slice Dr**

Straight: Hope St, first left: Camelot Ct, second left: Deep Spring La, third left: Nottingham Dr, first right: Eden Rd, E Cross Rd, second right: Broad Brook La, W Cross Rd, third right: Woodway Ridge La


**Smith St**
Greenwood Hill St, Schuyler Av, Stephen St

Straight: Mill River St, first left: W Broad St, first right: Main St, second right: Boston Post Rd 1, Greenwich Av
Straight: Stillwater Av, first left: Boston Post Rd 1, first right: Alden St, second right: Spruce St, third right: Fairfield Av

# The Stamford Streets AZ

**Smoke Hill Dr**

Straight: Arrow Head Dr, straight: Den Rd, first left: Old Orchard La, second left: Flint Rock Rd, third left: Hardesty Rd, first right: Long Ridge Rd 104


**Snow Crystal La**
Corn Cake La, Bradley Pl, Wild Horse Rd

Straight: Sun Dance Rd, first right: Shadow Ridge Rd


**Somerset La**
Dzamba Grove, Hampton La

Straight: Perna La, first left: High Ridge Rd 137


**Sound Av**
Cresthill Pl

Straight: Shippan Av, first left: Hobson St, second left: Rockledge Dr, third left: Ocean Dr W, first right: Fairview Av, second right: Westminster Rd, third right: Ocean Dr E, Ocean Dr W, Verplank Av

# The Stamford Streets AZ

Straight: Stamford Av, first left: Fairview Av, second left: Verplank Av, third left: Ocean Dr W, first right: Ocean Dr W, second right: Sagamore Rd, third right: Ralsey Rd


**Soundview Av**
Wallacks La, Wallacks Dr, Kenilworth Dr E, Kenilworth Dr W, Soundview Dr, Soundview Ct, Willowbrook Av, Carter Dr, Wascussee La, Tupper Dr, McMullen Av, James St, East Av, McMullen Av, Limerick St, Wardwell St

Straight: Cove Rd, first left: Lockwood Av, second left: Frederick St, third left: Shippan Av, Elm St, first right: Leeds St, second right: St Benedict Circle, third right: Raymond St


**Soundview Ct**

Straight: Soundview Av, first left: Soundview Dr, second left: Kenilworth Dr W, third left: Kenilworth Dr E, first right: Willowbrook Av, second right: Carter Dr, third right: Wascussee La

# The Stamford Streets AZ

## Soundview Dr

Straight: Soundview Av, first left: Soundview Ct, second left: Willowbrook Av, third left: Carter Dr, first right: Kenilworth Dr W, second right: Kenilworth Dr E, third right: Wallacks Dr

## Southerly Woods Rd

Straight: Northerly Woods Rd, straight: Barn Hill Rd, straight: E Middle Patent Rd, first left: Cherry Hill Rd, second left: Taconic Rd, first right: Ledge Rd, second right: Hidden Valley Way, third right: Hope's Farm La

## Southfield Av

Hickory Dr, Cook Rd, Davenport Dr, Top Gallant Rd, Burwood Av, Congress St, Wells Av, McClurg Av, Burley Av, Sunnyside Av, Taff Av, Homestead Av, Selleck St

Straight: Eureka Terrace, straight: Davenport Dr, first left: Hickory Dr, second left: Davenport Dr, third left: Southfield Av
Straight: Greenwich Av, Selleck St, first left: Orchard St, second left:

# The Stamford Streets AZ

Fairfield Av, third left: Fairfield Av, fourth left: Vassar Av, first right: Davenport St


**Southfield Village Ct**

Straight: Baxter Av, first left: Wilson St, second left: Fairfield Av, first right: Southwood Dr, second right: Southfield Village Ct, third right: E 6 Governor John Davis Lodge Tpke I-95, fourth right: West Av
Straight: Baxter Av, Southwood Dr, first left: Southfield Village Ct, second left: Wilson St, third left: Fairfield Av, first right: E 6 Governor John Davis Lodge Tpke I-95, second right: West Av, third right: Harvard Av, E 6 Governor John Davis Lodge Tpke I-95


**Southill St**

Straight: Cady St, Clearview Av, first left: Woodbury Av, first right: Buena Vista St, Bon Air Av, second right: Tower Av
Straight: Knickerbocker Av, first left: Short Hill St, second left: Clearview Av, third left: Bennett St, first right: St Charles Av, second right: Hartford Av, third right: Elizabeth Av

# The Stamford Streets AZ

### Southwest Dr

Straight: Hartswood Rd, first left: Beechwood Rd, second left: Meadowpark Av N, third left: Ayres Dr, first right: High Ridge Rd 137

### Southwood Dr
Montauk Dr

Straight: Peqout Dr, first left: Montauk Dr, first right: second right: Montauk Dr, Orlando Av
Straight: Baxter Av, Southfield Village Ct, first left: E6 Governor John Davis Lodge Tpke I-95, first right: Southfield Village Ct, second right: Waverly Pl, Wilson St

### Spinning Wheel La

Straight: Haviland Rd, first left: Scofieldtown Rd, first right: Hickory Farm, second right: Deerfield Dr, third right: Haviland Ct

### Spring Hill La E

Straight: Ingleside Dr, first left: Laurel Rd, Woodbine Rd, first right:

# The Stamford Streets AZ

Wynnewood La, second right: Shady Knoll Dr, third right: Briar Brae Rd, High Ridge Rd 137

**Spring Hill La N**

Straight: Laurel Rd, first left: High Ridge Rd 137, first right: Ingleside Dr, second right: Woodbine Rd, Reservoir La

**Spring St**

Straight: Summer St, first left: Broad St, second left: W Park Pl, Main St, Clark St, Bank St, first right: North St, second right: Hoyt St, third right: Oak St
Straight: Bedford St, Prospect St, first left: Forest St, second left: Walton Pl, third left: North St, first right: Broad St, Atlantic St

**Spruce St**
Boston Post Rd 1, Hazel St, Stillwater Av, Hillhurst St, Finney La

Straight: Wright St, straight: W Broad St, first left: Hinckley Av, second left: Hubbard Av, third left: St George Av, first right: Anderson St, second

# The Stamford Streets AZ

right: Stephen St, third right: Oak Hill St
Straight: Richmond Hill Av, first left: Ann St, Taylor St, second left: Rose Park, third left: Mission St, first right: Fairfield Av, second right: Boston Post Rd 1, Wilson St

**Square Acre Dr**
Olga Dr

Straight: High Ridge Rd 137, first left: Dunn Av, second left: Buxton Farm Rd, E 35 Merritt Pkwy 15, CT15, third left: E 35 Merritt Pkwy 15, CT15, first right: Olga Dr, second right: Cedar Heights Rd, Turn Of River Rd, third right: Vine Rd

**St Benedict Circle**
St Benedict Circle

Straight: Dale St, first left: Cove Rd, second left: Ursula Pl, third left: Ursula Pl
Straight: Cove Rd, first left: Leeds St, second left: Soundview Av, third left: Lockwood Av, first right: Raymond St, second right: Dale St, third right: Van Buskirk Av

# The Stamford Streets AZ

**St Charles Av**
Klondike Av, Woodbury Av, Marian St

Straight: Haig Av, first left: Joffre Av, second left: Todd La, Pershing Av, first right: Crestview Av, second right: Gray Farms Rd, third right: Nyselius Pl
Straight: Knickerbocker Av, first left: Short Hill St, second left: Clearview Av, third left: Bennett St, first right: Hartford Av, second right: Elizabeth Av


**St George Av**
W North St

Straight: W Broad St, first left: Hubbard Av, second left: Shelburne Rd, third left: Hinckley Av, fourth left: Wright St, fifth left: Anderson St, first right: Rachelle Av, Shelburne Rd, second right: Merrell Av, third right: Delaware Av


**St Marys St**
Gleason Av

Straight: Halloween Blvd, first left: Gleason Av, second left: Jefferson St
Straight: Magee Av, first left: Hanover St, second left: Pumping Station Rd,

# The Stamford Streets AZ

third left: Harbor Dr, Shippan Av, first right: Jefferson St

**Stafford Rd**

Straight: Ursula Pl, first left: Orange St, second left: Dale St, third left: Dale St, first right: Maher Rd
Straight: Orange St, first left: Maher Rd, first right: Ursula Pl, second right: Lockwood Av

**Stamford Av**
Ocean Dr W, Verplank Av, Fairview Av, Sound Av, Ocean Dr W, Sagamore Rd

Straight: Ralsey Rd, first left: Ralsey Rd S, first right: Shippan Av

**Stamford Plz**

Straight: E Main St, Elm St, first left: Grove St, second left: Suburban Av, first right: N State St, second right: E7 Governor John Davis Lodge Tpke I-95
Straight: Stamford Forum, Canal St, Greyrock Pl, first left: N State St, first right: E Main St

# The Stamford Streets AZ

**Stamford Rd N**
Cascade Rd, Lakeside Dr

Straight: Lakeside Dr, first left: Quarry Rd, second left: Interlaken Rd, third left: Newfield Av, Davenport Ridge Rd, first right: High Ridge Rd 137
Straight: High Ridge Rd 137, first left: Alma Rock Rd, second left: Stamford Rd N, third left: Brookdale Rd, first right: Skymeadow Dr, Bartlett La, second right: Pinner La, third right: Cedar Wood Rd

**Stamford Forum**
Town Center Dr

Straight: Greyrock Pl, Stamford Plz, Canal St, first left: E Main St, second left: Broad St, first right: N State St, second right: S State St, E 7 Governor John Davis Lodge Tpke I-95
Straight: Atlantic St, Tresser Blvd, first left: Federal St, second left: N State St, first right: Bell St, second right: Bank St

**Standish Rd**
Revere Dr

# The Stamford Streets AZ

Straight: Seaton Rd, first left: Boston Post Rd 1, Noroton Hill Pl, first right: Trumbull Gate, second right: Revere Dr, third right: Courtland Av 106
Straight: Boston Post Rd 1, first left: E 9 Governor John Davis Lodge Tpke I-95, second left: Courtland Av 106, E 6 Governor John Davis Lodge Tpke I-95, third left: Governor John Davis Lodge Tpke I-95, first right: Blachley Rd, second right: Maher Rd, third right: Lockwood Av


**Stanley Ct**

Straight: Franklin St, first left: North St, second left: Hoyt St, third left: Woodside St, first right: Broad St


**Stanton Dr**
Stanton La

Straight: Stillview Rd, straight: Stillwater Rd, first left: London La, second left: River Hill Dr, third left: Clover Hill Dr, first right: Pond Rd, second right: Cold Spring Rd, third right: Knoblock La, fourth right: Knobloch La

# The Stamford Streets AZ

**Stanton La**
Westwood Rd

Straight: Skyview Dr, first left: Westwood Rd, second left: Blueberry Dr, first right: Green Tree La, second right: Westwood Rd, third right: Stillwater Rd
Straight: Stanton Dr, first right: Stillview Rd


**Stanwick Circle**

Straight: Stanwick Pl, first right: Oaklawn Av


**Stanwich Club**

Straight: Taconic Rd, first left: E Middle Patent Rd, first right: Farms Rd
Straight: North St, first left: N Stanwich Rd, first right: Upper Cross Rd, Hekma Rd


**Stanwick Pl**
Stanwick Circle

Straight: Oaklawn Av, first left: Benstone St, second left: Northwoods Rd, third left: Old North Stamford Rd,

# The Stamford Streets AZ

Cantwell Av, first right: Camore St, second right: Dartley St, third right: Fairfield Memorial Park Cemetery, fourth right: Dann Dr

**Starin Dr**
Bayberrie Dr

Straight: Westover Rd, first left: Indian Hill Rd, second left: W Hill Rd, third left: Summit Ridge Rd, first right: Bayberrie Dr, second right: Emery Dr E, third right: Sycamore Terrace
Straight: Palmers Hill Rd, first left: Emery Dr, second left: Westover Rd, third left: Stillwater Rd, E Gaynor Brennan Golf Course, first right: Havemeyer La, second right: Hillcrest Park Rd, third right: Old Wagon Rd

**Stark Pl**

Straight: Long Ridge Rd 104, first left: Terrace Av, second left: McClean Av, third left: Cross Rd, first right: River Ridge Ct, second right: Brook Run La, third right: Wishing Well La
Straight: Jessup St, straight: Terrace Av, first left: High Ridge Rd 137, second right: Long Ridge Rd 104

# The Stamford Streets AZ

**State Hwy 104: SR 104: Long Ridge Rd**
Cross Rd, McClean Av, Terrace Av, Stark Pl, River Ridge Ct, Brook Run La, Wishing Well La, Woodridge Dr S, Three Lakes Dr, Clover Hill Dr, Roxbury Rd, Stillwater Rd, Buckingham Dr, Barnes Rd, Loughran Av, Maltbie Av, Vineyard La, Wire Mill Rd, E 34 Merritt Pkwy 15, CT15, E 34 Merritt Pkwy 15, CT15, Webbs Hill Rd, Northwood La, Midrocks Dr, Den Rd, Hazard La, Chestnut Hill Rd, Butternut La, Hunting Ridge Rd, Stone Hill Dr, Partridge Rd, Lakewood Dr, Sawmill Rd, Wildwood Rd, Mountain Wood Rd, Riverbank Rd, Old Long Ridge Rd, Grey Birch Rd, Erskine Rd, Parsonage Rd, N Lake Dr, Echo Hill Dr, Old Long Ridge Rd, Rockrimmon Country Club, White Birch Rd, NY

Straight: High Ridge Rd 137, Summer St, Bedford St, first left: Cold Spring Rd, second left: Halpin Av, third left: Oaklawn Av, first right: Hoover Av, second right: Forest Lawn Av, third right: 8th St

**State Hwy 106: SR 106: Courtland Av: Glenbrook Rd**
Seaton Rd, Hamilton Av, Tremont Av, Fairmont Av, Lenox Av, Taylor Reed Pl, Maple Tree Av, Glen Terrace, Glenbrook

# The Stamford Streets AZ

Rd, Research Dr, Oakdale Rd, Fresh Meadows La

Straight: Boston Post Rd 1, E 9 Governor John Davis Lodge Tpke I-95, first left: E 9 Governor John Davis Lodge Tpke I-95, second left: E 9 Governor John Davis Lodge Tpke I-95, third left: Seaside Av, first right: E 9 Governor John Davis Lodge Tpke I-95, second right: Standish Rd, third right: Blachley Rd
Straight: Middlesex Rd, Fresh Meadows La Darien, CT

## State Hwy 137: SR 137: Washington Blvd: Cold Spring Rd: High Ridge Rd 137

Bell St, Rippowam Pl, Main St, W Park Pl, Whittaker Pl, W Broad St, Broad St, North St, Linden Pl, Hoyt St, 2nd St, 2nd St, Bridge St, W Forest Lawn Av, Paragon La, Cold Spring Rd, Travis Av, Old Barn Rd S, Randall Av, Long Ridge Rd, Long Ridge Rd 104, Halpin Av, Oaklawn Av, Cross Rd, Dubois St, McClean Av, Terrace Av, High Ridge Rd, High Ridge Rd, Colony Ct, High Clear Dr, Brownley Dr, Unity Rd, Lakeview Dr, Loveland Rd W, Longview Av, Knollwood Av, Mercedes La, Dannell Dr, Yale Ct, Janice Rd, Ridge Park Av, Nichols Av, Emma Rd, Swampscott Rd, Bel Aire Dr, Hartswood Rd, Brandt Rd, Maplewood Pl,

## The Stamford Streets AZ

Tally Ho La, Bradley Pl, Donata La, Merriman Rd, Vine Rd, Cedar Heights Rd, Turn Of River Rd, Olga Dr, Square Acre Dr, Dunn Av, E 35 Merritt Pkwy 15, CT15, Buxton Farm Rd, High Ridge Rd, E 35 Merritt Pkwy 15, CT15, CT15, High Ridge Rd, Wire Mill Rd, Willard Terrace, Opper Rd, Brantwood La, Marva La, Pine Hill Terrace, Perna La, Blue Ridge Dr, Diamondcrest La, Meredith La, Scofieldtown Rd, High Ridge Rd, High Ridge Rd, Interlaken Rd, Bird Song La, Brookdale Rd, N Stamford Rd, Alma Rock Rd, N Stamford Rd, Skymeadow Dr, Bartlett La, Pinner La, Cedar Wood Rd, Hoyclo Rd, Acre View Dr, Hoyclo Rd, Bracchi Dr, Hickory Rd, Hickory Rd, Sunset Rd, Alexandra Dr, Ingleside Dr, Briar Brae Rd, Ingleside Dr, Briar Brae Rd, Russet Rd, Flora Pl, Laurel Rd, Mayapple Rd, Trinity Pass, Riding Stable Trail, Fairway Dr, Craig Ct, Pound Ridge Country Club NY

Straight: Tresser Blvd 1, first left: Atlantic St, second left: Town Center Dr, Stamford Forum, first right: Clinton Av, Boston Post Rd 1

# The Stamford Streets AZ

**State Hwy 15: Merritt Pkwy SR 15, CT15**
E 31: North Street, Greenwich, CT, E 33 : Den Rd, E 34 : Long Ridge Rd 104, E 35: High Ridge Rd 137, Buxton Farm Rd, E 36: Old Stamford Rd 106, E 37: Gerdes Rd, South Av, White Birch Rd, New Canaan, CT


**Station Pl**

Straight: Washington Blvd, first left: W Henry St, Henry St, second left: Pulaski St, third left: Atlantic St, first right: S State St, second right: E 8 Governor John Davis Lodge Tpke I-95, N State St, third right: N State St, fourth right: Richmond Hill Av
Straight: Atlantic St, first left: Manhattan St, second left: E 8 Governor John Davis Lodge Tpke I-95, S State St, third left: E 8 Governor John Davis Lodge Tpke I-95, N State St, first right: Rockland Pl, second right: Henry St, third right: Lipton Pl


**Stephen St**

Straight: W Broad St, first left: Anderson St, second left: Wright St, third left: Hinckley Av, first right:

# The Stamford Streets AZ

Oak Hill St, second right: Adams Av, third right: Schuyler Av
Straight: Smith St, first left: Schuyler Av, second left: Greenwood Hill St, Mill River St, W Main St, first right: Stillwater Av

**Sterling Farms Golf Course**

Straight: Newfield Av, first left: Patricia La, second left: Weed Hill Av, first right: Newfield Dr, second right: Intervale Rd E, Sweet Briar Rd

**Sterling Lake La**

Straight: Turn Of River Rd, first left: Intervale Rd, second left: Talmadge La, third left: Gerik Rd, first right: Buxton Farm Rd, second right: High Ridge Park

**Sterling Pl**

Straight: Weed Hill Av, first left: Hope St, first right: Elmer St, second right: Hickory Way, third right: Ridgeway St
Straight: Gaymoor Dr, first left: Gaymoor Circle, second left: Bouton St W, first right: Minivale Rd, second

# The Stamford Streets AZ

right: Salem Pl, third right: Prudence Dr

**Stillview Rd**

Straight: Stanton Dr
Stanton La
Straight: Stillwater Rd, first left: London La, second left: River Hill Dr, third left: Clover Hill Dr, first right: Pond Rd, second right: Cold Spring Rd, third right: Knoblock La

**Stillwater Av**
Smith St, Alden St, Spruce St, Spruce St, Fairfield Av, Finney La, Stillwater Pl, Liberty St, Colahan St, Virgil St, Merrell Av, Corbo Terrace, West Av, Progress Dr, Oxford Ct, W Broad St, Connecticut Av, Stillwater Rd

Straight: Boston Post Rd 1, first left: W Main St, Greenwich Av, second left: Clinton Av, Tresser Blvd 1, first right: Rose Park, second right: Ann St, third right: Spruce St
Straight: Stillwater Rd, Connecticut Av, first left: Myano La

# The Stamford Streets AZ

**Stillwater Pl**

Straight: Stillwater Av, first left: Finney La, second left: Fairfield Av, third left: Spruce St, first right: Liberty St, second right: Colahan St, third right: Virgil St


**Stillwater Rd**
Palmers Hill Rd, E Gaynor Brennan Golf Course, Halliwell Dr, Bridge St, Knobloch La, Knoblock La, Cold Spring Rd, Pond Rd, Stillview Rd, London La, River Hill Dr, Clover Hill Dr, Skyview Dr, Logan's Run, Westwood Rd, Long Hill Dr, Long Ridge Rd 104

Straight: Connecticut Av, Stillwater Av, first right: Myano La
Straight: Roxbury Rd, Long Ridge Rd, first left: W Hill Rd, second left: Overhill Rd, third left: Doral Farms Rd, first right: Long Ridge Rd 104, Buckingham Dr


**Stone Fence La**

Straight: Heming Way, straight: Old Long Ridge Rd, first left: Erskine Rd, second left: Shag Bark Rd, third left: Mill Rd, first right: Parsonage Rd, second right:

# The Stamford Streets AZ

Rock Rimmon Rd, third right: Long Ridge Rd 104

**Stone Hill Dr**

Straight: Long Ridge Rd 104, first left: Partridge Rd, second left: Lakewood Dr, third left: Sawmill Rd, first right: Hunting Ridge Rd, second right: Chestnut Hill Rd, Butternut La, third right: Hazard La

**Stone St**
Cedar St

Straight: Woodland Pl, first left: Elmcroft Rd, second left: Woodland Cemetery, first right: Pacific St

**Stone Wall Dr**

Straight: Lakeview Dr, first left: High Ridge Rd 137, first right: Coopers Pond Rd, second right: Brook Run La
Straight: Coopers Pond Rd, first left: Lakeview Dr

# The Stamford Streets AZ

**Stony Brook Dr**

Straight: W Hill Rd, first left: Carriage Dr, second left: Green Tree La, third left: Dancy Dr, first right: Greenleaf Dr, second right: Blueberry Dr, third right: Westgate Dr

**Strawberry Hill Av**
Hoyt St, Medical Center, Holcomb Av, Strawberry Hill Ct, Rock Spring Rd, Hackett Circle, 5th St, Colonial Rd, Holbrook Dr, Fieldstone La, Upland Rd, Crane Rd

Straight: Hoyt St, Hoyt St, Prospect St, Grove St, Hillandale Av
Straight: Newfield Av, Crane Rd, first left: Crane Rd N, second left: Crane Rd N

**Strawberry Hill Ct**
Strawberry Patch La

Straight: Strawberry Hill Av, first left: Rock Spring Rd, second left: Hackett Circle, third left: 5th St, first right: Medical Center, second right: Holcomb Av, third right: Medical Center

# The Stamford Streets AZ

Straight: Morgan St, first left: Medical Center, second left: Hoyt St, first right: 3rd St, second right: 5th St

**Strawberry Patch La**

Straight: Strawberry Hill Ct, first left: Strawberry Hill Av, first right: Morgan St

**Strawberry Woods**

Straight: Strawberry Hill Av, Colonial Rd, first left: Holbrook Dr, second left: Upland Rd, Fieldstone La, third left: Crane Rd, first right: 5th St, second right: Hackett Circle, third right: Rock Spring Rd

**Studio Ct**

Straight: Studio Rd, first left: Wire Mill Rd

**Studio Rd**
Studio Ct

Straight: Wire Mill Rd, first left: Red Fox Rd, second left: Linwood La, third

# The Stamford Streets AZ

left: Four Brooks Rd, first right: Gutzon Borglum Rd, second right: Blackwood La, third right: High Ridge Rd

**Suburban Av**

Straight: Forest St, first left: Greyrock Pl, second left: Prospect St, third left: Bedford St, first right: Grove St, second right: Ridge Pl, third right: Pleasant St

**Summer Pl**

Straight: Summer St, first left: Broad St, second left: Spring St, third left: North St, first right: W Park Pl, Main St, Clark St, Bank St

**Summer St**
Broad St, Spring St, North St, Hoyt St, Oak St, Woodside St, 1st St, 2nd St, 3rd St, 4th St, 5th St, 6th St, Bridge St, 7th St, 8th St, Forest Lawn Av, Hoover Av
Straight: W Park Pl, Main St, Clark St, Bank St, Main St
Straight: Long Ridge Rd, Bedford St, High Ridge Rd 137, first left: Cold Spring Rd, second left: Cross Rd, third

# The Stamford Streets AZ

left: McClean Av, first right: Locust La, second right: Marlou La, third right: Urban St

**Summit Pl**

Straight: Toms Rd, first left: Belltown Rd, first right: Central St, second right: Autumn La, third right: Dale Pl
Straight: Leonard St, first left: Central St, second left: Dale Pl, first right: Belltown Rd

**Summit Ridge Rd**
Victoria La

Straight: Westover Rd, first left: Westview La, second left: Bartina La, third left: Westover La, first right: W Hill Rd, second right: Indian Hill Rd, third right: Starin Dr

**Sun Dance Circle**

Straight: Sun Dance Rd
Shadow Ridge Rd, Snow Crystal La

**Sun Dance Rd**
Shadow Ridge Rd, Snow Crystal La

# The Stamford Streets AZ

Straight: Sun Dance Circle

**Sunnyside Av**
Orchard St

Straight: Fairfield Av, first left: Liberty Pl, second left: Melrose Pl, third left: Congress St, first right: Selleck St
Straight: Southfield Av, first left: Taff Av, second left: Homestead Av, third left: Selleck St, Greenwich Av, first right: Burley Av, second right: McClurg Av, third right: Wells Av

**Sunset Rd**
Princess Ct, West Trail

Straight: High Ridge Rd 137, first left: Alexandra Dr, second left: Ingleside Dr, third left: Briar Brae Rd, Ingleside Dr, first right: Hickory Rd, second right: Hickory Rd, third right: Hoyclo Rd, Bracchi Dr, fourth right: Hoyclo Rd, Acre View Dr
Straight: Scofieldtown Rd, Skyline La, first left: Northwind Dr, second left: Northwind Dr, third left: Skymeadow Dr

# The Stamford Streets AZ

**Sunset St**
Barholm Av

Straight: Hilltop Av, straight: Weed Hill Av, first left: Barholm Av, second left: Upper Haig Av, third left: Bouton St W, first right: Newfield Av
Straight: Bouton St W, first left: Minivale Rd, second left: Old Colony Rd, third left: Prudence Dr, first right: Gaymoor Dr, second right: Bouton Circle, third right: Weed Hill Av


**Surrey Rd**

Straight: Hunting Ridge Rd, first left: Boulder Brook Dr, second left: Long Ridge Rd, first right: Erickson Dr, second right: Lawrence Hill Rd, third right: Wildwood Rd, Konandreas Dr
Straight: Wellington Dr, first left: Haviland Rd


**Sussex Pl**

Straight: Joffre Av, first left: Joffre Ct, second left: Pershing Av, Ledge La, first right: Haig Av

# The Stamford Streets AZ

**Sutton Dr**

Sutton Pl, Sutton Dr

Straight: Judy La, Hamilton Av, first left: Maitland Rd, second left: Courtland Av, first right: Lawn Av, second right: Culloden Rd


**Sutton Dr E**

Straight: Sutton Pl, Sutton Dr W, first left: Sutton Dr, Sutton Dr E
Straight: Sutton Dr, Sutton Dr E, first left: Sutton Pl, first right: Hamilton Av, Judy La


**Sutton Dr W**

Straight: Sutton Pl, Sutton Dr E, first right: Sutton Dr
Straight: Sutton Dr, Sutton Dr E, first left: Sutton Pl, first right: Hamilton Av, Judy La


**Sutton Pl**

Straight: Sutton Dr W, Sutton Dr E, first left: Sutton Dr W, Sutton Dr, first right: Sutton Dr E, Sutton Dr

# The Stamford Streets AZ

**Swampscott Rd**

Straight: Meadowpark Av N, first left: Ayres Dr, second left: Nichols Av, third left: Meadowpark Av W, Meadowpark Av E, first right: Hartswood Rd

**Swan La**

Straight: Case Rd, Newfield Av, first left: Todd La, second left: Turner Rd, Belltown Rd, third left: Ogden Rd, first right: Sanford La, second right: Denicola Rd, third right: Megan La Straight: Hastings La

**Sweet Briar Ct**

Straight: Sweet Briar Rd, first left: Sweet Briar La, first right: Newfield Av, Intervale Rd E

**Sweet Briar La**

Straight: Sweet Briar Rd, first right: Sweet Briar Ct, second right: Intervale Rd E, Newfield Av

# The Stamford Streets AZ

**Sweet Briar Rd**
Sweet Briar La, Sweet Briar Ct

Straight: Newfield Av, Intervale Rd E, first left: Newfield Dr, second left: Sterling Farms Golf Club, third left: Weed Hill Av, first right: Emerald La, second right: White Oak La, third right: Wedgemere Rd


**Sycamore Terrace**

Straight: Halliwell Dr, first left: Hycliff Terrace, second left: Emery Dr E, third left: Bayberrie Dr, first right: Stillwater Rd, Bridge St, E Gaynor Brennan Golf Course
Straight: Westover Rd, first left: Coachlamp La, second left: Palmers Hill Rd, first right: Emery Dr E, second right: Bayberrie Dr, third right: Starin Dr


**Sylvan Knoll Rd**
Sylvan Knoll Rd, Sylvan Knoll Rd

Straight: Seaside Av, first left: Mathews St, second left: Bungalow Park, third left: Webb Av, first right: Cove Rd
Straight: Duffy St

# The Stamford Streets AZ

Givens Av, Palmer Av
Straight: Cove Rd, first left: Hobbie St, second left: George St, third left: Horton St, first right: Blachley Rd, Willowbrook Av, second right: Cove Rd, Ranson St, third right: Cove Rd

**Sylvandale Av**
Aberdeen St

Straight: West Av, Leon Pl, first left: Annie Pl, second left: Boston Post Rd 1, third left: Nurney St, first right: Ferris Av, second right: Piave St, third right: Grenhart Rd, E 6 Governor John Davis Lodge Tpke I-95

**Sunset Ct**

Straight: Sunset Rd, first left: Princess Ct, first right: West Trl, second right: High Ridge Rd

# The Stamford Streets AZ

**T**

**Taconic Rd**
Blue Spruce La, Cherry Hill Rd, E Middle Patent Rd, Stanwich Club, Farms Rd, N Stanwich Rd, Howard Rd, Crown La, Stanwich Rd, S Stanwich Rd, Skyridge Rd, Andrews Farm Rd, Hunting Ridge Rd, Interlaken Rd, Byfield La

Straight: Banksville Av, first left: Zygmont La, Round House Rd, second left: The Avenue, third left: Bedford Banksville Rd, Bates La, North St
Straight: North St, first left: Dempsey La, second left: North St, third left: Lindsay Dr, first right: North St, second right: Dewart Rd, third right: Red Coat La


**Taff Av**
Orchard St

Straight: Southfield Av, first left: Homestead Av, second left: Selleck St, Greenwich Av, first right: Sunnyside Av, second right: Burley Av, third right: McClurg Av

# The Stamford Streets AZ

**Tall Oaks Ct**

Straight: Tall Oaks Rd, first left: Round Hill Dr, second left: Laurel Ledge Rd

**Tall Oaks Rd**
Tall Oaks Ct, Round Hill Dr

Straight: Laurel Ledge Rd, first left: Laurel Ledge Ct, first right: Round Hill Dr, second right: Riverbank Rd

**Tally Ho La**

Straight: High Ridge Rd, first left: Maplewood Pl, second left: Brandt Rd, third left: Hartswood Rd, first right: Bradley Pl, second right: Donata La, third right: Merriman Rd

**Talmadge La**

Straight: Turn Of River Rd, first left: Gerik Rd, second left: Poppy La, third left: High Ridge Rd 137, Cedar Heights Rd, first right: Intervale Rd, second right: Sterling Lake La, third right: Buxton Farm Rd

# The Stamford Streets AZ

**Tanglewood La**

Straight: Mayapple Rd, first left: Boulderol Rd, second left: Country Club Rd, third left: Russet Rd, first right: Apple Valley Rd, second right: Rock Rimmon Rd

**Taylor Reed Pl**
Crescent St

Straight: Courtland Av 106, Maple Tree Av, first left: Glen Terrace, second left: Glenbrook Rd 106, first right: Lenox Av, second left: Fairfield Av, third left: Tremont Av

**Taylor St**
Perry St

Straight: Richmond Hill Av, Ann St, first left: Spruce St, second left: Fairfield Av, third left: Boston Post Rd 1, Wilson St, first right: Rose Park, second right: Mission St, third right: Greenwich Av
Straight: Fairfield Av, first left: Madison Pl, second left: First Stamford Pl, third left: Jackson St, first right: Hall Pl, second right: Perry St, third right: Richmond Pl

# The Stamford Streets AZ

**Teresa Ct**

Straight: Twin Brook Dr, first left: Eden Rd

**Terrace Av**
Jessup St

Straight: Long Ridge Rd 104, first left: McClean Av, second left: Cross Rd, third left: Cold Spring Rd 137, Cold Spring Rd, first right: Stark Pl, second right: River Ridge Ct, third right: Brook Run La
Straight: High Ridge Rd 137, first left: High Ridge Rd, second left: High Ridge Rd, third left: Colony Ct, High Clear Dr, first right: McClean Av, second right: Dubois St, third right: Cross Rd

**Terrace Pl**

Straight: Highland Rd, first left: Hillcrest Av, Lindale St, second left: Valley Rd, first right: Grove St

**Third St, 3rd St**
Bedford St, Revonah Av

# The Stamford Streets AZ

Straight: Summer St, first left: 2nd St, second left: Woodside St, 1st St, third left: Oak St, first right: 4th St, second right: 5th St, third right: 6th St

Straight: Morgan St, first left: 5th St, first right: Strawberry Hill Ct, second right: Medical Center, third right: Hoyt St


**Thornridge Dr**
Rambler La, Horse Shoe La, Rambler La

Straight: Davenport Ridge Rd, first left: Davenport Farm La E, second left: Thornridge Dr, third left: Davenport Farm La W, first right: Skyview La, second right: Ponus Ridge

Straight: Davenport Ridge Rd, first left: Davenport Farm La W, second left: Jeanne Ct, third left: Zora La, Davenport Ridge La, first right: Davenport Farm La E, second right: Thornridge Dr, third right: Skyview La


**Thornwood Rd**
Brushwood Rd, Bittersweet La

# The Stamford Streets AZ

**Thread Needle La**

Straight: Signal Rd, first left: Gatehouse Rd

**Three Lakes Dr**
Bridle Path Rd, Elaine Dr

Straight: Long Ridge Rd 104, first left: Wishing Well La, second left: Brook Run La, third left: River Ridge Ct, first right: Clover Hill Dr, second right: Stillwater Rd, third right: Roxbury Rd, Buckingham Dr

**Thunder Hill Dr**

Straight: Riverbank Rd, first left: Bangall Rd, second left: Windward La, third left: Fawnfield Rd, first right: Cow Path Dr, Westover Rd, Roxbury Rd

**Timber La**

Straight: Clay Hill Rd, first left: Cedar Heights Rd, first right: Archer La, second right: Arden La

# The Stamford Streets AZ

**Timber Mill Cir**

Straight: Timber Mill Rd, first left: Dundee Rd


**Timber Mill Rd**
Timber Mill Circle

Straight: Dundee Rd, first left: Forestwood Dr, first right: Sawmill Rd


**Tioga Pl**

Straight: Alton Rd, first left: Marie Pl, second left: Pine Tree Dr, first right: Norman Rd, second right: Upland Rd
Straight: Elmbrook Dr, first left: Glendale Rd, Glendale Circle, first right: Marie Pl, second right: Pine Hill Av


**Tod La**

Straight: Howard Rd, June Rd, first left: Taconic Rd, first right: Guinea Rd, second right: Riverbank Rd
Straight: Stanwich Rd, first left: Carrington Dr, second left: Stag La, third left: Carissa La, first right:

# The Stamford Streets AZ

Meeting House Rd, second right: Crown La, third right: Taconic Rd


**Todd La**
Edward Pl, Maryanne La, Pershing Av, Haig Av

Straight: Joffre Av, Ledge La, first left: Joffre Ct, second left: Sussex Pl, third left: Haig Av, first right: Ledge La, second right: Belltown Rd
Straight: Newfield Av, first left: Turner Rd, Belltown Rd, second left: Ogden Rd, third left: Hirsch Rd, first right: Case Rd, Swan La, second right: Sanford La, third right: Denicola Rd


**Toilsome Brook Rd**

Straight: West La, first left: East La, first right: Northwoods Rd, second right: East La


**Toms Rd**
Derwin St, Rutz St, Deleo Dr, Overbrook Dr, Dale Pl, Autumn La, Central St, Summit Pl

Straight: Hope St, first left: Viaduct Rd, second left: Edgewood Av, third

# The Stamford Streets AZ

left: Riverbend Dr S, first right: Glen Av, second right: Douglas Av, third right: Union St
Straight: Belltown Rd, first left: Fairland St, second left: Francis Av, third left: Leonard St, first right: Ledge La, second right: Pershing Av, third right: Newfield Av, Turner Rd


**Top Gallant Rd**
Gatehouse Rd, Dolphin Cove Quay

Straight: Fairfield Av, first left: Hendrie Ct, second left: Shore Rd, Cummings Point Rd, first right: Dee La, second right: Burwood Av, third right: Barry Pl
Straight: Southfield Av, Davenport Dr, first left: Burwood Av, second left: Congress St, third left: Wells Av, first right: Cook Rd, second right: Eureka Terrace


**Tower Av**
Palmer St, Bon Air Av, Lawton Av, Birchwood Rd

Straight: Clearview Av, first left: Knickerbocker Av, second left: Hope St, first right: Buena Vista St, Bon Air Av, second right: Cady St

# The Stamford Streets AZ

Straight: Woodbury Av, first left: Crestview Av, second left: Buena Vista St, third left: Cady St, first right: Lawton Av

**Town Center Dr**
Quintard Terrace

Straight: Atlantic St, first left: Bank St, second left: Bell St, third left: Tresser Blvd 1, Tresser Blvd, first right: Main St, second right: Luther St, third right: Broad St, Bedford St
Straight: Tresser Blvd, Stamford Forum 1, first left: Greyrock Pl, Stamford Pl 1, Canal St, first right: Atlantic St, second right: Washington Blvd 137, third right: Clinton Av, Boston Post Rd 1

**Trailing Rock Rd**

Straight: Riverbank Rd, first left: Erskine Rd, second left: Wildwood Rd, third left: Rocky Rapids Rd, first right: Harpsichord Tpke, second right: Laurel Ledge Rd, third right: Hedge Brook La

**Travis Av**
Duncanson St, Reynolds Av

# The Stamford Streets AZ

Straight: Cold Spring Rd 137, first left: Old Barn Rd S, second left: Randall Av, third left: Long Ridge Rd, Long Ridge Rd 104, first right: Washington Blvd, second right: Windsor Rd, third right: Severance Dr


**Treat Av**
Coolidge Av, Cowan Av, Hillandale Av

Straight: Hope St, first left: Frisbee St, second left: Kennedy La, third left: Faucett St, first right: Howes Av, second right: Wenzel Terrace, third right: Glenbrook Rd
Straight: Rock Spring Rd, first left: Mayflower Av, second left: Ardsley Rd, third left: Strawberry Hill Av, first right: Puritan La, Coolidge Av, second right: Hope St


**Tree La**

Straight: Putter Dr, first left: Hope St


**Tree Top Ct**

Straight: Long Hill Dr, first left: Clover Hill Dr, first right: Long Hill Dr, second right: Long Hill Dr, third

# The Stamford Streets AZ

right: Long Hill Dr, fourth right: Long Hill Dr, fifth right: Stillwater Rd


**Treglia Terrace**

Straight: Greenwich Av, first left: Boston Post Rd 1, W Main St, first right: Richmond Hill Av, second right: West St, third right: S State St, E 7 Governor John Davis Lodge Tpke I-95


**Tremont Av**
Field St

Straight: Courtland Av 106, first left: Hamilton Av, second left: Seaton Rd, third left: Boston Post Rd 1, E 9 Governor John Davis Lodge Tpke I-95, first right: Fairmont Av, second right: Lenox Av, third right: Taylor Reed Pl, Maple Tree Av
Straight: Midland Av, first left: Fairmont Av, second left: Lenox Av, first right: Hamilton Av, Courtland Hill St, second right: King St, third right: Hamilton Ct


**Tresser Blvd**
Washington Blvd, Atlantic St

# The Stamford Streets AZ

Straight: Boston Post Rd 1, Clinton Av, first left: Division St, second left: Richmond Hill Av, first right: Main St
Straight: Stamford Forum 1, Town Center Dr, first left: Quintard Terrace, second left: Atlantic St


**Trinity Pass**
Calass La, Black Rock Rd, Ponus Ridge

Straight: Rolling Meadows, Lower Trinity Pass New Canaan, Ct, first right: Trinity La, New Canaan, Ct
Straight: High Ridge Rd 137, first left: Mayapple Rd, second left: Laurel Rd, third left: Flora Pl, first right: Riding Stable Trail, second right: Fairway Dr, third right: Craig Ct


**Trumbull Gate**

Straight: Seaton Rd, first left: Revere Dr, second left: Courtland Av 106, first right: Standish Rd, second right: Boston Post Rd 1, Noroton Hill Pl
Straight: Lawn Av, first left: Sherman St, second left: Boston Post Rd 1, first right: Custer St, Helen Pl, second right: Leroy Pl, third right: Hamilton Av

# The Stamford Streets AZ

**Tupper Dr**

Straight: Soundview Av, first left: McMullen Av, second left: James St, third left: East Av, first right: Wascussee La, second right: Carter Dr, third right: Willowbrook Av
Straight: Carter Dr, first left: Soundview Av


**Turn Of River Rd**
Poppy La, Gerik Rd, Talmadge La, Intervale Rd, Sterling Lake La, Buxton Farm Rd

Straight: Cedar Heights Rd, High Ridge Rd 137, first left: Vine Rd, second left: Merriman Rd, third left: Donata La, first right: Olga Dr, second right: Square Acre Dr, third right: Dunn Av
Straight: High Ridge Park


**Turner Rd**
Sherwood Rd, High Clear Dr, Pepper Ridge Rd, Cody Dr, Barrett Av, Brinkerhoff Av

Straight: Dann Dr, first left: Oaklawn Av, first right: High Clear Dr
Straight: Newfield Av, Belltown Rd, first left: Todd La, second left: Case Rd, Swan La, third left: Sanford La,

# The Stamford Streets AZ

first right: Ogden Rd, second right: Hirsch Rd, third right: Newfield Ct

**Tuttle St**

Straight: West Av, first left: Leslie St, second left: Nobile St, Moore St, third left: Minor Pl, first right: Acosta St, Burr St, second right: Stillwater Av
Straight: Corbo Terrace
Burr St
Straight: Stillwater Av, first left: West Av, second left: Progress Dr, third left: Oxford Ct, first right: Merrell Av, second right: Virgil St, third right: Colahan St

**Twin Brook Dr**
Teresa Ct

Straight: Eden Rd, first left: Parry Rd, second left: Eden La, third left: Newfield Av, first right: Woodbrook Dr, second right: Old Well Rd, third right: Friars La

# The Stamford Streets AZ

**Twin Hills Rd**

Straight: Big Oak Rd, first left: Red Fox Rd, Big Oak La, first right: Big Oak Circle, second right: Wake Robin La

**Tyler Dr**

Straight: Fox Ridge Rd, first left: Foxwood Rd, second left: Fox Hill Rd, first right: Hunting Ridge Rd

# The Stamford Streets AZ

## U

**Uncas Rd**
Wascussee La

Straight: Willowbrook Av, first left: Caldwell Av, second left: Cove Rd, Blachley Rd, first right: Hale St, second right: Wascussee La E, third right: Soundview Av
Straight: Sachem Pl, first left: Wascussee La, first right: Van Buskirk Av


**Underhill St**
Arlington Rd

Straight: Hillandale Av, first left: Grove St, Prospect St, Hoyt St, Strawberry Hill Av, first right: Fenway St, Wenzel Terrace, second right: Holcomb Av, third right: Treat Av


**Union St**
Elm Tree Pl

Straight: Hope St, first left: Glendale Dr, second left: Pine Hill Av, Church St, third left: Rose St, first right: Douglas Av, second right: Glen Av, third right: Toms Rd

# The Stamford Streets AZ

Straight: Kirkham Pl, straight: Church St, first left: Glenbrook Rd, first right: Parker Av, second right: Elm Tree Pl, third right: Center St

**Unity Rd**
Kijek St

Straight: High Clear Dr, first left: Dann Dr, second left: Turner Rd, first right: Kijek St, second right: High Ridge Rd 137, Colony Ct
Straight: High Ridge Rd 137, first left: Brownley Dr, second left: Colony Ct, High Clear Dr, third left: High Ridge Rd, first right: Lakeview Dr, second right: Loveland Rd W, third right: Longview Av

**Upland Rd**
Pine Tree Dr, Norman Rd, Alton Rd

Straight: Burdick St, Belltown Rd, Bellmere Av, first left: Newfield Av, first right: Norman Rd
Straight: Strawberry Hill Av, Fieldstone La, first left: Holbrook Dr, second left: Colonial Rd, third left: 5th St, first right: Crane Rd, second right: Burdick St, third right: Oaklawn Av

# The Stamford Streets AZ

**Upper Haig Av**
Lund Av, Knox Rd

Straight: Knox Rd, Haig Av, first left: Upper Haig Av, first right: Lund Av, second right: Newfield Av
Straight: Weed Hill Av, first left: Barholm Av, second left: Hilltop Av, third left: Newfield Av, first right: Bouton St W, second right: Estwick Pl, third right: Ridgeway St


**Urban St**

Straight: Bedford St, first left: 6th St, Chester St, second left: 5th St, third left: 4th St, first right: Marlou La, second right: Locust La, third right: Summer St, Long Ridge Rd, High Ridge Rd
Straight: Revonah Av, first left: Revonah Circle, second left: East La, first right: Chester St, second right: 5th St, third right: 4th St


**Ursula Pl**
Stafford Rd, Orange St, Dale St

Straight: Maher Rd, first left: Boston Post Rd 1, first right: Orange St

# The Stamford Streets AZ

Straight: Dale St, first left: Cove Rd, second left: St Benedict Circle, first right: Ursula Pl, second right: Woodrow St, third right: William St

## US 1 Hwy

US 1 Hwy Greenwich, CT: Boston Post Rd: Havemeyer La, Laddin Rock Rd, Whitmore La, Myano La, Alvord La, Harvard Av, Aberdeen St, West Av, Diaz St, Virgil St, Victory St, Liberty St, Roosevelt Av, Wilson St, Richmond Hill Av, High St, Fairfield Av, Hazel St, Spruce St, Ann St, Rose Park, Stillwater Av, W Main St, Greenwich Av, Clinton Av, Tresser Blvd: Washington Blvd, Atlantic St, Town Center Dr, Stamford Forum: Greyrock Pl, Canal St, Stamford Plaza: Grove St, Elm St, Boston Post Rd: Broad St, Lindale St, Crandall St, Clarks Hill Av, Glenbrook Rd, Daly St, Lafayette St, Quintard Terrace, N State St, Crystal St, Myrtle Av, Maple Av, Lincoln Av, Lockwood Av, Grant Av, Lawn Av, Seaton Rd, Noroton Hill Pl, Maher Rd, Blachley Rd, Standish Rd, E 9 Governor John Davis Lodge Tpke I-95, Courtland Av, E 9 Governor John Davis Lodge Tpke I-95, Seaside Av, Home Ct, Houston Terrace, Hamilton Av, Waterbury Av, Weed Av, Brookside Dr, US 1 Hwy Darien, CT

# The Stamford Streets AZ

## V

**Valley Rd**

Straight: Arlington Rd, first left: Underhill St, first right: Fenway St, second right: Glenbrook Rd, Daskam Pl
Straight: Highland Rd
Lindale St, Terrace Pl
Straight: Grove St, first left: Greyrock Pl, second left: Forest St, third left: Broad St, first right: Hillcrest Av, second right: Prospect St, Hoyt St, Strawberry Hill Av, Hillandale Av


**Valley View Dr**
Flint Rock Rd E


**Van Buren Circle**

Straight: Holcomb Av, first left: Ardsley Rd, second left: Coolidge Av, third left: Cowan Av, first right: Strawberry Hill Av
Straight: Ardsley Rd, first left: Rock Spring Rd, first right: Holcomb Av


**Van Buskirk Av**
East Av, Sachem Pl, Caldwell Av

# The Stamford Streets AZ

Straight: Cove Rd, first left: Dale St, second left: Raymond St, third left: St Benedict Circle, first right: Cove Rd, second right: Cove Rd, Ranson St, third right: Blachley Rd, Willowbrook Av

## Van Rensselaer Av
Fairview Av

Straight: Verplank Av, first left: Stamford Av, second left: Shippan Av, Ocean Dr W, Ocean Dr E, first right: Ocean Dr W
Straight: Ocean Dr W, first left: Ralsey Rd S, second left: Fairview Av, third left: Lighthouse Way, first right: Stamford Av, second right: Woolsey Rd, third right: Shippan Av

## Vanech Dr

Straight: Oaklawn Av, first left: Sherwood Rd, second left: Dann Dr, third left: Fairfield Memorial Park Cemetery, first right: Pepper Ridge Rd, second right: Jamroga La, third right: Clifford Av
Straight: Rome Pl
Clifford Av

# The Stamford Streets AZ

Straight: Lindsey Av, S Lindsey Av, first left: Oaklawn Av, first right: Brighton Pl, second right: Crane Rd N


**Vassar Av**

Straight: Selleck St, first left: Fairfield Av, second left: Fairfield Av, third left: Orchard St, first right: Irving Av, Bonner St, second right: Durant St, Montauk Dr, third right: Betts Av
Straight: Pressprich St, first left: Irving Av, second left: Wilson St, first right: Fairfield Av


**Vernon Pl**
Renwick St


**Verplank Av**
Van Rensselaer Av, Stamford Av

Straight: Shippan Av, Ocean Dr E, Ocean Dr W
Straight: Ocean Dr W, first left: Saddle Rock Rd, second left: Stamford Av, third left: Verplank Av, Shippan Av, Ocean Dr E, first right: Rogers Rd, second right: Lighthouse Way, third right: Fairview Av

# The Stamford Streets AZ

**Very Merry Rd**

Straight: Larkspur Rd, first left: Skymeadow Dr, first right: Cousins Rd, second right: Hannahs Rd

**Viaduct Rd**
Poplar St, Viaduct Rd

Straight: Larkin St, Research Dr, first left: Poplar St, first right: Glenbrook Rd 106
Straight: Hope St, first left: Toms Rd, second left: Glen Av, third left: Douglas Av, first right: Edgewood Av, second right: Riverbend Dr S, third right: Chatfield St

**Victoria La**

Straight: Summit Ridge Rd, first right Westover Rd

**Victory St**
Piave St

Straight: Boston Post Rd 1, first left: Virgil St, second left: Diaz St, third left: West Av, first right: Liberty St,

# The Stamford Streets AZ

second right: Roosevelt Av, third right: Wilson St, Richmond Hill Av
Straight: Grenhart Rd, first left: Wilson St, first right: Diaz St, second right: E 6 Governor John Davis Lodge Tpke I-95, third right: West Av


**Vincent Av**
Vincent Ct


**Vincent Ct**

Straight: Vincent Av
Straight: 5th St, first left: Strawberry Hill Av, first right: Morgan St, second right: Revonah Av, third right: Bedford St


**Vine Pl**
Saxon Ct, Donata La


**Vine Rd**
Kane Av, Vine Pl, Barmore Dr, Pamlynn Rd, Brandywine Rd, Malvern Rd, Pepper Ridge Rd, Kerr Rd, Simsbury Rd

Straight: High Ridge Rd 137, first left: Merriman Rd, second left: Donata La, third left: Bradley Pl, first right:

# The Stamford Streets AZ

Turn Of River Rd, Cedar Heights Rd, second right: Olga Dr, third right: Square Acre Dr
Straight: Newfield Av, first left: Club Rd, second left: Knox Rd, third left: Weed Hill Av, first right: Gray Farms Rd, second right: Megan La, third right: Denicola Rd


**Vineyard La**

Straight: Long Ridge Rd 104, first left: Maltbie Av, second left: Loughran Av, third left: Barnes Rd, first right: Wire Mill Rd, second right: E 34 Merritt Pkwy 15, CT15, third right: E 34 Merritt Pkwy 15, CT15
Straight: Hunting La, first left: Wire Mill Rd, Cedar Tree La


**Virgil St**
Dryden St, Minor Pl

Straight: Stillwater Av, first left: Merrell Av, second left: Corbo Terrace, third left: West Av, first right: Colahan St, second right: Liberty St, third right: Stillwater Pl
Straight: Boston Post Rd 1, first left: Victory St, second left: Liberty St, third left: Roosevelt Av, first right:

# The Stamford Streets AZ

Diaz St, second right: West Av, third right: Aberdeen St

**Vista St**

Straight: Anderson St, first left: W Broad St, first right: Chestnut St, second right: W North St, Woodcliff St
Straight: Adams Av, first left: Green St, second left: Chestnut St, third left: W North St, Powell Pl, first right: W Broad St, Schuyler Av

**Vuono Dr**

Straight: Golf View Circle
Straight: Hubbard Av, first left: Charles Mary La, second left: Prince Pl, third left: Pellom Pl, first right: Grandview Av, second right: W North St, third right: W Broad St

# The Stamford Streets AZ

## W

### W Bank La

Straight: W Glen Dr, first left: Westover Rd, first right: Bend of River La, second right: Benenson Dr, Shelter Dr

### W Broad St
Mill River St, Hanrahan St, Schuyler Av, Adams Av, Oak Hill St, Stephen St, Anderson St, Wright St, Hinckley Av, Hubbard Av, St George Av, Shelburne Rd, Rachelle Av, Merrell Av, Delaware Av

Straight: Washington Blvd 137, Broad St, first left: North St, second left: Linden Pl, Hoyt St, third left: 2nd St, fourth left: 2nd St, first right: Whittaker Pl, second right: W Park Pl, third right: Main St, fourth right: Rippowam Pl
Straight: Stillwater Av, first left: Oxford Ct, second left: Progress Dr, third left: West Av, first right: Connecticut Av, second right: Palmers Hill Rd, E Gaynor Brennan Golf Course, third right: Halliwell Dr, Bridge St

# The Stamford Streets AZ

**W Forest Lawn Av**

Straight: Washington Blvd 137, first left: Paragon La, second left: Cold Spring Rd, first right: Bridge St, second right: 2nd St, third right: 2nd St, fourth right: Linden Pl, Hoyt St


**W Glen Dr**
W Bank La, Bend of River La

Straight: Westover Rd, first left: Long Close Rd, second left: Merriebrook La, third left: Long Close Rd, first right: Mianus Rd, second right: Westover Av, third right: Westover La, fourth right: Bartina La
Straight: Benenson Dr
Shelter Dr, Serenity La


**W Haviland La**
Bennington Ct

Straight: Haviland Rd, first left: E Hunting Ridge Rd, second left: Wellington Dr, third left: Haviland Dr, first right: Cross Country Trail, second right: Haviland Ct, third right: Deerfield Dr
Straight: Chestnut Hill Rd, first left: Eagle Dr, second left: Ethan Allen La,

# The Stamford Streets AZ

third left: Scofieldtown Rd, first right: Jordan La, second right: Chestnut Hill La, third right: Webbs Hill Rd, fourth right: Long Ridge Rd 104, Butternut La

**W Henry St**

Straight: Washington Blvd, Henry St, first left: Station Pl, second left: S State St, third left: E8 Governor John Davis Lodge Tpke I-95, first right: Pulaski St, second right: Atlantic St

**W Hill Cir**

Straight: W Hill Rd, first left: Bartina La, second left: Westview La, third left: Westover Rd, first right: Wyndover La, second right: Wesgate Dr, third right: Blueberry Dr

**W Hill La**

Straight: W Hill Rd, first left: Roxbury Rd, first right: Drum Hill La, second right: MacGregor Dr, third right: Dancy Dr

# The Stamford Streets AZ

**W Hill Rd**
W Hill La, Drum Hill La, MacGregor Dr, Dancy Dr, Green Tree La, Carriage Dr, Stony Brook Dr, Greenleaf Dr, Blueberry Dr, Wesgate Dr, Wyndover La, W Hill Circle, Bartina La, Westview La

Straight: Roxbury Rd, first left: Overhill Rd, second left: Doral Farms Rd, third left: Barncroft Rd, first right: Stillwater Rd, second right: Long Ridge Rd 104, Buckingham Dr
Straight: Westover Rd, first left: Indian Hill Rd, second left: Starin Dr, third left: Bayberrie Dr, first right: Summit Ridge Rd, second right: Westview La, third right: Bartina La


**W Main St**
Main St

Straight: Boston Post Rd 1, Tresser Blvd 1, Greenwich Av, first left: Clinton Av, second left: Washington Blvd, third left: Atlantic St, first right: Stillwater Av, second right: Rose Park, third right: Ann St
Straight: Mill River St
Greenwood Hill St, Smith St
Straight: W Broad St, first left: Hanrahan St, second left: Schuyler Av,

# The Stamford Streets AZ

first right: Washington Blvd 137, Broad St

**W North St**
Rachelle Av, St George Av, Hubbard Av, Hinckley Av, Woodcliff St, Anderson St, Hillside Av, Powell Pl, Adams Av

Straight: North St

**W Rock Trl**

Straight: Knobloch La, first left: Emery Dr E

**W Park Pl**
Washington Blvd 137

Straight: Summer St, Main St, Bank St, Clark St, Main St

**W Washington Av**
Linden Pl

Straight: Court St
Straight: North St, first left: Hollywood Ct, second left: W North St, first right: Washington Ct, second

# The Stamford Streets AZ

right: Renwick St, third right: Washington Blvd 137

**Wake Robin La**
Big Oak Rd

Straight: Four Brooks Rd, first left: Four Brooks Circle, second left: Wire Mill Rd
Straight: Red Fox Rd, first left: Big Oak Rd, Big Oak La, second left: White Fox Rd

**Wallenberg Dr**

Straight: S Lake Dr, first right: Lisa La

**Wallace St**
Nelson St

Straight: Shippan Av, first left: Iroquois Rd, second left: Mariners La, third left: Rippowam Rd, first right: Mitchell St, second right: Lanell Dr, third left: Auldwood Rd

**Wallacks Dr**
Burns Rd

# The Stamford Streets AZ

Straight: Soundview Av, first left: Kenilworth Dr E, second left: Kenilworth Dr W, third left: Soundview Dr, first right: Wallacks La

**Wallacks La**

Straight: Soundview Av, first right: Wallacks Dr, second right: Kenilworth Dr E, third right: Kenilworth Dr W
Straight: Euclid Av, straight: Cove Rd, first left: Dora St, second left: Dean St, third left: Seaside Av, first right: Albin Rd, second right: Island Heights Dr, third right: Weed Av

**Walter La**

Straight: Den Rd, first left: E33 Merritt Pkwy 15, CT15, first right: Doolittle Rd, second right: Roxbury Rd

**Walter Wheeler Dr**

Straight: Atlantic St, first left: Washington Blvd, first right: Lipton Pl, second right: Woodland Av, third right: Lipton Pl, fourth right: Henry St
Straight: Pacific St, E Walnut St, first left: Woodland Pl, second left: Woodland

# The Stamford Streets AZ

Av, Ludlow St, third left: Henry St, first right: Remington St, second right: Crosby St, third right: Belden St


**Walton Pl**

Straight: Bedford St, first left: Forest St, second left: Spring St, Prospect St, third left: Broad St, Atlantic St, first right: North St, second right: Dolsen Pl, third right: Hoyt St
Straight: Prospect St, first left: North St, second left: Hoyt St, Strawberry Hill Av, Hillandale Av, Grove St, first right: Forest St, second right: Bedford St, Spring St


**Wampanaw Rd**

Straight: Rippowam Rd
Mohegan Av, Ponus Av, Algonquin Av
Straight: Shippan Av, first left: Mariners La, second left: Iroquois Rd, third left: Wallace St, first right: Lindstrom Rd, second right: Harbor Dr, Magee Av, third right: Seaview Av
Straight: Iroquois Rd
Mohegan Av, Ponus Av, Algonquin Av
Straight: Shippan Av, first left: Wallace St, second left: Mitchell St, third left: Lanell Dr, first right:

# The Stamford Streets AZ

Mariners La, second right: Rippowam Rd, third right: Lindstrom Rd

## Warchol La

Straight: Brandt Rd, straight: High Ridge Rd 137, first left: Maplewood Pl, second left: Tally Ho La, third left: Bradley Pl, first right: Hartswood Rd, second right: Bel Aire Dr, third right: Swampscott Rd

## Ward La

Straight: Woodbrook Dr, first left: Eden Rd, first right: Parry Rd

## Wardwell St
Shippan Av, Cummings Av, Frederick St, Soundview Av

Straight: Elm St, first left: Jefferson St, Myrtle Av, second left: Cherry St, third left: Elm Ct, first right: Shippan Av, Cove Rd

## Warren St
Maple Av, Lee St, Shippan Av

# The Stamford Streets AZ

Straight: Lockwood Av, first left: Woodrow St, second left: William St, third left: Lillian St, first right: Cove Rd
Straight: Myrtle Av, first left: Frederick St, second left: Elm St, Jefferson St, first right: William St, second right: Gregory St, third right: E 8 Governor John Davis Lodge Tpke I-95

## Warshaw Pl

Straight: West Av, first left: Ardmore Rd, second left: Baxter Av, first right: Orlando Av, second right: Outlook St
Straight: Harvard Av, Brown House Rd, first left: Selleck St, first right: Ardmore Rd, second right: Baxter Av, E 6 Governor John Davis Lodge Tpke I-95

## Warwick La

Straight: Buckingham Dr, first left: Buckingham Ct, second left: Long Ridge Rd 104, Roxbury Rd
Straight: Amherst Pl, first left: Amherst Ct, first right: Woodridge Dr S

# The Stamford Streets AZ

**Wascussee La E**

Straight: Wascussee La, first left: Soundview Av, first right: Sachem Pl, second right: Uncas Rd
Straight: Willowbrook Av, first left: Hale St, second left: Uncas Rd, third left: Caldwell Av, first right: Soundview Av


**Wascussee La**
Wascussee La E, Sachem Pl

Straight: Soundview Av, first left: Carter Dr, second left: Willowbrook Av, third left: Soundview Ct, first right: Tupper Dr, second right: McMullen Av, third right: James St
Straight: Uncas Rd, first left: Sachem Pl, first right: Willowbrook Av


**Washington Blvd 137**
Crosby St, Atlantic St, Pulaski St, W Henry St, Henry St, Station Pl, S State St, E 8 Governor John Davis Lodge Tpke I-95, N State St, E 8 Governor John Davis Lodge Tpke I-95, Richmond Hill Av, Division St, Tresser Blvd 1, Bell St, Rippowam Pl, Main St, W Park Pl, Whittaker Pl, Broad St, W Broad St, North St, Linden Pl, Hoyt St, 2nd St,

# The Stamford Streets AZ

2nd St, Bridge St, W Forest Lawn Av, Paragon La

Straight: Pacific St, first left: Dyke La, second left: Belden St, third left: Crosby St
Straight: Cold Spring Rd 137, first left: Windsor Rd, second left: Severance Dr, third left: Windsor Rd, first right: Travis Av, second right: Old Barn Rd S, third right: Randall Av


**Washington Ct**

Straight: North St, first left: W Washington Av, second left: Hollywood Ct, third left: Adams Av, Powell Pl, first right: Renwick St, second right: Washington Blvd, third right: Franklin St


**Water St**

Straight: Pulaski St, first left: Greenwich Av, first right: Berkeley St, second right: Washington Blvd


**Waterbury Av**
Birch St

# The Stamford Streets AZ

Straight: Mathews St, first left: Cambridge Rd, second left: Weed Av, first right: Houston Terrace, second right: Webb Av, third right: Seaside Av
Straight: Boston Post Rd 1, Hamilton Av, first left: Houston Terrace, second left: Home Ct, third left: Seaside Av, first right: Weed Av, second right: Brookside Dr, third right: Purdy La

**Waterford La**
7th St

Straight: 8th St
Weil St
Straight: Summer St, first left: Forest Lawn Av, second left: Hoover Av, third left: Long Ridge Rd, High Ridge Rd, Bedford St, first right: 7th St, second right: Bridge St, third right: 6th St

**Waterside Pl**

Straight: Greenwich Av, first left: Davenport St, second left: Milton St, third left: Selleck St, Southfield Av, first right: First Stamford Pl, second right: S State St, E 7 Governor John Davis Lodge Tpke I-95
Straight: Pulaski St, first left: Greenwich Av, first right: Water St,

# The Stamford Streets AZ

second right: Berkeley St, third right: Washington Blvd

**Waverly Pl**

Straight: Fairfield Av, first left: Jackson St, second left: First Stamford Pl, first right: Pressprich St, second right: Selleck St
Straight: Wilson St, Baxter Av, first left: Pressprich St, first right: Grenhart Rd, second right: Madison Pl

**Webb Av**
Home Ct, Mathews St, Middlebury St

Straight: Seaside Av, first left: Bungalow Park, second left: Mathews St, third left: Sylvan Knoll Rd, first right: E 9 Governor John Davis Lodge Tpke I-95, second right: E 9 Governor John Davis Lodge Tpke I-95, third right: Boston Post Rd 1
Straight: Dora St
Neponsit St
Straight: Cove Rd, first left: Euclid Av, second left: Albin Rd, third left: Island Heights Dr, first right: Dean St, second right: Seaside Av, third right: Avery St

# The Stamford Streets AZ

**Webbs Hill Rd**

Huckleberry Hollow, Lynam Rd, Jeffrey La, Dogwood La, Dogwood La, Pheasant La

Straight: Chestnut Hill Rd, first left: Long Ridge Rd 104, Butternut La, first right: Chestnut Hill La, second right: Jordan La, third right: W Haviland La
Straight: Long Ridge Rd, first left: E 34 Merritt Pkwy 15, CT15, second left: E 34 Merritt Pkwy 15, CT15, third left: E 34 Merritt Pkwy 15, CT15, first right: Northwood La, second right: Midrocks Dr, third right: Den Rd


**Webster Rd**

Straight: Middlebury St, first left: Webb Av, Dora St, first right: Andover Rd, second right: Cambridge Rd
Straight: Neponsit St, Albin Rd, first left: Andover Rd, second left: Island Heights Dr, third left: Cambridge Rd, first right: Dora St


**Wedgemere Rd**

Straight: Newfield Av, first left: White Oak La, second left: Emerald La, third left: Intervale Rd E, Sweet Briar Rd, first right: Eden Rd, second right: N

# The Stamford Streets AZ

Meadows La, third right: Lakeside Dr, Davenport Ridge Rd

**Weed Av**
Weed Circle, Mathews St, Holly Cove Circle, Birch St

Straight: Cove Rd
Straight: Boston Post Rd 1, first left: Hamilton Av, Waterbury Av, second left: Houston Terrace, third left: Home Ct, first right: Brookside Dr, second right: Purdy La

**Weed Circle**

Straight: Weed Av, first left: Cove Rd, first right: Mathews St, second right: Holly Cove Circle, third right: Birch St

**Weed Hill Av**
Hilltop Av, Barholm Av, Upper Haig Av, Bouton St W, Estwick Pl, Ridgeway St, Hickory Way, Elmer St, Sterling Pl

Straight: Newfield Av, first left: Knox Rd, second left: Club Rd, third left: Vine Rd, first right: Patricia La, second right: Sterling Farm Golf Course, third right: Newfield Dr

# The Stamford Streets AZ

Straight: Hope St, first left: Minivale Rd, second left: Mead St, third left: Bouton St, Bouton St W, first right: Mulberry St, second right: Camp Av, third right: Greenway St, Knapp St

**Weil St**

Straight: 7th St, first left: Summer St, first right: Waterford La
Straight: 8th St, first left: Waterford La, first right: Summer St

**Wellington Dr**
Surrey Rd

Straight: Haviland Rd, first left: Haviland Dr, second left: Crofts La, third left: Hunting Ridge Rd, first right: E Hunting Ridge Rd, second right: W Haviland La, third right: Cross Country Trail

**Wells Av**

Straight: Southfield Av, first left: McClurg Av, second left: Burley Av, third left: Sunnyside Av, first right: Congress St, second right: Burwood Av,

# The Stamford Streets AZ

third right: Davenport Dr, Top Gallant Rd
Straight: Carlisle Pl, first left: Congress St, first right: Liberty Pl, McClurg Av, second right: Burley Av


**Wenzel Terrace**

Straight: Fenway St, Hillandale Av, first left: Arlington Rd, first right: Holcomb Av, second right: Treat Av
Straight: Hope St, first left: Howes Av, second left: Treat Av, third left: Frisbee St, first right: Glenbrook Rd, Lafayette St, Clovelly Rd


**Wesgate Dr**

Straight: W Hill Rd, first left: Blueberry Dr, second left: Greenleaf Dr, third left: Stony Brook Dr, first right: Wyndover La, second right: W Hill Circle, third right: Bartina La


**West Av**
Winsted St, Selleck St, Orlando Av, Warshaw Pl, Ardmore Rd, Baxter Av, Grenhart Rd, E 6 Governor John Davis Lodge Tpke I-95, Piave St, Ferris Av, Sylvandale Av, Leon Pl, Annie Pl, Boston

# The Stamford Streets AZ

Post Rd 1, Nurney St, Minor Pl, Nobile St, Moore St, Leslie St, Tuttle St, Acosta St, Burr St

Straight: Stillwater Av, first left: Progress Dr, second left: Oxford Ct, third left: W Broad St, first right: Corbo Terrace, second right: Merrell Av, third right: Virgil St

**W Cross Rd**

Straight: Hope St, Broad Brook La, first left: Eden Rd, E Cross Rd, second left: Slice Dr, third left: Camelot Ct, first right: Woodway Ridge La, second right: Running Brook La, third right: Hawks Hill Rd
Straight: Hawks Hill Rd, first left: Ponus Ridge, first right: E Cross Rd

**West La**
Toilsome Brook Rd, Northwoods Rd

Straight: East La, first right: West La, second right: Revonah Circle, third right: Urban St
Straight: East La, first right: Revonah Circle, second right: Urban St, third right: Chester St

# The Stamford Streets AZ

**West St**
Brown Av

Straight: Greenwich Av, first left: Richmond Hill Av, second left: Treglia Terrace, third left: Boston Post Rd 1, W Main St, first right: S State St, E 7 Governor John Davis Lodge Tpke I-95, second right: First Stamford Pl, third right: Pulaski St
Straight: Mission St, first right: Richmond Hill Av


**West Trail**
Mountain Trail, Fishing Trail, Settlers Trail

Straight: Sunset Rd, first left: High Ridge Rd 137, first right: Princess Ct, second right: Skyline La, Scofieldtown Rd


**Westcott Rd**

Straight: Rockledge Dr, first left: Ocean Dr E, second left: Hobson St, Sea Beach Dr, first right: Shippan Av
Straight: Ocean Dr E, first left: Shippan Av, first right: Sea Beach Dr, second right: Rockledge Dr, third right: Hobson St, fourth right: Fairview Av

# The Stamford Streets AZ

**Westminster Rd**

Straight: Shippan Av, first left: Fairview Av, second left: Sound Av, third left: Hobson St, first right: Verplank Av, second right: Ocean Dr W, Ocean Dr E


**Westover Av**

Straight: Westover Rd, first left: Mianus Rd, second left: W Glen Dr, third left: Long Close Rd, first right: Westover La, second right: Bartina La, third right: Westview La
Straight: River Rd
Sweet Briar La, Hillcrest Park Rd


**Westover La**

Straight: Westover Rd, first left: Westover Av, second left: Mianus Rd, third left: W Glen Dr, first right: Bartina La, second right: Westview La, third right: Summit Ridge Rd


**Westover Rd**
Coachlamp La, Sycamore Terrace, Emery Dr E, Bayberrie Dr, Starin Dr, Indian Hill Rd, W Hill Rd, Summit Ridge Rd, Westview

# The Stamford Streets AZ

La, Bartina La, Westover La, Westover Av, Mianus Rd, W Glen Dr, Long Close Rd, Merriebrook La, Long Close Rd, Canfield Dr, Canfield Dr, Nathan Hale Dr, High Line Trail, Winding Brook La, Old Mill La

Straight: Palmers Hill Rd, first left: Stillwater Rd, E Gaynor Brennan Golf Course, first right: Emery Dr, second right: Starin Dr, third right: Havemeyer La
Straight: Cow Path Dr, Roxbury Rd, Riverbank Rd, first right: Roxbury Terrace, second right: Den Rd, third right: Munko Dr

**Westview La**

Straight: Westover Rd, first left: Summit Ridge Rd, second left: W Hill Rd, third left: Indian Hill Rd, first right: Bartina La, second right: Westover La, third right: Westover Av, fourth right: Mianus Rd
Straight: W Hill Rd, first left: Bartina La, second left: W Hill Circle, third left: Wyndover La, first right: Westover Rd

# The Stamford Streets AZ

**Westwood Ct**

Straight: Westwood Rd, first left: Stanton La, second left: Skyview Dr, first right: Skyview Dr, second right: Westwood Pl, third right: Stillwater Rd


**Westwood Pl**

Straight: Westwood Rd, first left: Stillwater Rd, first right: Skyview Dr, second right: Westwood Ct, third right: Stanton La


**Westwood Rd**
Stanton La, Westwood Ct, Skyview Dr, Westwood Pl

Straight: Skyview Dr, first left: Blueberry Dr, first right: Stanton La, second right: Green Tree La, third right: Westwood Rd
Straight: Stillwater Rd, first left: Long Hill Dr, second left: Long Ridge Rd 104, third left: Roxbury Rd, first right: Logan's Run, second right: Skyview Dr, third right: Clover Hill Dr

# The Stamford Streets AZ

**Whistler Pl**

Straight: Edward Pl, first left: Albert Pl, second left: Todd La


**White Birch La**
Deer La

Straight: Loveland Rd, first left: Loveland Rd W, Silver Hill La, first right: Lantern Circle, second right: Dannell Dr
Straight: Pepper Ridge Rd, first left: Kensington Rd, second left: Crestwood Dr, third left: Pepper Ridge Pl, first right: Silver Hill La, second right: Fara Dr, third right: Turner Rd


**White Birch Rd S**

Straight: White Birch Rd, first left: Shad Rd W, first right: Long Ridge Rd


**White Fox Rd**

Straight: Red Fox Rd, first left: Big Oak Rd, Big Oak La, second left: Wake Robin La, third left: Wire Mill Rd

# The Stamford Streets AZ

### White Oak La

Straight: Newfield Av, first left: Emerald La, second left: Intervale Rd E, Sweet Briar Rd, third left: Newfield Dr, first right: Wedgemere Rd, second right: Eden Rd, third right: N Meadows La

### Whitmore La

Straight: W Main St, first left: Myano La, second left: Alvord La, first right: E Putnam Av, Laddin Rock Rd, Havemeyer La
Straight: Catoona La, first left: Havemeyer La, first right: Myano La, second right: Alvord La

### Whittaker Pl

Straight: Washington Blvd 137, first left: W Broad St, Broad St, second left: North St, third left: Linden Pl, Hoyt St, first right: W Park Pl, second right: Main St, third right: Rippowam Pl

### Whittaker St

Straight: Ralph St, first right: Downs Av

# The Stamford Streets AZ

Straight: Downs Av, first left: Ralph St, first right: Shippan Av

**Wild Duck Rd**
Woodchuck Rd

Straight: Partridge Rd, first left: Long Ridge Rd 104

**Wild Horse Rd**

Straight: Shadow Ridge Rd, first left: Sun Dance Rd, first right: Lancaster Pl, second right: Cedar Heights Rd
Straight: Snow Crystal La, first left: Bradley Pl, second left: Corn Cake La, first right: Sun Dance Rd

**Wilder Rd**

Straight: Crystal Lake Rd, first right: Ashton Rd, second right: Beechwood Rd

**Wildwood Rd**
Indian Rock Rd, High Rock Rd, Harpsichord Tpke, Rocky Rapids Rd, Long Ridge Rd 104

# The Stamford Streets AZ

Straight: Riverbank Rd, first left: Rocky Rapids Rd, second left: Farms Rd, third left: Deep Valley Rd, first right: Erskine Rd, second right: Trailing Rock Rd, third right: Harpsichord Tpke
Straight: Hunting Ridge Rd, Konandreas Dr, first left: Haviland Rd, second left: Foxwood Rd, third left: Fox Ridge Rd, first right: Lawrence Hill Rd, second right: Erickson Dr, third right: Surrey Rd


**Willard Terrace**
Brantwood La

Straight: High Ridge Rd 137, first left: Wire Mill Rd, second left: E 35 Merritt Pkwy 15, CT15, High Ridge Rd, third left: E 35 Merritt Pkwy 15, CT15, first right: Opper Rd, second right: Brantwood La, third right: Marva La


**William St**
Lockwood Av, Lee St, Maple Av

Straight: Dale St, first left: Lillian St, second left: Frank St, first right: Woodrow St, second right: Ursula Pl, third right: Ursula Pl
Straight: Myrtle Av, first left: Warren St, second left: Frederick St, third

# The Stamford Streets AZ

left: Elm St, Jefferson St, first right: Gregory St, second right: E 8 Governor John Davis Lodge Tpke I-95, third right: Boston Post Rd 1

**Willoughby Rd**

Straight: Barclay Dr, first right: Den Rd

**Willowbrook Av**
Soundview Av, Wascussee La E, Hale St, Uncas Rd, Caldwell Av

Straight: Cove Rd, Blachley Rd, first left: Ranson St, Cove Rd, second left: Cove Rd, third left: Van Buskirk Av, first right: Duffy St, second right: Hobbie St, third right: George St

**Willowbrook Ct**

Straight: Hale St, Willowbrook Pl, first left: Willowbrook Av, first right: Ferro Dr, Martin St

# The Stamford Streets AZ

**Willowbrook Pl**

Straight: Hale St, Willowbrook Ct, first left: Ferro Dr, Martin St, first right: Willowbrook Av


**Wilson St**
Baxter Av, Grenhart Rd, Madison Pl, Hall Pl, Richmond Hill Av

Straight: Boston Post Rd 1, Richmond Hill Av, first left: Roosevelt Av, second left: Liberty St, third left: Victory St, first right: High St, second right: Fairfield Av, third right: Hazel St, Spruce St
Straight: Pressprich St
Irving Av, Vassar Av


**Wind Mill Cir**

Straight: Sawmill Rd, first left: Cider Mill Rd, second left: Long Ridge Rd 104, first right: Mill Stone Circle, second right: Dundee Rd, third right: Mill Stream Rd

# The Stamford Streets AZ

**Windell Pl**

Straight: Glenbrook Rd, first left: Frankel Pl, second left: Ely Pl, third left: Howes Av, first right: Scofield Av, second right: Crescent St, third right: Church St

**Windermere La**

Straight: High Line Trail, first left: High Line Trail S, second left: Westover Rd

**Winding Brook La**
Eljays La

Straight: Westover Rd, first left: High Line Trail, second left: Nathan Hale Dr, first right: Old Mill La, second right: Cow Path Dr, Roxbury Rd, Riverbank Rd

**Windsor Rd**

Straight: Cold Spring Rd, first left: Severance Dr, second left: Windsor Rd, third left: Cold Spring Rd 137, Washington Blvd 137, Paragon La, first right: Stillwater Rd

# The Stamford Streets AZ

Straight: Cold Spring Rd, first left: Cold Spring Rd 137, Washington Blvd 137, Paragon La, first right: Severance Dr, second right: Windsor Rd, third right: Severance Dr, fourth right: Stillwater Rd

**Winesap Rd**
Crab Apple Pl, McIntosh Rd, Merriland Rd

Straight: Shady La, straight: Briar Brae Rd, first left: High Ridge Rd 137, first right: Briar Wood Trail, second right: Rock Rimmon Rd
Straight: Russet Rd, first left: McIntosh Rd, second left: Mayapple Rd, first right: High Ridge Rd 137

**Winslow Dr**

Straight: Rock Rimmon Rd, first left: Old Long Ridge Rd, Long Ridge Rd 104, first right: Pond View La, second right: Rock Meadow La, third right: Mayapple Rd

**Winsted St**

Straight: Outlook St, straight: Selleck St, first left: Harvard Av, second left: Brown House Rd, first right: West Av,

# The Stamford Streets AZ

second right: Betts Av, third right: Durant St, Montauk Dr
Straight: West Av, first left: Selleck St, second left: Orlando Av, third left: Warshaw Pl

**Winter St**

Straight: Dunn Av, first left: Dunn Ct, second left: Finch St, third left: Cedar Heights Rd, first right: Derry St, second right: Peak St, third right: Alpine St

**Winthrop Pl**

Straight: Broad St, first left: Washington Blvd 137, W Broad St, first right: Franklin St, second right: Summer St, third right: Bedford St, Atlantic St

**Windward La**

Straight: Riverbank Rd, first left: Fawnfield Rd, second left: June Rd, third left: Riverbank Dr, first right: Bangall Rd, second right: Thunder Hill Dr, third right: Cow Path Dr, Roxbury Rd, Westover Rd

# The Stamford Streets AZ

**Wire Mill Rd**
Blackwood La, Gutzon Borglum Rd, Studio Rd, Red Fox Rd, Linwood La, Four Brooks Rd, Cedar Heights Rd, Cedar Tree La, Hunting La

Straight: Long Ridge Rd 104, first left: Vineyard La, second left: Maltbie Av, third left: Loughran Av, first right: E 34 Merritt Pkwy 15, CT15, second right: E 34 Merritt Pkwy 15, CT15, third right: E 34 Merritt Pkwy 15, CT15, fourth right: Webbs Hill Rd
Straight: High Ridge Rd 137, first left: Willard Terrace, second left: Opper Rd, third left: Brantwood La, first right: E 35 Merritt Pkwy 15, CT15, High Ridge Rd, second right: High Ridge Rd, third right: E 35 Merritt Pkwy 15, CT15, Buxton Farm Rd


**Wishing Well La**

Straight: Long Ridge Rd 104, first left: Brook Run La, second left: River Ridge Ct, third left: Stark Pl, first right: Woodridge Dr S, second right: Three Lakes Dr, third right: Clover Hill Dr

# The Stamford Streets AZ

**Wood La**

Straight: Brownley Dr, first left: Deacon Hill Rd, first right: High Ridge Rd 137

**Wood Ridge Dr**
Brookvale Pl, Ridge Park Av

Straight: Rosano Rd, Ridge Park Av, first left: Hillview La, second left: Longview Av, third left: Knollwood Av

**Woodbine Rd**
Woodbine Way, Mather Rd, Pinewood Rd, Brushwood Rd, Cedar Wood Rd, Round Lake Rd, Bittersweet La, Fernwood Dr, Reservoir La

Straight: Cascade Rd, first left: Ponus Ridge, first right: Frost Pond Rd, second right: Michael Rd, third right: Pembroke Dr
Straight: Laurel Rd, Reservoir La, first right: Ponus Ridge

**Woodbrook Dr**
Ward La

# The Stamford Streets AZ

Straight: Eden Rd, first left: Old Well Rd, second left: Friars La, third left: Hope St, E Cross Rd, first right: Twin Brook Dr, second right: Parry Rd, third right: Eden La
Straight: Parry Rd, first left: Eden Rd, first right: Parry Ct

**Woodbury Av**
Cady St, Buena Vista St, Crestview Av, Tower Av

Straight: Marian St, first left: St Charles Av, second left: Knickerbocker Av, first right: Klondike Av, second right: Haig Av
Straight: Lawton Av, first left: Knapp St, Sleepy Hollow La, first right: Birchwood Rd, second right: Woodledge Rd, third right: Bennett St

**Woodchuck Rd**

Straight: Wild Duck Rd, first right: Partridge Rd

**Woodcliff St**
Grandview Av

# The Stamford Streets AZ

Straight: W North St, Anderson St, first left: Hillside Av, second left: Powell Pl, Adams Av, third left: Hollywood Ct, W Washington Av, first right: Hinckley Av, second right: Hubbard Av, third right: St George Av
Straight: Hubbard Ct, Ivy St, first right: Hillside Av, second right: Powell Pl

**Woodland Av**

Straight: Pacific St, Ludlow St, first left: Henry St, second left: Market St, third left: Manhattan St, first right: Woodland Pl, second right: Walter Wheeler Dr, E Walnut St, third right: Remington St
Straight: Atlantic St, first left: Lipton Pl, second left: Walter Wheeler Dr, third left: Washington Blvd, first right: Lipton Pl, second right: Henry St, third right: Henry St

**Woodland Cemetery**

Straight: Woodland Pl
Elmcroft Rd, Stone St, straight: Pacific St, first left: Walter Wheeler Dr, E Walnut St, first right: Woodland Av, Ludlow St

# The Stamford Streets AZ

**Woodland Pl**
Elmcroft Rd, Stone St

Straight: Woodland Cemetery
Straight: Pacific St, first left: Walter Wheeler Dr, E Walnut St, second left: Remington St, Crosby St, first right: Woodland Av, Ludlow St, second right: Henry St, third right: Market St

**Woodledge Rd**
Northill St

Straight: Lawton Av, first left: Bennett St, second left: Tower Av, first right: Birchwood Rd, second right: Woodbury Av, third right: Knapp St

**Woodley Rd**

Straight: Scofieldtown Rd, first left: Middle Ridge Rd, second left: Janes La, third left: Old Logging Rd, first right: Campbell Dr, second right: Georgian Ct, third right: Chestnut Hill Rd

**Woodmere Rd**
Bridge St

# The Stamford Streets AZ

Straight: Hubbard Av, first left: Pellom Pl, second left: Prince Pl, third left: Charles Mary La, first right: Bridge St, second right: Riverside Av
Straight: Riverside Av, first left: Hubbard Av, first right: Bridge St


**Woodridge Dr S**
Amherst Pl, Bridle Path Rd

Straight: Elaine Dr, first left: Florence Ct, second left: Clorinda Ct, third left: Three Lakes Dr
Straight: Long Ridge Rd 104, first left: Wishing Well La, second left: Brook Run La, third left: River Ridge Ct, first right: Three Lakes Dr, second right: Clover Hill Dr, third right: Stillwater Rd


**Woodrow St**
Leeds St

Straight: Lockwood Av, first left: Warren St, second left: Cove Rd, first right: William St, second right: Lillian St, third right: Frank St
Straight: Dale St, first left: William St, second left: Lillian St, third left: Frank St, first right: Ursula Pl, second right: Ursula Pl, third right: Cove Rd

# The Stamford Streets AZ

### Woods End Rd
Janice Rd

Straight: Dannell Dr, first left: Loveland Rd, second left: Crestwood Dr, third left: Crestwood Dr, first right: High Ridge Rd 137, Mercedes La
Straight: Berrian Rd, first left: Rolling Wood Dr, second left: Little Hill Dr, first right: Idlewood Dr, second right: Pepper Ridge Rd

### Woodside Green

Straight: Bridge St, first left: Washington Blvd, second left: Riverside Av, third left: Woodmere Rd

### Woodside St
Franklin St

Straight: Summer St, 1st St, first left: 2nd St, second left: 2nd St, third left: 3rd St, first right: Oak St, second right: Hoyt St, third right: North St

### Woodway Rd
Highview Av, Hidden Brook Dr, Regent Ct

# The Stamford Streets AZ

Straight: Hope St, first left: Bouton St W, Bouton St, second left: Mead St, third left: Minivale Rd, first right: Robinhood Rd, second right: Putter Dr, third right: Mary Violet Rd Straight: Hoyt St 106, first left: Woodway Country Club, second left: Leeds La, third left: Country Club Rd, first right: Greenwood Av, second right: Proccaccini La, third right: Wakemore St

**Woody Trail**

Straight: Fishing Trail, first left: West Trail, first right: Short Trail

**Woolsey Rd**

Straight: Sagamore Rd, first left: Stamford Av, second left: S Sagamore La, third left: Ralsey Rd S, first right: Shippan Av Straight: Ocean Dr E, first left: Shippan Av, first right: Stamford Av, second right: Van Rensselaer Av, third right: Ralsey Rd S

# The Stamford Streets AZ

**Wright St**

Straight: W Broad St, first left: Hinckley Av, second left: Hubbard Av, third left: St George Av, first right: Anderson St, second right: Stephen St, third right: Oak Hill St
Straight: Spruce St
Finney La, Hillhurst St, Stillwater Av, Boston Post Rd 1, Hazel St
Straight: Richmond Hill Av, first left: Ann St, Taylor St, second left: Rose Park, third left: Mission St, first right: Fairfield Av, second right: Boston Post Rd 1, Wilson St


**Wyndover La N**

Straight: Wyndover La, first left: Hemlock Dr, first right: Phaiban La, second right: W Hill Rd


**Wyndover La**

Phaiban La, N Wyndover La, Hemlock Dr

Straight: W Hill Rd, first left: W Hill Circle, second left: Bartina La, third left: Westview La, first right: Wesgate Dr, second right: Blueberry Dr, third right: Greenleaf Dr

# The Stamford Streets AZ

**Wynnewood La**

Straight: Ingleside Dr, first left: Shady Knoll Dr, second left: High Ridge Rd 137, Briar Brae Rd, third left: High Ridge Rd 137, first right: Spring Hill La E, second right: Laurel Rd


**Woodbine Way**

Straight: Woodbine Rd, first left: Mather Rd, first right: Cascade Rd

# The Stamford Streets AZ

## Y

**Yale Ct**

Straight: High Ridge Rd 137, first left: Janice Rd, second left: Ridge Park Av, third left: Nichols Av, first right: Mercedes La, Dannell Dr, second right: Knollwood Av, third right: Longview Av

# The Stamford Streets AZ

## Z

**Zora La**

Straight: Davenport Ridge Rd, Davenport Ridge La, first left: Jeanne Ct, second left: Davenport Farm La W, third left: Thornridge Dr, first right: Lakeside Dr, Newfield Av


September 2014, Stamford, CT


**Edited streets**

**Apple Tree La**

Straight: Cedar Heights Rd, first left: Duke Dr, first right: Alpine St


**Mid River Run**

Straight: Maltbie Av, first right: Loughran Av

# The Stamford Streets AZ

Paperback database print handbook edition printed in 2014- *The Stamford Streets AZ by Lev Vozchikov* © Copyright 2008. Any part of this publication being retrieved, copied in any means should have written permission author. Annotation: second edition 2014, improved, developed, and updated. Hypertext Database is electronics future digital version paperback edition. Compilation presented genuine encyclopedic collection of Stamford, CT streets in the borders of it's owns original physical geo locations, within Stamford highway regional merge.

www.ingramcontent.com/pod-product-compliance
Lightning Source LLC
Chambersburg PA
CBHW071432300426
44114CB00013B/1405